CANADIANA

JAN 30 1997

DEFENCE RESEARCH ESTABLISHMENT VALCARTIER

1945-1995

50 YEARS OF HISTORY AND SCIENTIFIC PROGRESS

by
Alain Gelly
and
H. P. Tardif

© Minister of Public Works and Government Services Canada 1995
ISBN 0-662-23567-3
Catalogue No. D2-96/1-1995E

Legal Deposit - 4th trimester 1996
National Library of Canada
Bibliothèque nationale du Québec

Also available in French

NOTES ON THE AUTHORS

ALAIN GELLY, a historian, holds a Master's degree in history from Laval University, where he specialized in the history of the munitions industry in Quebec City from 1879 to 1946. He has been working in the field of institutional history for several years and his works include a monograph on the sixtieth anniversary of the Cultural Property Commission of Quebec, *La passion du patrimoine*, another marking the 125 years of the Jeffery Hale hospital, and his most recent one on the history of the city of Cap-Rouge. He has also acted as a historian for research projects on various subjects.

HENRI P. TARDIF holds degrees from Laval University (B.A.Sc.), the Carnegie Institute of Technology, Pittsburgh (M.Sc.), and the University of Birmingham, United Kingdom (Ph.D.). With a Ph.D. in metallurgy, he joined DREV in 1953 as a researcher in the field of materials. In 1966 he was named Deputy Chief, Canadian Defence Research Staff, in London. Three years later he returned to DREV as Director, Armaments Division. Awarded a degree in 1973 by the National Defence College in Kingston, Ontario, he occupied senior management positions at DREV, becoming its Chief in 1984, a post he held until his retirement in 1990. This co-author has also written a number of publications and is a member of several scientific societies.

TABLE OF CONTENTS

FOREWORD xiii
LIST OF ABBREVIATIONS xviii
INTRODUCTION 1

PART ONE

ESTABLISHMENT OF A SCIENCE BASIS AND ORGANIZATION OF MILITARY RESEARCH IN CANADA

1   CANADA AND MILITARY RESEARCH BEFORE 1945
- 1.1   DEFENCE POLICY AND MILITARY RESEARCH IN CANADA   9
- 1.1.1   Overview of Canadian Defence Policy during the Interwar Years and up to 1941   9
- 1.1.2   The Opening of the Scientific Front in Canada   12
- 1.1.2.1   The National Research Council of Canada and Military Research prior to 1939   13
- 1.1.2.2   The National Research Council of Canada and Military Research during the Second World War   16
- 1.2   FORMATION OF THE VALCARTIER RESEARCH ESTABLISHMENTS DURING THE WAR   19
- 1.2.1   The Location Factor: Proximity of the Dominion Arsenal   19
- 1.2.2   Creation of a Military Technology Complex in Valcartier   21
- 1.2.3   A Precursor to CARDE: The Ballistics Laboratory   24

2   ARMAMENTS AT THE FORE: THE CANADIAN ARMAMENT RESEARCH AND DEVELOPMENT ESTABLISHMENT (CARDE) 1945-1950
- 2.1   THE POST-WAR PERIOD AND THE IMPORTANCE OF MILITARY RESEARCH   31
- 2.1.1   Defence Research Policy in the Immediate Post-War Period   32
- 2.1.2   An Innovative Notion: The Fourth Service   34
- 2.1.3   Founding of the Defence Research Board (DRB)   38
- 2.2   THE CREATION OF CARDE   39

	2.2.1	Steps Taken by the Director of Artillery	39
	2.3	CARDE'S FIRST INITIATIVES UNDER ARMY MANAGEMENT	41
	2.3.1	Administrative Integration	43
	2.3.2	Difficulties Experienced by the Army in Recruiting Scientists	44
	2.3.3	Research Conducted at CARDE under Army Authority	46
	2.4	CARDE: AN ORGANIZATION MANAGED BY CIVILIANS	47
	2.4.1	Consolidation of CARDE with the Defence Research Board	47
	2.4.2	DRB Considers Transforming CARDE into an Explosives Research Establishment	52
	2.4.3	Amalgamation of the Inspection Board of Canada Artillery Proof and Experimental Establishment with CARDE	53
	2.4.4	A Difficult Task: Recruiting Defence Scientists	54
	2.4.5	The Establishment's Budget	58
	2.4.6	The Establishment's Construction Program	58
	2.5	CARDE'S FIRST SUCCESS IN CONVENTIONAL WEAPONS	60

PART TWO

THE GOLDEN YEARS: ALMOST TWO DECADES OF GREAT PROJECTS AT DREV

3		THE START OF A NEW ERA FOR CARDE: VELVET GLOVE AND HELLER	
	3.1	OVERVIEW OF CANADIAN DEFENCE POLICY AFTER THE SECOND WORLD WAR	69
	3.1.1	Formulation of Policies and Programs for Defence Research	75
	3.2	CARDE AND GUIDED MISSILES	78
	3.2.1	Canada and Research on Guided Missiles	78
	3.2.2	Why an Air-to-Air Missile?	80
	3.2.3	CARDE's Role in Conducting an Opportunity and Feasibility Study on an Air-to-Air Missile	82
	3.3	CARDE AND THE EVOLUTION OF THE VELVET GLOVE PROGRAM	84
	3.3.1	Complexity of the Air-to-Air Missile	84
	3.3.2	Some of the Organizational Challenges posed by the Velvet Glove Program to CARDE Management	85

	3.3.3	The Participation of Industry and other Government Research Establishments in the Velvet Glove Project	88
	3.3.4	Initial Preparations	91
	3.3.5	Evolution of the Velvet Glove Program at CARDE	92
	3.3.6	The Velvet Glove Missile is Abandoned	96
	3.3.7	The Impact of the Velvet Glove Project on CARDE's Budget and Personnel	98
	3.4	CONVENTIONAL WEAPONS DEVELOPMENT AT CARDE, 1950 TO 1955	100
	3.4.1	Heller	100
4	APPLIED RESEARCH PROGRAM ON ACTIVE DEFENCE AGAINST INTERCONTINENTAL BALLISTIC MISSILES, 1955-1970		
	4.1	DEFENCE AGAINST INTERCONTINENTAL BALLISTIC MISSILES	109
	4.1.1	General Historical Context	109
	4.1.2	A Major Change in Military Strategy: The Introduction of Strategic Missiles	115
	4.1.3	CARDE Scientists Seek a Replacement Program for Velvet Glove	118
	4.1.4	A Period of Change in CARDE's other Research Activities: 1954-1956	122
	4.2	AEROSPACE RESEARCH	124
	4.2.1	The Role of Dr. Gerald Vincent Bull	124
	4.2.2	Prelude to the Joint Program with the United States: The Administrative Reorganization of 1958	132
	4.2.3	The Joint Canada/United States Aerophysics Program: The Physics of Projectile Re-entry into the Earth's Atmosphere	135
	4.2.4	Changes Following the End of the Re-entry Physics Program	141
	4.2.5	The Study of Infrared Radiation in the Upper Atmosphere	141
	4.2.6	Project Lookout	144
	4.2.7	The Cold Can Project: Atmospheric Research	146
	4.2.8	Upper Atmosphere Research using Stratospheric Sounding Balloons	147
	4.2.9	CRAM Collaboration in Upper Atmospheric Research	150
	4.3	THE DEVELOPMENT OF THE BLACK BRANT HIGH ALTITUDE RESEARCH ROCKET	151

	4.3.1	Composite Propellants for Rocket Motors	151
	4.3.2	Design of the Black Brant Rocket	152

5 RESTRUCTURING OF RESEARCH ACTIVITIES AT DEFENCE RESEARCH ESTABLISHMENT VALCARTIER

	5.1	REORGANIZATION OF NATIONAL DEFENCE	179
	5.1.1	Defence at the Centre of Political Upheaval	179
	5.1.2	The Glassco Commission and the Department of National Defence	181
	5.1.3	Reorganization of the Department of National Defence	183
	5.2	ONE CONSEQUENCE OF UNIFICATION OF THE CANADIAN FORCES: RESTRUCTURING OF RESEARCH ACTIVITIES AT CARDE	185
	5.3	RENEWED EMPHASIS ON WEAPON SYSTEMS STUDIES AND RESEARCH ON CONVENTIONAL ARMAMENTS	188
	5.3.1	Weapon Systems Studies	188
	5.3.2	The Creation of the Armament Engineering Wing	190
	5.3.3	The Main Activities of the Armament Engineering Wing	191
	5.3.4	The Canadian Forces Special Projects Laboratory	192
	5.4	DREV BECOMES A WORLD LEADER IN LASER RESEARCH: THE DEVELOPMENT OF THE TEA-CO_2 LASER	193
	5.4.1	CARDE Research on Military Applications of Lasers	193
	5.4.2	A Shift in Research Emphasis: From Solid-State Lasers to Electrically-Excited CO_2 Lasers	195
	5.4.3	Invention of the Transversely-Excited Atmospheric Carbon Dioxide (TEA-CO_2) Laser	197
	5.4.4	Project LOTION	199
	5.4.5	World-Wide Renown for the Invention of the TEA-CO_2 Laser	200
	5.4.6	Spin-off from the Invention of the TEA-CO_2 Laser	202

PART THREE
AN ERA OF CHANGE: DREV ON THE EVE OF THE THIRD MILLENIUM

6	CANADA'S DEFENCE POLICY DURING THE PAST 25 YEARS	
6.1	STATE OF CANADA'S PUBLIC FINANCE	209
6.2	THE IMPACT OF BUDGETARY POLICY ON CANADA'S DEFENCE POLICY SINCE 1969	214
6.2.1	Defence Policy in the Early 1970's and the 1971 Defence White Paper	215
6.2.2	The Mid-1970's: A Change in Course Dictated by *Realpolitik*	217
6.2.3	The 1987 White Paper: *Challenge and Commitment*	220
6.2.4	The 1994 Defence White Paper: The Impact of Fiscal Policy and the End of the Cold War on Defence Policy in the 1990's	223

7	REORGANIZATION OF DEFENCE RESEARCH IN CANADA	
7.1	DEVELOPMENT OF NATIONAL SCIENCE POLICY	229
7.1.1	The Glassco Commission and Scientific Activities within Government	229
7.1.2	The Development of Organizational Mechanisms for Managing	231
7.2	TRANSFORMATION OF CANADA'S DEFENCE ESTABLISHMENT AND THE DEFENCE RESEACH BOARD	234
7.2.1	The Glassco Commission and the Defence Research Board	234
7.2.2	Impact of the Integration of the Armed Forces on the Defence Research Board	235
7.3	NEW DISTRIBUTION OF RESPONSIBILITIES FOR DEFENCE RESEARCH ACTIVITIES WITHIN DND, OR THE END OF THE FOURTH SERVICE CONCEPT	237
7.3.1	Restructuring Provides for Better Coordination of Research and Development Programs within DND	240
7.4	SCIENTIFIC ACTIVITIES OF DREV FROM 1970 TO 1974	241
7.4.1	Research in the Field of Lasers	246
7.4.1.1	The TEA-CO_2 Laser	246

	7.4.1.2	Chemically-Excited Lasers	247
	7.4.2	Armaments Research	249
	7.4.2.1	The CRV7 Rocket	251
	7.4.3	Surveillance	253
	7.5	CHANGES IN ORIENTATION OF DREV RESEARCH FOLLOWING THE DEMISE OF DRB AND THE RESTRUCTURING OF DEFENCE RESEARCH UNDER CRAD	255
	7.6	SCIENTIFIC ACTIVITIES AT DREV SINCE 1974	258
	7.6.1	Energetic Materials	259
	7.6.2	Armaments	261
	7.6.3	Information Technologies	263
	7.6.4	Electro-Optics	264
	7.6.5	Development of Scientific Infrastructures	266
8		IMPACT OF DREV'S PARTICIPATION IN DEFENCE RESEARCH	
	8.1	SOME EXAMPLES OF THE MAIN SPIN-OFFS FROM DREV SCIENTIFIC ACTIVITIES	271
	8.1.1	Patents, Inventions and Licences	271
	8.1.2	The Make-or-Buy Policy	274
	8.1.3	Exploitation of DREV's Research	277
	8.1.4	Industrial Benefits	280
	8.1.5	Scientific Benefits	282
	8.2	AN OUTLINE OF THE ECONOMIC BENEFITS TO QUEBEC FROM THE PRESENCE OF DREV AT VALCARTIER	283
	8.3	INTERNATIONAL PARTICIPATION	285
	8.3.1	The Technical Cooperation Program (TTCP)	286
	8.3.2	NATO	286
	8.3.3	NATO Industrial Advisory Group (NIAG)	287
	8.3.4	The Franco-Canadian Accord	287

PART FOUR
MAJOR DEVELOPMENTS IN DREV ADMINISTRATION

9		EVOLUTION OF THE ADMINISTRATIVE STRUCTURE OF DEFENCE RESEARCH ESTABLISHMENT VALCARTIER	
	9.1	ADMINISTRATIVE STRUCTURE OF DREV UNDER DRB	291
	9.1.1	Importance of the "Wing" or "Divisional" Structure in CARDE	291
	9.1.2	Successive Structural Reorganizations	293
	9.1.2.1	Computerization of Administrative Data	296
	9.1.2.2	Project Coordination	299
	9.1.2.3	Reorganization of Administrative Services	300
	9.2	THE CHANGE OF STATUS FROM SEPARATE EMPLOYER TO AN ORGANIZATION SUBJECT TO THE REGULATIONS OF THE FEDERAL PUBLIC SERVICE	301
	9.3	RESHAPING OF DREV ADMINISTRATION	305
	9.3.1	Changes in DREV Management	306
	9.3.2	Integration of DREV Staff within the Public Service: A New Classification Structure and Formal Position Descriptions	307
	9.3.3	The Loss of Separate Employer Status and its Impact on Staff Relations at DREV	310
	9.3.4	The Attempt to Integrate Certain Establishment Services into the Valcartier Base	311
	9.4	ADMINISTRATION STRUCTURE OF DREV DURING THE 1980's	312
	9.5	DREV HUMAN RESOURCES	318
	9.5.1	Recruitment of Scientists	318
	9.5.2	The Women of DREV	323
	9.6	DREV FINANCIAL RESOURCES	327
CONCLUSION			335
ANNEX			351
BIBLIOGRAPHICAL SCOPE			358

FOREWORD

In a human lifetime, dates live on through memories. In the history of a research organization such as DREV, however, they are associated with the triumphs and enduring contributions of men and women that have punctuated its development. The slice of history presented in this book vividly demonstrates that DREV has a long scientific tradition that is far from ordinary or commonplace. In this golden anniversary year it is readily acknowledged that the scientific heritage it represents today has become one of the driving forces of our economic prosperity while continuing to be an essential component of our defence science culture. Buildings, however, are merely silent witnesses of this past and warily avoid revealing the exploits of the men and women who, through their past and present activities, have contributed to the emergence of DREV and earned it an international reputation. This book has been written to draw attention to the work of these pioneers and pay them special homage. They are clearly deserving of our unqualified gratitude and admiration.

In science, boundaries become blurred. It will be seen that the accomplishments of DREV have been at the heart of the world-wide scientific reality in which distinctions of nationality, colour and race are set aside and meld in a common unity of thought and mind. It was doubtless quite natural for us to have this historical tribute to a noble organization which, while certainly upholding the dignity and efficacy of its role and mission, has established its credibility in the eyes of the allied defence community and become a magnificent symbol of Canada. Needless to say, DREV has served the cause of research and development brilliantly and with distinction over the past five decades. As Director General, I am delighted that a successful effort has been made to reconstruct the most significant milestones of its activities through this historical fresco. I therefore take pride and extreme satisfaction in introducing this history as part of the celebration of DREV's golden anniversary.

The history of DREV coincides with the accelerated revolutionary movements of modern science. To return to the source of its activities in order to identify its main features is also to witness, to a great extent, the origin of defence science in Canada since the post-war years. In 50 years, DREV has grown and increased its visibility, leaving as a legacy a period that has been immensely rich and intensely productive. However, the purpose of this history was not merely to shed light on and measure the progress that has been made. It was also to indicate the motives and intentions of the builders. To do this, it was necessary to grasp the significance of DREV's major achievements and seek to determine their origins and how they occurred to its research scientists and technicians. If it was not possible to foresee or promote future accomplishments, it was fitting at least to endeavour to trace their roots in past and recent achievements. Indeed, the authors have excelled in this task, and this effort is clearly equal to their objective. It should therefore arouse widespread interest, not only because of the quality of its format, but also because of the aptness of its content. History, however, is never obvious at first sight. For those who wish to become acquainted with it and appreciate it, it must first of all be aged a little and then savoured and allowed to ferment like a good wine.

DREV has undoubtedly played a major role in technological development in the Quebec City area. It is evident today that it has succeeded over the years in gaining an excellent degree of exposure vis-à-vis the industrial, university and government partners actively engaged in this highly specialized field of research and innovation. Nonetheless, its origins are, in fact, largely unknown among the general population, although the subject is often raised. The numerous concepts that the layman may have of it are in general fragmented like the pieces of a puzzle that is difficult to assemble. Because of their concern about meeting the needs of a broader public than one consisting of specialists — historians or scientists — the authors have endeavoured to write a simple, comprehensible book and constantly striven to be clear, methodical and helpful. In the interests of clarity, they have omitted minor details without setting aside what is essential; in an effort to be methodical, they have attempted to follow chronological order, while placing the reality of the research activities and their development in their proper context in terms of their causes and effects; and finally, in an attempt to be helpful, they have included bibliographical data that the more specialized reader may consult at his/her leisure if he/she wishes to know more about certain specific topics.

This book therefore provides us with a complete panorama and a coherent view of the history of the Establishment from its creation in 1945 up to the present day. Indeed, it fills a gap that the scientific community of Quebec and all of Canada have long deplored. Through their excellent spadework, the authors have done an admirable job of collecting an abundance of information hitherto scattered throughout a host of publications, and have produced a lucid synthesis that succeeds in identifying the relationships between each event and the one that preceded it. Needless to say, history can be clarified, but unfortunately, it cannot be altered. The reader will simply wonder whether it is possible, in a few hundred pages, to provide a satisfactory account of 50 years of significant events associated with science, culture and traditions. We boldly answer yes. Indeed, this book is intended for popular consumption and is designed to meet the expectations of our founders and fulfil the desires of the defence community. In a number of places, occurrences and events are shown from an angle that has heretofore been unknown or unrecognized, and this helps to elucidate the facts and promote an understanding of what enlivens lifeless historical matter. Despite all the care devoted to these details, a book such as this would inevitably have been somewhat dry in appearance and flavour had the authors confined themselves to simply reconstituting the facts.

To avoid this pitfall, they resisted the temptation to merely recite the litany of its accomplishments and have painted instead a vivid picture of the richness and durability of DREV's heritage, thereby paying a stirring tribute to those who have shaped its reputation and expanded its influence.

I must say that I accepted enthusiastically and with great pleasure the invitation extended to me by the authors, Messrs. Gelly and Tardif, to compose the foreword for this history of DREV which was being written at the time. However, once I had received the manuscript, I felt some apprehension in view of the scope and excellence of the book and, consequently, the distinct honour that had been bestowed upon me. After perusing the initial drafts, my confidence quickly returned and I ultimately yielded to the pleasure and enthusiasm of adding my modest contribution to this unique work. What struck me as interesting about this book and its authors was the fact that Mr Gelly's experience and vision as a professional historian were combined with Mr Tardif's experience as a man of science who has himself served as Chief of DREV, besides having contributed as a research scientist to its development over the past few decades. Needless to say, this is highly unusual in this age of compartmentalization when historians are increasingly removed from the figures of the past. The authors are therefore able, on the one hand, to adopt the temporary intellectual detachment of the highly professional historian in order to identify the fundamental main themes and, on the other, to highlight them, through the personal reminiscences and first-hand evidence of a scientist concerning a period of history in which he himself was associated with the events. At the risk of offending Mr Tardif's proverbial modesty, it is a pleasure for me to pay tribute to him as a leader in the field of historical research on DREV. His unflagging perseverance at a time when this concern appeared to be of very minor importance succeeded in establishing the need to take an interest in its history and publicize it better.

This book, which is well thought out and well written, also deals with the history of science and technology in Canada and should serve as a pioneer in the essential yet much neglected field of the history of defence sciences. It no doubt bears repeating that it is primarily because of a desire to pay special tribute to all the men and women who, through their ideas and efforts, have helped the Establishment to earn its reputation that this book has been produced. Many have made their mark here, and others have passed through more unobtrusively and left no tangible trace. Be that as it may, a collective undertaking such as the Defence Research Establishment Valcartier would not have been able to endure and extend its influence beyond our borders had not everyone made a significant contribution to the fabric of its progress and development. It is therefore due to the efforts of all of these men and women that we can boast, after this first half-century, of a record of achievements that is as impressive as it is diversified. Those who consult this memoir will readily observe that it owes a great deal to all these pioneers for what is great and enduring in its content. It is all here in crystal clarity: men, women, setting, success and discoveries, placing DREV in its general, scientific, economic and military context. Endowed with the grandeur of its heritage and traditions, DREV must, in this final decade of the present century which is rife with uncertainty, steadfastly steer a course towards the future. Let us hope that our future generations will be able to follow in the footsteps of the authors of past accomplishments and master the skills of tomorrow that will be essential to take us to the dawn of the 21st century in a blaze of glory.

In closing, I hope that this book will be favourably received by its target audience. That will be the most fitting reward for the pains that the authors have taken with it. Let us take this opportunity to express our gratitude to them.

Jacques Gilbert
7/7/95

LIST OF ABBREVIATIONS

ADEE	Armament Development and Experimental Establishment
ADM(Mat)	Associate Deputy Minister (Materiel)
ADM(Pol)	Associate Deputy Minister (Policy)
AEP	Aid to Employees Program
APEE*	Artillery Proof and Experimental Establishment
ADEE*	Artillery Proof and Development Establishment
ARGMA	Army Rocket and Guided Missile Agency
ARPA	Advanced Research Projects Agency
BAL	Bristol Aerospace Ltd
BVAR	Bureau de valorisation des applications de la recherche (Laval U.)
CADEE	Canadian Armament Development and Experimental Establishment
CARDE	Canadian Armament Research and Development Establishment
CDC	Computing Devices of Canada Limited
CEPE	Central Experimental and Proofing Establishment
CETO	Coordonnateur des études sur les techniques opérationnelles

CPDL	Canadian Patent Development Limited
CRAD	Chief Research and Development
CRAM	Centre de recherches sur les atomes et les molécules
CRIM	Centre de recherches en informatique de Montréal
CRIQ	Centre de recherches industrielles du Québec
CSCE	Conférence sur la sécurité et la coopération en Europe
CSST	Commission de la santé et de la sécurité du travail
D.-A.	Director-Artillery
DAA	Directorate of Artillery Ammunition
DARPA	Defense Advanced Research Projects Agency
DIR	Defence Industrial Research
DND	Department of National Defence
DRB	Defence Research Board
DRTE	Defence Research Telecommunications Establishment
DS	Defence Scientist
DSSO	Defence Scientific Service Officer

EEE	Explosives Experimental Establishment
IBEW	The International Brotherhood of Electrical Workers
IBRL	Internal Ballistics Research Laboratory
ICBM	Intercontinental Ballistic Missile
IRAP	Industrial Research Assistance Programme (NRC)
ITM	Institut de technologie du magnésium
LMRC	Labor Management Relations Committee
MICSTQ	Ministère de l'Industrie, du Commerce de la Science et de la Technologie du Québec
MRG	Management Review Group
NAE	National Aeronautical Establishment
NOI	National Optics Institute
NORAD	North American Aerospace Defense
NRC	National Research Council
OCDE	Organisation pour la coopération et le développement économique
ORAE	Operational Research and Analysis Establishment
PIPSC	Professional Institute of the Public Service of Canada

PSAC	Public Service Alliance of Canada
PSC	Public Service Commission
RCAF	Royal Canadian Air Force
TTCP	The Technical Cooperation Program
UBC	University of British Columbia
UNDE	Union of National Defence Employees
UNO	United Nations Organization
USAF	United States Air Force

(*) The two names were used to define the same centre.

INTRODUCTION

The intention of the Canadian government in authorizing the formation of the Canadian Armament Research and Development Establishment by Order-in-Council in 1945 was to preserve the main elements of the military technological complex in Valcartier which had been developed during the Second World War. But the effect of the decision was far-reaching, for through this Order-in-Council the Government created one of the most prestigious research institutions in Canada. For the past half-century, the personnel of CARDE (now DREV) have enriched the totality of defence science in Canada through the quality of their scientific work. It can be said, therefore, that for 50 years DREV has contributed to the development of Canadian science.

Interest of the Establishment in its history is not new. On the occasion of CARDE's 25th Anniversary, the event was highlighted through the inclusion of a brief history of the Establishment in the Annual Report. In an imaginative move, CARDE management also persuaded the Canadian Broadcasting Corporation to broadcast a series of telecasts on the main research activities of the Establishment. Over recent years, Dr. Henri P. Tardif, former Chief of the Establishment, has maintained a continuing interest in DREV's history.

In view of the richness of DREV's history, historian Alain Gelly and Dr. Henri P. Tardif were asked to author a book recounting the main activities of the Establishment from its beginnings up to the present day. The authors quickly decided to make maximum use of annual reports, available records and other unclassified administrative documentation. These sources constituted an excellent source of information on the development of the Establishment's decision-making process, mission, mandate and main research activities.

The annual reports were highly relevant, but unfortunately did not cover the entire fifty-year period of the Establishment's existence. Additional material was needed and, to this end, research was undertaken on the holdings of the National Archives of Canada (NAC). Series RG 24 of the Department of National Defence proved to be particularly useful in elucidating the circumstances surrounding the creation of CARDE and the activities conducted in the early years. Dr. Tardif's press clipping collection and his extensive literature review of the subject matter was of great value in the production of this book. But its content was enriched by the willingness of key individuals to provide their own personal perspectives on important aspects of the Establishment's history. These persons included Mr. Bobyn, Dr. Gilbert, Dr. Lemay and Mr. Letarte.

DREV's history was shaped as much by the Canadian government's defence policies as by its defence research policies, and to exclude these contextual aspects of DREV's history would be to discard the key to a good understanding of the evolution of defence science in Valcartier. It is, therefore, important to place the subject matter in proper context in order to ensure a good understanding of the major directions that DREV has taken and the changes it has experienced since its creation. The authors decided, therefore, to outline the Canadian government's defence policies and defence research policies before describing the main phases of DREV's history.

This book, as the history of an institution, deals with the Establishment's administration, mission, organizational structure and research activities. It also deals with the relationships developed by the Establishment with its parent organizations, first DRB and later CRAD, and with its sole client and master, the Department of National Defence. Because of the influence exerted by these bodies on the Establishment's development, the main elements of their evolution are briefly outlined, but only to the extent that they shed light on the history of DREV; any further elaboration would be beyond the scope of this book. The approach adopted thus merges the history of an organization with that of defence, of military research and of science.

Because the richness and complexity of DREV's history called for a rigorous approach, the subject has been treated not only chronologically but also thematically so as to segregate the important from the non-essential. Thus, the first part of the book outlines military research prior to 1945, from the formation of a scientific front to its institutionalization, in order to expose the foundations that led to the emergence of a major scientific complex in Valcartier. The circumstances surrounding the creation this complex, and subsequently the creation of CARDE, are then described at length. The discussion also focuses on the main elements of defence research policy in the immediate post-war period and especially on the unique concept of organizing military research as the fourth Service of the Department of National Defence with the same rights and prerogatives as the other three Services. Against this backdrop, the consequences of CARDE's integration within the Defence Research Board are more clearly discernible. The second part of the book outlines the major projects that left an indelible mark on the history of DREV, specifically, the Velvet Glove air-to-air missile project, the applied research program on ballistic missile defence and the TEA-CO_2 laser development, together with a general overview of Canada's defence and defence research policies. The third part examines the reasons underlying the decision to reassign responsibilities for defence research in 1974 - which appears to be the cornerstone for DREV's activities ever since - and the profound implications of this decision for the Establishment. Finally, the fourth part focuses on the main elements of the Establishment's administrative development from the early beginnings up to the present time. Although these latter aspects appear throughout the book, it seemed important to group them in a separate part.

The authors used a thematic approach to go deeper into aspects that were specific to DREV's history. This methodology had many advantages, one being to study this history more systematically. Another unquestionable advantage of this methodology is that it is directed to all types of readers, whether one is interested by DREV's entire history or only by some specific aspects. Many events related to the evolution of the Establishment are multidimensional. They must often be pointed out in this book to be better understood. Also, the authors, only once, confined themselves to a detailed analysis of these events. To help the selective reader or the one who wishes to refresh his/her memory, they made a synthesis of these events in the conclusion of this book. And finally, it must be mentioned that the authors deemed it necessary to translate the numerous quotations in English for the French version of this book.

The authors wish to thank the following persons: Dr. Jacques Gilbert, Director General DREV, for his unfailing support; Pierre St-Onge, Head, Program Management and Strategic Planning, for coordinating this effort; Mr. P. Twardawa for critically reviewing the final text of the English version; Mr. E.J. Bobyn, Dr. André Lemay, Mr. Marcel Letarte and again Dr. Jacques Gilbert who were ready to provide, during the course of interviews, first-hand accounts of events at DREV in which they played a part, and without whose assistance this book could not have been written. The authors also wish to thank a number of Establishment personnel whose comments and participation enabled the authors to improve the book's content. In particular, thanks are due to the following Division Directors: Mr. D. Smith (Command and Control); Mr. R. Corriveau (Electro-Optics); Mr. P. Twardawa (Energetic Materials); and Mr. M. Clark (Armaments), who kindly provided comments on the part dealing with the development of the R&D program over the last two decades. The assistance of Dr. G. Otis, who contributed significantly to the part dealing with lasers, is gratefully acknowledged. It would be remiss not to mention the invaluable collaboration of Dr. M. Gravel, Dr. J. Beaulieu, Dr. R. Lavertu, Mr. D. Ouellet, Mr. G. Drouin, Mr. C. Carrier, Mr. G.D. Watson and Mr. Y. Noël who provided vital information on some specific topics. Finally, thanks are due to Mrs. Johanne Cantin for her tireless work and logistic support, to Mr. Jacques Leblanc for editing the French text, to Mrs. Jocelyne

Audy for the graphic design of this book, to all personnel of Graphic Arts for their great collaboration, and to Mrs. Lise Ladouceur to whom we are greatly endebted for provinding editorial advice and coordinating of the final production of this work.

PART ONE

ESTABLISHMENT OF A SCIENCE BASIS AND ORGANIZATION OF MILITARY RESEARCH IN CANADA

> *"The battle line of tomorrow runs through the research laboratories of today."* (Sir Winston Churchill)
>
> *"I think the work being done in Canada on explosives will prove to be a bright spot in our many achievements."*
> (Dr. Chalmers Jack Mackenzie)

1

CANADA AND MILITARY RESEARCH BEFORE 1945

1.1   DEFENCE POLICY AND MILITARY RESEARCH IN CANADA

1.1.1   Overview of Canadian Defence Policy during the Interwar Years and up to 1941

At the end of the First World War, the warring nations emerged badly scarred by the scale and duration of the conflict. Following the horrors of the Great War, pacifism was on the rise throughout most of the world. At home, many Canadians embraced this doctrine,[1] whilst Borden's Unionist government faced a heavy national debt and the beginning of an economic recession. In such a context, most Canadians "were opposed to increased defence expenditures"[2] although the Unionist government appeared to be somewhat favourably disposed towards maintaining a permanent military force. In 1921, the Liberal Party under Mackenzie King gained power and adopted a policy of reducing military expenditures.

In the 1922 Session of Parliament, the National Defence Act was passed and took force on 1 January 1923. Under this Act, the

Naval Service, the Department of Militia and Defence and the Air Board were all integrated within one single department, and the Prime Minister could rationalize the whole defence sector and reduce budgets de facto. These economies of scale nevertheless still appeared inadequate, and the government imposed a tight financial policy on the new department. In 1927, the military budget started to rise under the Liberals, but the stock market crash of 1929 put a swift end to it. In 1930, the Conservatives took office. Although reputedly favourable towards the military,[3] they made no changes at all to the draconian reductions imposed on the defence budget: "It would have been political suicide for any government to have voted money for military purposes with a large body of people clamouring for help to earn a decent living."[4] Then, by 1935, as the economic crisis endured, Canada's defence fell into unbelievable decay. Military equipment was outdated and very scarce[5] and the members of the armed forces were far too few. Indeed, Canada appeared to be virtually disarmed.[6]

The situation was even more critical since, at the time, the country had no defence industry apart from the Dominion Arsenal and could not rearm itself alone. According to Donald James Goodspeed, Canada's policy of purchasing British rather than Canadian equipment was not extraneous to this situation. For its part, the Canadian Army had undertaken no armaments research of any consequence. In brief, "as a result [...] no research or development on armament problems was done in Canada during the 1920's and 1930's and there was, in effect, no Canadian armament industry."[7]

In 1935, the rearmament issue was the order of the day in most Western capitals. In Canada, the defence situation was alarming and Major General McNaughton confirmed, in a confidential memorandum, the state of unpreparedness of the Canadian Armed Forces.[8] Mackenzie King, back at the helm of government, remained hesitant to embark on a rearmament program. In fact, King sought to avoid engaging the country in any action that could be interpreted by his French-speaking compatriots as a willingness to go to war again. But the international context left him little choice and, in the end, the Liberal government adopted a rearmament program for its Armed Forces. Faithful to his policy of appeasement, King downplayed the significance of the rearmament program by emphasizing defence of national territory and refusing to equip an overseas expeditionary force.[9] Viewing the infantry as a drain on manpower, he was more disposed towards modernization of the Air Force and, to a lesser extent, the Navy. In 1936, another factor - the money supply - favoured the RCAF as the main beneficiary of rearmament in the Canadian Armed Forces: "money is scarce [in Canada] and the government cannot simultaneously modernize the equipment of the three Services; a choice has to be made and the RCAF has the vote."[10]

The adoption of the rearmament program did not, however, solve all the problems, "for it was difficult for private enterprise in Canada to develop a strong armament industry."[11] Thus, Canada settled for an aeronautical industry which built British-designed aircraft under licence that were ill-adapted to Canadian needs. More importantly, the industry was plagued with delays and the aircraft leaving the factories were already obsolescent.[12] To compensate for the shortcomings of its rudimentary defence industry, Canada then turned for help to its usual supplier, but without any luck. Great Britain was also in full pursuit of its own rearmament program and could not deliver equipment quickly.[13] By the summer of 1939, it became increasingly obvious to military observers that war was imminent. Despite all efforts since 1936, the Canadian Armed Forces remained under-equipped.[14]

On 1 September 1939, Germany invaded Poland. On 3 September, Britain then France declared war on Germany. Canada was forced to take a position. Prime Minister Mackenzie King convened Parliament and, on 10 September, Canada joined the ranks of the Allies by declaring war on Nazi Germany. At the time, Canada was not really prepared to enter the war which was rapidly assuming global dimensions. In any event, Canada advocated a "policy of limited engagement". The main advantage of this policy was that it did not "pressure [the Canadian economy] to the last dollar"[15] and it allowed the Canadian Government to maintain the war effort "within the limits of careful economic calculations made by the Department of Finance."[16] This did not prevent Canada from laying the foundations for a future mobilization of the Canadian economy through the creation, in September 1939, of the Department of Munitions and Supply. This new department was accorded unprecedented powers, but could not exercise them until the proclamation of 9 April 1940.

Despite all his powers, the Minister of Munitions and Supply, Clarence Decatur Howe, could not have organized war production efficiently had it not been for a significant change in the Allied strategic situation. The rout of the French in 1940 obliged Great Britain to order enormous quantities of military materiel from Canada, and this tolled the knell of Canada's policy of "limited engagement". As the Acting President of the National Research Council, Dr. Chalmers Jack Mackenzie, observed: "[the nation] embarked upon an all-out programme of military preparation, industrial production, and financial commitments that staggered the imagination."[17]

1.1.2 The Opening of the Scientific Front in Canada

After their victory over Poland, the Germans held back their attack against the allied nations. Between September 1939 and May 1940, the situation was stagnating between the belligerent parties on the western front, such that this would later be called the "phony war". The end of the "phony war" marked the turning point in British-Canadian scientific collaboration. Beforehand, Great Britain had serious reservations about sharing all its military secrets with Canada: the risk of having its know-how and inventions exploited by North American industry after the war seemed too high in relation to the advantages that could be gained from total collaboration with its former Dominion.[18] The surrender of France ended all hesitations of the British Government, which henceforth was willing to reveal, unconditionally, all its defence science secrets in exchange for Canadian and American support for its war effort.

This was the context in which Sir Henry Tizard, Rector of Imperial College and Chairman of the Aeronautical Research Committee, was charged with heading a scientific mission to North America. During August and September 1940, he paved the way for the fullest and freest collaboration between Britain and the two North American powers. In addition to making arrangements for basic information exchange between the three countries, the mission established a list of priorities for military research. Canada was invited to participate to the extent of its scientific potential. In fact, Canada's contribution proved to be particularly notable in the areas of radar, RDX explosives, nuclear physics, medical research, aerodynamics, etc.

Canada's success was due in large part to the National Research Council (NRC) which was responsible for coordinating and directing military research throughout the Second World War and for maintaining scientific liaison with the Allies. This role properly belonged to NRC since, "apart from scientific activities concerning national resources, Canada had had little competence and no international standing in the field of 'big science'. The only establishment of any size in this category was at the National Research Council."[19] It was understandable, therefore, that "when war broke out in 1939 its function as the scientific arm of government became increasingly apparent,"[20] with the Army, Navy and Air Force comprising the government's military arm.

1.1.2.1 The National Research Council of Canada and Military Research prior to 1939

The role of NRC during the war can only be properly understood in the context of its origins, which date back to the

First World War when Great Britain was forced to react to the scientific and technical superiority of Germany. In July 1915, Britain established a permanent scientific and industrial research committee with the aim of coordinating and mobilizing the collectivity of scientific and industrial resources.[21] In Canada, there were increasing calls throughout 1915 for the establishment of a similar body. Early in 1916, the government of Great Britain suggested to the Dominion Government that a committee be formed "in order that the ingenuity and skill of Canadian scientists in all branches might be brought to bear on the many urgent problems"[22] which appeared as the war unfolded. Bowing to these internal and external pressures, the Canadian Government, on 6 June, created a committee charged with studying the issue. In November, after receiving the committee's recommendations, Ottawa established an Honourary Advisory Committee for Scientific and Industrial Research to "foster, stimulate and coordinate scientific and industrial research in Canada."[23] This body would also be responsible for contributing to the war effort.

The embryonic state of Canadian science was, however, a serious impediment to the fulfilment of the Committee's mandate. In 1916, Canada had no "government laboratories or research facilities"[24] and industrial research was practically non-existent.[25] Indeed, only the universities had "research laboratories of any consequence" but the chronic lack of funds often prevented them from bringing their research efforts to fruition.[26] To compound the problem, Canada suffered at the time from an acute shortage of people with sufficient post-graduate training to "permit any general application of [independent] scientific research to Canadian industrial problems."[27]

The Committee reacted swiftly to redress this state of affairs, mainly by providing the laboratories with equipment and qualified technicians, and by setting up advisory committees.[28] However, as Goodspeed observes, the scientific infrastructure was in such an embryonic state that the "committee could, for a considerable time, do little more than make a survey of the problem."[29] Be that as it may, Canada's scientific potential remained rudimentary until the end of hostilities. The Council simply could not make up for lost time in the short time frame available.

On the other hand, from the time of their first meetings, the members of the Committee undertook to provide Canada with the means to rectify the situation and thus fulfilled their primary mission. The Committee adopted a series of measures to support national research and to foster better post-graduate education opportunities for Canadian researchers. Due, in part, to this scientific support program, Canada was to witness the emergence of an experienced scientific group and the creation of "strong, scientific, graduate schools."[30]

In 1918, to compensate for Canada's deficient scientific infrastructure, the Committee proposed that a national research institute be built in Ottawa. Although the government showed interest, no action was taken because of the unfavourable budgetary environment. Canada had to wait until 1924 before Parliament adopted the Research Council Act. During the following year, temporary laboratories were built, but it was only in 1928 that the government authorized the construction of permanent laboratories. The NRC immediately set about drawing up plans for its "temple of science" and recruiting scientific staff to make it operational.[31] In 1930, in the midst of economic crisis, the construction work started. At the time of its formal inauguration in 1932, the laboratory consisted of five Divisions: Chemistry, Applied Biology, Research Information, Electrical Engineering, and Physics. Four years later, the Division of Mechanical Engineering was added.[32]

In 1935, with Major General McNaughton as its new President, the NRC took a major turn in the orientation of its research. A former military researcher, General McNaughton reintroduced a clearly military flavour to new research projects undertaken by the Council and injected new impetus to projects already underway. Earlier, in 1926, General McNaughton had co-invented a method "of using the cathode-ray tube for radio direction-finding ... [and] had obtained a patent on a device which, with some extension of the meaning, might be called a radar."[33] Not surprisingly, he was fully familiar with the work of Henderson in the Radio Section on long-wave cathode-ray direction-finders. In 1938, Henderson undertook work for the RCAF "on an instrument suitable for use by [the Aviation] at ground stations for direction finding on signals from aircraft." As a result, Canada was not caught off guard in March 1939 when asked to participate in developmental work on radar (Radio Direction and Ranging).[34] According to Eggleston, McNaughton had even anticipated the essentials of military research for the Second World War by initiating a series of scientific projects in the areas of ballistics, chemical warfare and, of course, radio detection.[35]

On the other hand, it would be erroneous to believe that NRC's actions were adequate to redress the effects of inertia in defence research that Canada had experienced throughout these long years. Undoubtedly, Major General McNaughton's initiatives helped to develop internal expertise in some particular areas of military research but, even by 1939, Canada had only a limited number of experts in these areas. Nonetheless, Canada was in a much better position in 1939 than in 1914 to help its allies on the scientific front because its scientific potential was appreciably greater, in terms of both personnel and scientific infrastructure.

1.1.2.2 The National Research Council of Canada and Military Research during the Second World War

In September 1939, NRC had its own research centre and some 300 public servants, of whom 80 were scientists, with which to pursue its research program.[36] Its annual budget at the time was a little less than one million dollars. The members of the Council quickly buckled down to the task and authorized the construction of buildings needed for conducting studies on aeronautical engineering problems. While increasing its capacity to conduct research, NRC did not lose sight of its primary mission, i.e. to achieve the highest possible degree of coordination in research. This was accomplished by conducting a survey of the potential of all the research organizations across the country. NRC then proceeded to seek close collaboration with departmental laboratories, industrial organizations, universities and the Armed Forces so as to direct the combined effort "to the solution of new and urgent problems arising out of the War."[37] But the "phony war" on the European Front and Canada's defence policy slowed the momentum because research programs received less than adequate funding.[38]

But things changed radically after the fall of France. Great Britain negotiated a scientific cooperation agreement with the United States and Canada, which gave us access to a phenomenal amount of scientific information. For their part, Canadian businessmen spontaneously contributed significant sums for scientific research. According to Dr. Chalmers Jack Mackenzie, this venture capital immediately provided scientists with the necessary financial means to conduct their research programs. At the same time, the Canadian Government recognized that the war against Germany would be total war, and spared no effort in optimizing the nation's scientific potential. NRC adopted new research policies which would guide research efforts throughout the war. As NRC's Acting President, Dr. Mackenzie, so vividly put it: "The pure scientist becomes an engineer overnight. It's not a matter of different techniques but a matter of nearness of objective. Long-term fundamental research is for times of peace. In a war for survival, we live on our capital and work for today."[39]
In addition, NRC pursued its role as "a central coordinating body directing scientific research in Canada"[40] by strengthening its partnership with the three Services of the Canadian Armed Forces and their respective headquarters. This is an important point because, in July 1940, the Department of National Defence (DND) was split into "three departments, each presided over by a separate minister of the Crown, all however, cooperating in closest relationship with each other."[41] The government confirmed the

importance of NRC for the three Services by officially designating it "the civilian research establishment of the Navy, Army and Air Force."[42]

For all these reasons, military research in Canada enjoyed an unprecedented boom in a multitude of often unexplored directions. For example, Canada was a participant in the scientific challenge to build "a first atomic reactor, required for developing the atomic bomb"[43], in the laboratories of the Université de Montréal. Under NRC supervision, this research resulted, in September 1945, in the first operational atomic pile outside the United States. Canada was also the first nation "to achieve mass-production of microwave radar fire-control instruments".[44] Canadian scientists also discovered a new formula for producing an extremely powerful explosive, known as RDX, based on "the reaction of ammonium nitrate with hexamine in the presence of acetic anhydride."[45] Canada's scientific contribution was not, however, confined to these single successes; it was recognized worldwide in many areas:

> "aids to the Navy in mine and submarine detection, control of gunfire and other ballistics problems, new and more powerful explosives, emergency methods of food storage and transport under war conditions, development of special types of clothing and other equipment for Navy, Army and Air Force requirements. Problems relating to the physical well-being of troops involved studies in nutrition, housing, sanitation, medical examination of recruits and treatment of the injured and sick."[46]

As impressive as this list of accomplishments may be, it is still only a pale reflection of Canada's actual contribution; most Canadian scientific laboratories contributed to the war effort, and space precludes any detailed description.[47]

According to Eggleston, 20 major associate research

Some of the original scientists. From left to right: Dr. Don C. Rose, who would later become the first Chief Superintendent of CARDE; an unidentified individual; Dr. Keith Laidler; Mr. Gordon D. Watson. (Gordon D. Watson collection).

committees and about a hundred sub-committees were operated under the aegis of the National Research Council of Canada. It also contributed to 280 research projects spread across 30 independent laboratories and cooperated in joint research programs with Great Britain and the United States. To fulfil all its responsibilities, NRC built 21 additional laboratories[48] and employed, for its own purposes, over 2,000 persons including 450 scientists.[49]

1.2 FORMATION OF THE VALCARTIER RESEARCH ESTABLISHMENTS DURING THE WAR

1.2.1 The Location Factor: Proximity of the Dominion Arsenal

In the pervading climate of urgency to mobilize all national resources, scientists quickly sought the expertise that had been developed by Canada's sole government arsenal. The Dominion Arsenal, owned and operated by the government since its foundation in 1879, mostly produced military munitions. Its main activities were concentrated at a location inside the Quebec fortifications, although some were conducted at a laboratory built in 1881 and located on the Plains of Abraham. Just prior to the war, a new arsenal was built in Valcartier as part of an unemployment relief project, and which gradually established its operations during the summer of 1938. In August 1939, the Department of National Defence (DND) decided to consign all production of small arms ammunition to the Dominion Arsenal. Faced with this influx of orders, its management acquired the Saint-Malo Factories and proceeded to triple the production area. This allowed the management to rationalize production by assigning specific work to each of the three components. The

Construction work on the Explosives Experimental Establishment (EEE) in 1943.

Quebec Arsenals produced the munitions while the Valcartier Arsenal charged and assembled them. The latter site was selected for these dangerous operations because of its relative isolation.[50]

Military Inspection Services, which were responsible for quality control of munitions, had a small Proof Establishment at Little River (Duberger), close to the Dominion Arsenal in Quebec City. In the late 1930's, because of the apparent dilapidation of this facility, it was decided to relocate the establishment to Valcartier.[51] Construction work on the establishment was accelerated in January 1940 to accommodate the mounting need for proofing of ammunition.[52] In October of the same year, the Dominion Arsenal passed under the jurisdiction of the Department of Munitions and Supply.

1.2.2   Creation of a Military Technology Complex in Valcartier

In October 1940, in a climate of frenzied munitions production, the United Kingdom and Canada decided to establish a single inspection organization to be known as the Inspection Board of the United Kingdom and Canada.[53] In the context of total war, the facilities of the Valcartier Proof Establishment were inadequate, to say the least, and the Inspection Board decided to construct a number of additional facilities. These were designed to improve artillery proofing and also accommodate small arms proofing. With the impetus given by the Inspection Board, the Artillery Proof and Development Establishment (APDE) burgeoned and the Small Arms Proof and Experimental Establishment (SAPEE) was born.[54]

According to Goodspeed, the APDE facilities were completed in early 1942, and construction of the SAPEE facilities were well underway. One of the main functions of the APDE was "to see that the propellants which go to the gunners in the field have been adjusted to give the greatest possible accuracy when fired."[55] SAPEE augmented testing and experimentation on small arms and collaborated with the APDE in testing grenades and projectiles for the Projector Infantry Anti-Tank (PIAT) weapon. Interestingly enough, SAPEE conducted many firing tests on small arms exceeding 20-mm calibre without any "sand range and accuracy strip" throughout the entire war.[56]

During this period:

> "many new instruments for measurement and new experimental techniques were introduced and adopted to speed up proof and inspection and to meet the accuracies required by more modern types of weapons. Instruments developed in the NRC were placed at the Artillery Proof Establishment at Valcartier and it soon became apparent that a qualified scientist was essential to keep these in operation and to assist with problems in external ballistics as they arose. Changes in basic ingredients in propellants so that materials available could be used to meet the rapidly rising supply requirement introduced new problems in internal ballistic solutions and measurements."[57]

Clearly, "with the application of new electronic instruments to ballistic proof and the rapid introduction of propellant materials"[58], the support of one resident NRC expert supplemented with frequent visits from other NRC experts, was no longer adequate to resolve all the problems which arose in the work of the Inspection Board Proof Establishment at Valcartier (proof, corrective development and experimental investigations). The Establishment needed an increased level of permanent scientific assistance. Accordingly, NRC and the British each assigned two scientists to the Establishment, while the Canadian Army and the University of Manitoba each assigned one.[59] The Inspection Board decided to hire these scientists directly, mainly because "they had more freedom in making appointments and paying acceptable salaries for scientific work than had the NRC."⁶⁰ This scientific section formed the nucleus around which the Internal Ballistics Research Laboratory (IRBL) would later be structured.

In August 1942, the Army Technical Development Board approved a grant of $450,000 for the construction of an Explosives Experimental Establishment (EEE) under the aegis of NRC. The Acting President of NRC considered many possible sites for the Establishment, but two in particular attracted his attention. The first was the new site for the Council's laboratories in Ottawa, and the second was Valcartier.⁶¹ Dr. Chalmers J. Mackenzie finally opted for the Valcartier site for the following reasons. First, he held the work of the Dominion Arsenal in high esteem and he was assured of the assistance of its superintendent, Brigadier Thériault.⁶² Second, the site would be close to the other Valcartier facilities. Finally, Mackenzie was sufficiently far-sighted to recognize that such a concentration of scientific expertise held the potential for creating "a valuable centre of scientific interest in that part of Quebec which could be carried on after the war."⁶³

Once the decision was taken, NRC set about planning the construction and creation of this establishment. Construction began in 1943. One year later, the laboratories for physical and chemical research on explosives were opened, together with a pilot plant for the manufacture of explosives and propellants.⁶⁴ According to Goodspeed, NRC quickly secured the technical assistance of the British who considered this project so important that they sent one of their scientists, Dr. Harold Poole, to Canada to direct the new research establishment. A small research group was already in place when Poole arrived. His task was to plan and supervise the work of this group and to foster the development of the Establishment. From the start, Dr. Poole ensured that the Establishment would be able "to develop new manufacturing processes for explosives and to develop analytical methods for process control and for the control of material quality of the explosives being made in Canadian factories."⁶⁵ According to Goodspeed, the researchers progressively used the facilities to study the stability of explosives and their compatibility with other materials with which they came into contact. Eventually, research activities encompassed all phases "from fundamental organic chemistry" to pilot-plant fabrication of explosives and propellants to test "methods of manufacture on an economical scale."[66]

Finally, at the end of the war, the Armed Forces completed this military technology complex by adding a Trials Wing which reported to the Director of Artillery and was responsible for conducting tests on military equipment.

1.2.3   A Precursor to CARDE: The Ballistics Laboratory

Canada reached the pinnacle of its extraordinary war effort in 1943; it was the fourth largest supplier of armaments and munitions amongst the allied nations and the second largest exporter in the world.[67] Military equipment orders started to decline, however, around the turn of 1944 and the activities of the Inspection Board of the United Kingdom and Canada slowed down. During this period also, there was a profound shake up in the senior management and organizational structure. As a result, the Artillery Proof Establishment was repositioned under the authority of the Directorate of Artillery Ammunition (DAA)[68] and the Small Arms Proof and Experimental Establishment was attached to another directorate.

This was the context in which the new Director of Artillery Ammunition expressed the desire for greater cooperation between the Department of National Defence and the Inspection Board so as to exercise better control over research and engineering development.[69] Whether Colonel Abinett had the Valcartier Proof and Development Establishment specifically in mind is not known. We do know, however, that the Proof Officer at Valcartier was experiencing increasing difficulty in coordinating and controlling the relentlessly mounting flow of demands for research and testing from the Director Artillery (DA) on behalf of the Master General of Ordnance of the Canadian Army.

Senior officers of the Inspection Board of the United Kingdom and Canada together with the concerned Services of the Department met in Ottawa on 5 January 1944 to resolve this problem. Abinett's precise position during this discussion is not known. We are aware, however, of the general understanding that was reached on that day. Both parties identified the priorities of the Establishment in greater detail, and agreed that the test program would always take precedence over the research work.

Members of the NRC Propellants Subcommittee photographed at the entrance to the Internal Ballistics Research Laboratory of the Inspection Board of the United Kingdom and Canada in March 1944. From left to right, back row: Mr. Gordon D. Watson, Dr. Nathan Mendlesohn, Dr. Jason Greenblatt, LCol Caddy. Centre row: Dr. Humphrys, Capt Halperin, Mr. Miller, Dr. Keith Laidler, Mr. Leslie Barnes. Front row: Mr. Cheetham, Prof. G.F. Wright, Dr. Harold J. Poole, Committee Chairman, and Dr. J.S. Tapp, Committee Secretary. (Gordon D. Watson collection)

Once this principle was accepted, the military would try to better control the flow of work by defining everyone's responsibilities.

First, they considered it appropriate to appoint a representative of the Director Artillery of the Canadian Army at Valcartier who would submit, in writing, all Service requests for research and testing to the Proof Officer.[70] They then specified that the Proof Officer would be responsible for authorizing the start of research work. Finally, according to one of the participants, the representative of the DA "will act as liaison officer in carrying out the work."[71] Following this agreement, the DA asked the Valcartier Proof Officer to authorize the initiation of a research program on the effects of low temperature on munitions, and detailed several other programs to be conducted subsequently.[72]

This compromise solution proved to be temporary, for the Deputy Controller of the Inspection Board, the DA and the Master General of Ordnance of the Department reached a new agreement in March 1944. On this occasion they arrived at the conclusion that the best solution would be to make the Establishment's scientific section a separate unit directly under the control of the Department, and decided that this unit would henceforth be known as the Ballistics Laboratory.

Once this was agreed in principle, they had to concede to the reality of circumstances. The Department of National Defence was not, at the time, administratively prepared to absorb this laboratory. Faced with this situation, both parties agreed that the scientific section would be organized in the following way. The Director Artillery of the Canadian Army would be responsible for supervision and technical direction, while the Inspection Board of the United Kingdom and Canada would retain administrative control and assume the operational costs. This agreement was effective from 1 May 1944 to 1 October 1944. At the end of this period, the laboratory would either be absorbed by the Department or return to the fold of the Inspection Board.[73]

1	Desmond Morton, *Canada and War: A Military and Political History*, Toronto, Butterworths, 1981, p. 82.
2	George F.G. Stanley, *Canada's Soldiers, 1604-1954, The Military History of an Unmilitary People*, Toronto, Macmillan, 1954, p. 327.
3	Desmond Morton, *op. cit.*, p. 97.
4	George F.G. Stanley, *op. cit.*, p. 330.
5	Col C.P. Stacey, *Arms, Men and Governments: The War Policies of Canada 1935-1945*, Ottawa, Queen's Printer, p. 3.
6	Brian Cuthbertson, *Canadian Military Independence in the Age of the Superpowers*, Don Mills Ontario, Fitzhenry & Whiteside, 1977, p. 9.
7	Capt D.J. Goodspeed, *A History of the Defence Research Board*, Ottawa, Queen's Printer, 1958, p. 112.
8	Col C.P. Stacey, *op.cit.*, p. 3.
	Brian Cuthbertson, *op. cit.*, p. 9.
10	Rénald Fortier, *Intervention gouvernementale et industrie aéronautique: L'exemple canadien 1920-1945*, Doctoral Thesis, Québec, Université Laval, 1990, p. 108.
11	George F.G. Stanley, *op. cit.*, p. 335.
12	Rénald Fortier, *op. cit.*, p. 618.
13	Desmond Morton, *op. cit.*, p. 101-102.
14	George F.G. Stanley, *op. cit.*, p. 339. C.P. Stacey, *op. cit.*, p. 6.
15	J.L. Granatstein, "Indépendance et dépendance. La politique étrangère du Canada pendant la Seconde Guerre mondiale", *Revue d'histoire de la deuxième guerre mondiale*, Vol. 104 (October 1976), p. 50.
16	Col C.P. Stacey, *op. cit.*, p. 11.
17	Wilfrid Eggleston, *Scientists at War*, London, Oxford University Press, 1950, p. 17.
18	*Ibid.*, p. 15.
19	Gen. A.G.L. McNaughton and C.J. Mackenzie, *The Mackenzie-McNaughton Wartime Letters*, Toronto, University of Toronto Press, 1975, p. 135.
20	Canada, *Year Book 1940*, Ottawa, Dominion Bureau of Statistics/Department of Trade and Commerce, 1941, p. 980.
21	J.H. Parkin, *Aeronautical Research in Canada 1917-1957*, Ottawa, NRC, 1983, p. 317.
22	Canada, *Year Book 1947*, Dominion Bureau of Statistics/Department of Trade and Commerce 1948, p. 300.
23	Canada, *Year Book 1945*, Ottawa, Dominion Bureau of Statistics/Department of Trade and Commerce 1946, p. lii.
24	Capt D.J. Goodspeed, *op. cit.*, p. 5.
25	Canada *Year Book 1947*, p. 300.
26	Canada, *Year Book 1932*, Ottawa, Dominion Bureau of Statistics/Department of Trade and Commerce 1933, p. 867.

27 Canada, *Year Book 1947*, p. 300.
28 Canada, *Year Book 1932*, p. 867.
29 Capt D.J. Goodspeed, *op. cit.*, p. 5.
30 Canada, *Year Book 1945*, p. lii.
31 Wilfrid Eggleston, *National Research in Canada: The NRC 1916-1966*, Toronto, Clarke Irwin, 1978, p. 21-55.
32 Canada, *Year Book 1947*, p. 300.
33 J.J. Brown, *Ideas in Exile: A History of Canadian Invention*, Toronto/Montreal, McClelland & Steward, 1967, p. 253.
34 Wilfrid Eggleston, *NRC...*, p. 147.
35 Wilfrid Eggleston, *Scientists...*, p. 13.
36 O.M. Solandt, "Scientific Research in the Modern World", *Dalhousie Review*, No. 27 (Summer 1957), p. 142.
37 Canada, *Year Book 1943-44*, Ottawa, Dominion Bureau of Statistics/Department of Trade and Commerce 1945, p. xlvii.
38 Wilfrid Eggleston, *Scientists...*, p. 15-16.
39 Wilfrid Eggleston, *NRC...*, p. 173-174.
40 Canada, *Year Book 1943-44*, p. xlvii.
41 *House of Commons Debates*, 8 July 1940, p. 1398; see also *Statutes of Canada 1940*, Chap. 21.
42 Canada, *Year Book...1947*, p. 301.
43 Luc Chartrand et al., *Histoire des sciences au Québec*, Boréal, Montreal, 1987, p. 141.
44 Wilfrid Eggleston, *Scientists...*, p. 22.
45 C.J.S. Warrington and R.V.V. Nicholls, *A History of Chemistry in Canada*, Toronto, Pitman Publishing in Canada, 1949, p. 317.
46 Canada, *Year Book...1947*, p. 301.
47 The interested reader is referred to the two volumes of Eggleston.
48 Wilfrid Eggleston, *Scientists...*, p. 13-14.
49 O.M. Solandt, "Scientific Research...", *Dalhousie Review*, p. 143.
50 Alain Gelly, *Importance et incidence de l'industrie des munitions sur la structure industrielle de Québec 1879-1946*, Master's Thesis, Québec, Université Laval, 1989.
51 J. Mackay Hitsman, *Military Inspection Services in Canada 1855-1950*, Ottawa, DND Inspection Services, 1962, p. 40.
52 *Ibid.*, p. 52.
53 J. de N. Kennedy, *History of the Department of Munitions and Supply: Canada in the Second World War*, Volume 2, Ottawa, Queen's Printer, 1950, p. 438.
54 Capt D.J. Goodspeed, *op. cit.*, p. 114.
55 *Ibid.*
56 J. Mackay Hitsman, *op. cit.*, p. 101.

57	D.C. Rose, *Historical Background of CARDE*, Valcartier, undated, p. 1.
58	*DREV Annual Report 1969*, p. 1.
59	Capt D.J. Goodspeed, *op. cit.*, p. 115.
60	D.C. Rose, *op. cit.*, p. 1.
61	Wilfrid Eggleston, *NRC...*, p. 245.
62	Gen. A.G.L. McNaughton and C.J. Mackenzie, *op. cit.*, p. 101 and 122.
63	*Ibid.*, p. 122.
64	*DREV Annual Report 1969*, p. 1.
65	Capt D.J. Goodspeed, *op. cit.*, p. 117.
66	*Ibid.*
67	NAC, RG 28, Vol. 1, *Release 478A*, p. 1.
68	J. Mackay Hitsman, *op. cit.*, p. 80 and 85.
69	*Ibid.*, p. 68.
70	NAC, Reel C-5170, HQS 8236-5, Vol. 1, *Deputy MGO to Controller-General of I.B. of U.K. and Canada*, 7 January 1944.
71	NAC, Reel C-5170, HQS 8236-5, Vol. 1, *Lt. Halperin, Directorate of Artillery to Director of Artillery*, 19 January 1944.
72	*Ibid.*, 7 and 19 January 1944.
73	NAC, Reel C-5170, HQS 8236-5, Vol. 1, *Appendix "G" Minute 1038*, and *Ransford to MGO*, 2 April 1944.

> *"If politics is the art of the possible, research is surely the art of the soluble. Both are immensely practical-minded affairs."* (Sir Peter Medewar)
>
> *"Research and development of new weapons must, therefore, be one of the fundamental principles of our new defence policy."* (Gen Charles Foulkes)[1]

2

ARMAMENTS AT THE FORE: THE CANADIAN ARMAMENT RESEARCH AND DEVELOPMENT ESTABLISHMENT (CARDE) 1945-1950

2.1 THE POST-WAR PERIOD AND THE IMPORTANCE OF MILITARY RESEARCH

With the Allies advancing relentlessly on all fronts, it was clear that victory was at hand. In Canada, orders for military equipment declined dramatically, as did the need for military research. The time for making decisions was drawing near. Canada had to decide whether the scientific potential so meticulously developed during the war should be allowed to collapse. Action had to be taken quickly, for the scientific teams would soon start to disperse throughout North America.

Since the start of hostilities, scientists had frequently demonstrated the importance of technological advance as a decisive factor determining victory or defeat on the battlefield. In 1944, Nazi propaganda threatened the Allies with imminent attack by Hitler's famous "secret weapons", and London was bombarded with V1 and V2 missiles. Succinctly,

> "in matters of national defence the scientist now had to

play a role of equal importance to that played by the soldier, the sailor or the airman, and that the difference between victory or defeat in the future would depend, far more than ever before in the past, upon the preparations which had been made before the outbreak of hostilities."[2]

In his book, Goodspeed recounts the events which led to the creation of an organization structure for Canadian military research in the immediate post-war era. Only the main elements will be summarized herein. In July 1944, the Director General of Air Research suggested the formation of a Committee on Research for Defence in order to prepare for Canada's next research endeavours. The Cabinet War Committee examined the issue and agreed in principle in October 1944. An ad hoc committee was struck in January 1945 to determine the composition of the proposed committee and, in August 1945 the government approved its formation. The new committee had to answer the crucial question: "What form should defence research take in Canada after the war?"[3]

2.1.1 Defence Research Policy in the Immediate Post-War Period

According to Goodspeed, the appointment of General Charles Foulkes as Chief of the General Staff in August 1945 was an important factor in the events that were to follow. During the 1939-1945 conflict, General Foulkes had become aware of the importance of military research in the conduct of warfare. He considered that Canadian military research should not focus on marginal improvements to existing weapons but instead on developing weapons systems and equipment for the decade ahead.[4]

At the end of the Second World War, a great number of military planners seem to have believed that military research could be conducted jointly by the three fighting Services and NRC. General Foulkes was not convinced that this would be the best solution because "the military scientific effort of the nation was too vital a thing for it to be influenced by inter-Service rivalries."[5] Remembering the lessons of the past, he also envisaged the possible imposition of cutbacks in the defence budget which would induce the various Services "in hard times to economize on those expenditures which did not produce an immediate and tangible result."[6] In any event, the latter approach was hardly viable since NRC intended to concentrate all its efforts on structuring Canadian research towards meeting peacetime needs. The President of NRC considered that military research and civilian research each required special attention and that NRC could not manage both at once.[7] He asked, therefore, that NRC be released from its military research responsibilities so that it could concentrate on civilian research.

The issue was further complicated by the fact that one of the basic principles in Canadian defence policy was the traditional alliance with Great Britain. During the Second World War, however, Canada had drawn appreciably closer to the United States. By the end of the war, the Canadian Armed Forces still used British equipment but the Canadian defence industry used North American production methods. Under these circumstances, Canada could only hope for standardization of military materiel between its two allies.[8] As well, the human and material resources that Canada could apply to defence research "were very limited."[9] To make the best use of its resources, Canada had to limit its number of areas of research. This was the perspective from which Canada proposed pursuing scientific collaboration with its Anglo-American partners and dividing the effort in accordance with the potential of the each nation. In other words, Canada sought to pursue a lower level of scientific effort and collaboration during peacetime than that set in motion by the three nations during the Second World War.

2.1.2 An Innovative Notion: The Fourth Service

This was the situation when Colonel W.W. Goforth, Director of Staff Duties (Weapons), sent General Foulkes a document entitled *The Future of Canadian Army Research and Development*. In it, Goforth painted an excellent picture of the situation surrounding Canadian defence research in 1945, and submitted four proposals for the future framework of military research. The first proposal envisaged assigning all defence research and development, except for operational research, to NRC. The second envisaged the creation of a new government department responsible for applied industrial and defence research. The third envisaged affirming Army responsibility for the research infrastructures that it had recently set up. These first three proposals were not entirely unanticipated and, as Goodspeed observes, did not appear as a bolt from the blue. It was just the opposite for Goforth's fourth proposal, which was:

> "to regard research for defence as a single concept and to reorganize research and development for all Services with appropriate scientific representation into a new (fourth) sub-department of National Defence with a representative on the Chiefs of Staff Committee but with a vote of public funds separate from the Service votes."[10]

The concept of a fourth Service was born, and it was this last proposal that won support.

For Goforth, the first proposal had many advantages but was virtually impossible to implement because NRC would not consider it. He considered the second proposal as equally impractical, because the responsibility for the defence of the nation was essentially indivisible. The technological functions of defence could not be separated from the strategic, tactical and administrative duties without impairment to the defence program in general. In the third proposal, Goforth put forward the possibility of consolidating scientific research infrastructures under Army responsibility. Amongst the advantages of this approach was that it paralleled the British and American structures and ensured the retention of a team of military researchers. Goforth argued, however, that this solution did not take account of the realities of the atomic age, nor "take adequate account of the essential inter-Service character of research and development for defence."[11] Goforth considered, therefore, that the only possible solution was the fourth, for it recognized that "details might well be questioned, but never the need for the application of scientific knowledge to the whole peacetime defence problem."[12] It would lessen the difficulties of recruiting civilian scientists and avoid the risk of duplication inherent to the existing military research structure. Goforth was well aware, however, of the difficulties that would be encountered in convincing the two other Services of his point of view and of the time that would be needed - at least 18 months - to establish this fourth service.

According to Goodspeed, Goforth's appreciation found immediate favour with General Foulkes, who sent copies of the document to the Chief of the Naval Staff and the Chief of the Air Staff. On 5 October, he gave them in writing his agreement in principle for the integration of the research and development establishments controlled by their respective Services and asked for their approval. This was the context in which the Chief of the Naval Staff gave his consent to this principle. Goodspeed observes, however, that there was no indication that he had any intention of relinquishing the Halifax establishment. As for the position of the Chief of the Air Staff, Goodspeed found no formal record confirming his agreement with Foulkes' suggestions. But the position held by the Royal Canadian Air Force was that "the control of research projects could best be implemented by the establishment of working groups under the Committee on Research for Defence and that a separate vote of funds would be required."[13]

In any event, General Foulkes sent a note to his Minister entitled Post-War Policy for Scientific Research and Development in the Canadian Army. In this short text, Foulkes stressed the four principles that should underpin military research and sought ministerial approval for a three-phase implementation plan, being careful to explain that it had received the approval of the other Chiefs of Staff. The first phase of this plan called for the consolidation of the research infrastructure established by the three Services.[14] This phase was, in fact, well underway, judging by the number of research and development establishments already in operation relative to the number planned. Indeed, the Army alone, which controlled six such establishments at the time, had plans for two additional establishments, while the Air Force already operated five and the Navy operated one.[15]

Figure 1- Research Establishments Managed by One of the Three Services of the Canadian Armed Forces or Jointly Managed with the United States at the End of the Second World War.

Research Establishments managed by the Army:

Canadian Armament Research and Development Establishment, Valcartier

Vehicle Design and Development Establishment, Ottawa

Chemical Warfare Laboratories, Ottawa

Canadian Signals and Radar Development Establishment, Ottawa

Inter-Service Research and Development Establishment (General Stores), Ottawa

No. 1 Airborne Research and Development Centre, Shilo (Manitoba)

Research Establishments planned by the Army:

Royal Canadian Engineers Research Establishment

Small Arms Design and Development Section

Research Establishments managed by the Royal Canadian Navy:

Naval Research Establishment, Halifax

Research Establishments managed by the Royal Canadian Air Force:

Test and Development Establishment, Rockliffe

Winter Experimental Establishment, Edmonton

Photographic Research Establishment and Radio Wave Propagation Unit, Ottawa

Institute of Aviation Medicine, Toronto

Research Establishment operated by NRC with Royal Canadian Air Force involvement:

Flight Research Station, Arnprior

Joint Canada/United States Research Project:

War Disease Control Station, Grosse Île (Québec)

Research Establishment under joint Canada/United States responsibility:

Chemical Warfare Experimental Station, Suffield (Alberta)

Source: Goodspeed, D.J., *A History of the Defence Research Board*, Ottawa, Queen's Printer, 1958, p. 9.

Foulkes planned to implement Goforth's recommendation in January 1947 during the second phase. Finally, Foulkes suggested, in the third phase, the creation of a new department, the Department of Research, which would regroup defence related research.[16] After Foulkes sent the document to the Minister, the number of meetings between the three Service Chiefs of Staff and the President NRC multiplied.

On 4 December 1945, the Cabinet Committee on Research for Defence met in the office of the Minister, C.D. Howe. The members concluded that Goforth's proposal amounted to no more than a reorganization within the Department of National Defence. They considered, therefore, that a Cabinet submission was not required and that the appointment of the first Director General of Defence Research could be approved by Order-in-Council.[17] Fifteen days later, the Cabinet confirmed this judgement.

2.1.3   Founding of the Defence Research Board (DRB)

According to Goodspeed, following the 4 December meeting of the Cabinet Committee on Research for Defence, a few members met privately to list the potential candidates for the position of Director General of Defence Research. After some deliberation, the nomination went to Colonel Omond M. Solandt, then stationed in England. Solandt accepted the challenge and was appointed by Order-in-Council on 28 December 1945. For Goodspeed, this was the first official act heralding the formation of the Defence Research Board (DRB).

Since the new Director General of Defence Research had to be a civilian, no time was lost in demobilizing the Colonel and repatriating him to Canada.[18] On 15 February 1946, shortly after his return to Canada, Solandt officially assumed his duties. His first task was to develop guidelines for instituting the new organization. In July, open opposition to the project from the Royal Canadian Air Force (RCAF) put everything back into question. In October, after three different organizational models had been contemplated, it was decided that the Defence Research Board should have powers similar to those of NRC, but that it would be closely linked to the Department. Despite negotiations, latent resistance to the project persisted.[19]

On 12 December 1946, the Minister of National Defence for Naval Services and the Minister of National Defence for Air relinquished their functions and Brooke Claxton was appointed as the one and only Minister of National Defence. Claxton merged all personnel, including the headquarters of all three Services, in one physical location.[20] According to the Annual Report of DND, this regrouping was aimed at furthering the expansion of defence research work. Claxton, the energetic politician that he was, came down in favour of a separate defence research organization. To legalize his decision, Claxton tabled a Bill, on 7 February 1947, to amend the National Defence Act. On 28 March 1947, the Act to Amend the National Defence Act received royal assent.

This authorized the creation of a Defence Research Board and designated the Director General of Defence Research as its Chairman.[21] Earlier, "an interim advisory board known as the Defence Research Board" had been formed to assist the Director General and his staff.[22] The mandate of the new organization was to advise the Minister on all matters relating to scientific, technical and other research and development which affect national defence. It was also responsible for conducting defence research and development programs and for providing financial support for both defence-related basic research conducted in Canadian universities and defence-related applied research conducted in Canadian industry.[23]

2.2 THE CREATION OF CARDE

2.2.1 Steps Taken by the Director of Artillery

In 1944, officers of the Department of National Defence (Army) became concerned that the expertise developed by Canada in the area of military research could disperse, and that a major part of the scientific infrastructure built up during the war could collapse. They had to act swiftly, for "the dissipation of these unique teams would probably require not less than ten years to replace, in the slower tempo of peace."[24] The key pieces of scientific infrastructure were quickly identified and ways were sought to retain them. One priority was to preserve the integrity of the Valcartier research establishments.

It was clear to observers at the time that NRC would not

continue to operate its Explosives Experimental Establishment, and moreover the fate of the Ballistics Laboratory had still to be decided. Senior military officers intensified the frequency of their inter-Service meetings and came to the conclusion that the Valcartier research centres had to be integrated within a single major establishment. They decided also that such an establishment should be operated by the Director Artillery on behalf of the Master General of Ordnance of the Canadian Army. It was only a matter of time before the Canadian Armament Research and Development Establishment (CARDE) would see the light of day.

Shortly before the end of September 1944, the military interests surrounding the formation of the establishment had been decided. On 1 October, the Department of National Defence confirmed them by ministerial order. Plans for the Canadian Armament Research and Development Establishment (or the future CARDE) in Valcartier took shape. The project could not be finalized, however, until issues surrounding the employment of civilians had been resolved, and the Privy Council deliberated on the matter in order to establish all the parameters.[25]

As a number of administrative documents show, the Department did not remain inactive during this waiting period. The Director of Artillery, Colonel W.E. van Steenburgh, appointed Major MacAulay as the Establishment Administrative Officer, responsible for all outstanding administrative problems. MacAulay was also responsible, in collaboration with Major Leslie, for supervising the development of the administrative structure of the Establishment and the preparation of plans for new construction.

While Majors MacAulay and Leslie were busy planning for the future, Colonel van Steenburgh concerned himself with maintaining the existing integrity of the Ballistics Laboratory, even though the matter of hiring civilians still remained unsettled. Towards the end of September 1944, the Inspection Board published a list of scientists and technicians soon to be released from the Ballistics Laboratory. Van Steenburgh contacted the Controller General of the Inspection Board and obtained an eleventh-hour reprieve on the termination of their services. In January 1945, he wrote to physicist K.J. Laidler to confirm his appointment as Chief Scientist and Head of the Laboratory, and to outline the approach that Laidler should take in future research programs. Also in this letter, van Steenburgh hastened to confirm that seven particular Laboratory specialists would be retained. Aside from this attempt to consolidate personnel, he started to identify Canadian scientists who would likely want to work at the Laboratory.[26]

In parallel, the Department tried to fill a number of vacant positions at the future research establishment by recruiting personnel from the three Services of the Canadian Armed Forces. According to Lieutenant General Murchie, Chief of General Staff, the new establishment had been authorized a strength of 36 officers and 153 personnel of all ranks and ratings.[27] On 6 March 1945, the Committee of the Privy Council authorized the formation of the Canadian Armament Research and Development Establishment (CARDE). On 8 March 1945, Order-in-Council P.C. 1640 was approved.[28]

2.3 CARDE'S FIRST INITIATIVES UNDER ARMY MANAGEMENT

The mission of the new establishment, as its name indicates, was to conduct scientific research in the area of armaments. This research and development centre "was planned to be inter-Service but operated by the Army."[29] It was the Army, therefore, or more specifically the Artillery Directorate, that assumed the task of integrating within a single organization all the staff of the Internal Ballistics Research Laboratory (IBRL), the Explosives Experimental Establishment (EEE) and the Army's Field Trials Wing. Most of the details concerning this integration are unknown, but it is fair to assume that it had its share of difficulties and that the approach adopted by the Army was able to iron them out.

It was a tall challenge for the Army, because each of the three organizations that had to be integrated within CARDE had its own culture. The Army had a number of options. It could ignore this aspect and distribute the personnel on a new basis. In doing so, it would destroy the autonomy of the organizations but have a better integrated establishment. Another possibility was to group the three agencies in a way that would respect their origins, so allowing them to operate as quasi-autonomous entities within a central supervisory structure. This was the option that the Army finally selected.

The Army favoured a "divisional" structure in which the respective researchers and specialists were grouped in the Ballistics Wing, the Explosives and Propellants Wing and the Trials Wing. Such a structure involved a certain decentralization of power, since the Wing Superintendents had to have the necessary authority to manage their operations. The responsibilities of the Chief Superintendent included exercising control over the Wings by assessing their performance, and ensuring liaison between the research establishment and the external community. Given such a structure, some observers including Solandt gained the impression that the Valcartier Research and Development Establishment "had been formed on paper by the union of several pre-existing organizations, but had never really existed in fact."[30]

Whether the new structure was dictated by circumstance is not known. On the other hand, one cannot help thinking that one of the major factors contributing to the decision to group researchers by field of activity was the perceived need to minimize any negative impact that total integration could have on the scientific work of the research teams. This hypothesis is appealing from more than one standpoint. If true, it might suggest that the administrators, right from the start, adopted the principle that the organizational structure should adapt to the needs of the scientists and not vice versa.

Starting up CARDE was a delicate operation. First of all, the Army had to form a single administrative entity from three different organizations. It then had to recruit the requisite scientific personnel and build the lacking scientific infrastructures. Finally, it had to fulfil its primary mission of setting a program of armaments research in motion. The Army had to find a competent scientist to direct this program, and selected Dr. Donald C. Rose. Dr. Rose had worked for many years at the National Research Council of Canada and, significantly, had acted as Scientific Advisor to the Chief of the General Staff from 1943 to 1945. The first Chief Superintendent of CARDE was "the fire control expert in Canada, from the theoretical standpoint at least"[31] and, by the same token, one of the leading specialists in ballistics in the country. The appointment of Dr. Rose illustrates the importance that the Army attached to the success of the Establishment.

2.3.1   Administrative Integration

The integration of the Ballistics Laboratory and its staff with CARDE started in October 1944 and was completed by mid-April 1945.[32] In 1945, the Army realized that state-of-the-art facilities and equipment meant that trials would be extremely costly to conduct. At the time, the Suffield Experimental Station, the Inspection Board of the United Kingdom and Canada, and the Army were conducting armament trials.[33] In response to the situation, the Army decided to group its activities at Valcartier, under E Wing, with the Army's Field Trial Wing as its core.[34] Integration of the Explosives Experimental Establishment, however, was not as straightforward. In a letter to the Master General of Ordnance dated May 1945, Chief Superintendent Rose indicated that the formation of the Chemistry Wing was not completely finalized. It would appear that the presence of Dr.

Harold Poole was not an irrelevant factor. The Chief Superintendent was not immediately ready to dispense with the services of Poole who was the guiding spirit of the Explosives Experimental Establishment. For that reason, he advanced a series of scenarios which served to delay the effective integration of the EEE with CARDE. Rose could not, however, delay the departure of the British scientist indefinitely, and the EEE had to be integrated with CARDE at the time of Poole's departure, presumably in August 1945.[35] In 1945, a group of eight civil and military engineers joined the ranks of CARDE. According to a DRB report, these researchers were specialists in "army requirements on weapon design and improvements in existing weapons" and they formed "the nucleus and the beginning of the present D Wing."[36] With the arrival of this group, the Establishment then comprised four scientific Wings: the Ballistics Wing, the Chemistry Wing, the Design Wing and the Experimental Wing (see Figure 2 - Organization Chart). An Administrative Wing was subsequently added to relieve "the Superintendents of the Scientific Wings of as many administrative problems as possible."[37] The Administrative Wing was responsible for providing Library, Publications and Security services.

2.3.2 Difficulties Experienced by the Army in Recruiting Scientists

Despite every effort to recruit scientists, the CARDE management had to come to terms with an extremely difficult situation. The number of scientific researchers in the Valcartier military technological complex was relatively small during the war, and many of the uniformed scientists wanted to return to civilian life. As well, most of the component establishments included scientists on loan from Britain, and it was only a matter of time before they returned home. The situation was even more difficult since these scientists often held key positions.

Management had to use all means possible to fill these positions. In June 1945, the Master General of Ordnance (MGO) sought the assistance of the President of Defence Industries Ltd., in solving a difficult problem. A replacement had to be found for Dr. Harold Poole, and this was no easy challenge since the British scientist had been the guiding spirit of the Explosives Experimental Establishment since 1942. The MGO asked the President of Defence Industries for the loan of one of the company's renowned chemists for a year or so in order to train one of the Laboratory's chemists as a successor. To secure the President's support, the MGO wrote: "I feel it essential that research in Canada in this field should be developed on a sound scientific and industrial basis and an experienced scientist is required as soon as possible".[38] Three days later, the company responded favourably to the call of duty. This exceptional step characterized the problems experienced by CARDE in recruiting scientists to fill key positions, and attests to the relative scarcity of scientists in Canada at that time.

In his study on post-war military research, Goforth, an economist by profession, identifies two major reasons for the reluctance of scientists and technicians to work in the field of defence research. First, many uniformed scientists wanted either to resume their pre-war university research activities or to seek employment in industry. Second, prospects of employment in the Army at the time were, to say the least, uncertain.[39] Goforth proposed the creation of a research organization managed by civilians specifically to remedy this situation. In his view, such an organization would be more likely to attract qualified scientists as well as graduates fresh from the universities because the environment would be better suited to their interests. The significant impact of the advent of the Defence Research Board on recruitment of scientists at the Establishment will be discussed later. For now, suffice it to say that "the majority of its key scientific and technical staff had left before the Board took over."[40]

2.3.3 Research Conducted at CARDE under Army Authority

Organizational challenges notwithstanding, the Army had to ensure the success of its research program at the Canadian Armament Research and Development Establishment. Infrastructures were lacking, and the Army began some construction work in 1945. When the Defence Research Board took over, the Establishment infrastructure was geared for research and development work on projectiles, propellants, high explosives, fuzes, rockets and components of various types of munition, including "the design of gun barrels, carriages and other weapon items; the proof, modification and testing of such items."[41]

During this period, in addition to its ongoing activities, the Establishment participated in research leading to the development of three new weapon systems: the "Sabot" series of anti-tank projectiles, the "Heller" anti-tank rocket and the light artillery "Pack Howitzer" equipment (75 mm). Two types of projectile were developed in the "Sabot" series. The first was known under the code name ATDB Project 74 "17-pounder 'pot' type Sabot projectile" and the second under that of ATDB Project 44 "25-pounder Sabot."[42] According to Solandt, General McNaughton had a real passion for sabot projectiles throughout the war.[43] It must be admitted that armour-piercing projectiles enjoyed great success on the battlefield. It is not surprising, therefore, to find McNaughton's name listed amongst the high ranking officials interested in the development of this type of projectile. According to Goodspeed, "CARDE was working on the design of a new type of sabot shot, the "pot sabot" whose distinguishing characteristic was that the discarded portion fell off all in one piece, thus minimizing the hazard to our own troops and increasing the stability of the round."[44] In 1946, "Heller" was still only in the design stage, because D Wing had only just begun studying the principle of the "Hammer" anti-tank weapon developed by the Germans during the Second World War. As for the "Pack-How", the Canadian Armament Research and Development Establishment at Valcartier did pioneering work by undertaking, for the first time in Canada, "the design of a complete artillery equipment". According to Goodspeed, "this indeed was the major reason why the project was adopted, for the training and experience to be gained from it were essential to the development of Canadian technical knowledge."[45]

2.4 CARDE: AN ORGANIZATION MANAGED BY CIVILIANS

2.4.1 Consolidation of CARDE with the Defence Research Board

During the summer of 1946, the Director General of Defence Research undertook the groundwork in anticipation of the formation of the fourth Service. In particular, he engaged in negotiations with the Army concerning the transfer of administrative responsibility for CARDE. His efforts were successful, for the Army agreed to transfer "responsibility for the direction of [CARDE], and [its] transfer to a civilian basis about 15 Sep. 1946."[46] However, the transfer did not occur as planned because of the hubbub surrounding the creation of the Defence Research Board. But shortly afterwards, during the winter of 1946-1947, the Master General of Ordnance for the Army progressively handed over responsibility to DRB for coordination of the scientific work at the Establishment.[47] Since the Defence Research Board did not officially exist until 28 March 1947, it must be assumed that this responsibility fell on the shoulders of the Director General for Defence Research, Dr. O.M. Solandt. Another bridge was crossed when financial responsibility for CARDE was accorded to Dr. Solandt on 1 April 1947.[48]

On 30 April, the Canadian Armament Research and Development Establishment at Valcartier was placed under DRB direction by Order-in-Council.[49] As the press reported, so Canada "becomes the first democratic nation to give a civilian full supervisory control of the development of weapons, equipment, for the three armed forces."[50] Also in 1947, the Suffield Experimental Station and the Chemical Warfare Laboratories in Ottawa were integrated within the administrative structure of DRB. The Order-in-Council of 30 April specified, however, that this was an interim measure and that the Board had to obtain government approval for "post-war organizations for the research and development establishments therein mentioned."[51]

During this transition period, the Board counted on the assistance of the Chief Superintendent, Dr. Donald C. Rose, who remained in office until October 1947.[52] Earlier, in May 1947, the Chairman of DRB took stock of the potential of each of the four scientific wings at CARDE. In broad terms, Solandt considered that the facilities of C Wing were excellent, in that they allowed scientists to pursue studies of propellants and explosives of all types. For Solandt, the work of this Wing proved extremely useful for the chemical industries and the Canadian Arsenals, citing as evidence "the further development of a new process for the manufacture of picrite", one of the ingredients of a propellant.[53] Since the British were planning to use picrite, "it was decided to apply the process to a small-scale production in order to have a perfect knowledge of engineering processes and corresponding costs", as stated in Dr. Solandt's semi-annual report of November 1947. In August 1948, the Army made a formal request to DRB that this work continue, and the CARDE chemists concentrated on trying to find a new method of synthesis. One year later, the results obtained by CARDE were sufficiently conclusive to justify the initiation of test and evaluation of an improved process for manufacturing nitroguanidine using the pilot plant of the Consolidated Mining and Smelting Company. In 1954, the Company confirmed that the results warranted the use of this process in commercial production. Two years later, the Defence Research Board granted an award to Dr. Jean-Louis Boivin for his contribution to the development of the new process. This was the first such award made by DRB to one of its defence scientists. The fact that "a considerable contribution had been made to basic chemical knowledge"[54] was no doubt an important consideration in the decision to honour this CARDE chemist.

Ceremony marking the presentation of the merit award conferred upon Dr. Jean-Louis Boivin by DRB at Valcartier on 23 January 1956.

Solandt considered that the activities of B Wing were less spectacular, because they were focused strictly "on filling in certain gaps in the theory of rocket design". He believed, however, that the relatively low number of scientists in the Wing largely explained the Wing's modest accomplishments, and that there were, therefore, mitigating circumstances. To remedy this situation, he recommended that the requisite staff be hired in order to concentrate effort "in the development and use of a free-flight

Figure 2- Organisation Chart Illustration of the General Organizational Structure for Research in the Department of National Defence and the Particular Organizational Structure of CARDE in the Early 1950's.

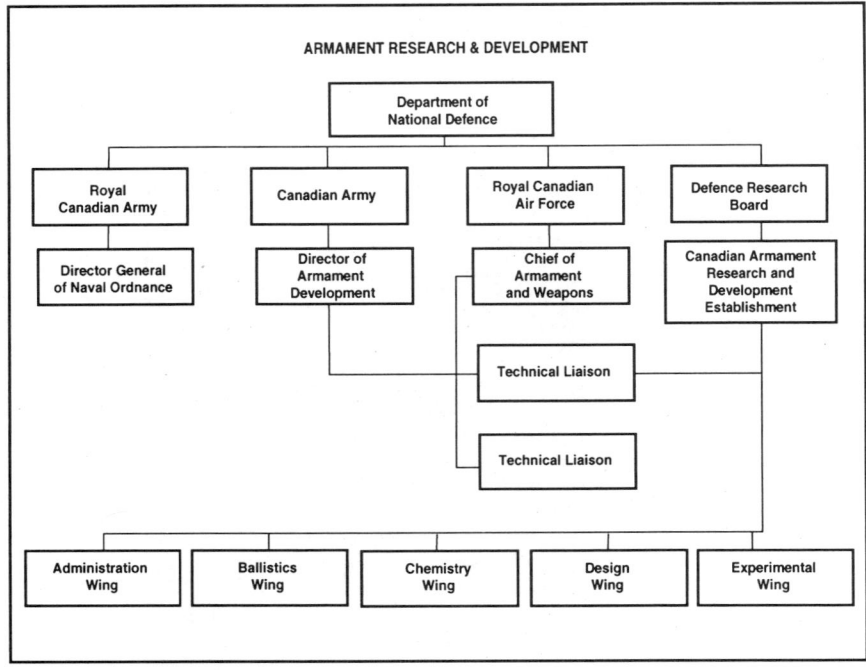

Source: Third Annual Report of DREV

range for the study of the problem of supersonic ballistics and aerodynamics". Solandt noted that the scientists in D Wing were largely preoccupied with the development of the Pack Howitzer. He proposed that, once this work was completed, the Wing should devote most of its time to providing technical assistance to the other CARDE Wings. Finally, realizing that E Wing was conducting a large number of tests on behalf of the United Kingdom Artillery Board, Solandt proposed that its activities be reoriented towards providing technical support to the Suffield Experimental Station, to the three Services of the Canadian Armed Forces[55] and to the other Wings of CARDE.

In parallel with undertaking this assessment of CARDE's activities, Board authorities took the necessary steps to ensure a smooth transition from an organization managed by the Army to an organization administered by civilians. As part of this process, they determined "the basic minimum of personnel required to carry out efficiently the duties and functions presently assigned to the Establishment."[56] In mid-July, DRB estimated that the civilian personnel requirement for the Establishment at Valcartier totalled 413, comprising 74 professionals and 339 non-professionals. Seventy-one of the 74 professionals would be scientists and 44 of the non-professionals would be technicians. There was also a requirement for 5 Army personnel, comprising 3 officers having professional status and 2 master gunners having non-professional status.[57] DRB submitted these estimates to the Canadian Government together with an attachment describing the functions for each of the 28 occupational groups, the number of personnel designated to each group, the number of levels within the groups and the corresponding salary scales. DRB did not stand still while

The members of the Defence Research Board with most of the professionals employed at CARDE, taken on 27 September 1948.

awaiting government approval. According to Goodspeed, "job analyses were initiated in all branches of the Board, and the task of reclassifying all the Board's employees was begun."[58]

2.4.2 DRB Considers Transforming CARDE into an Explosives Research Establishment

In November 1947, the Chairman of the Defence Research Board, Dr. Solandt, had some doubts about his first ideas on the mission of CARDE which envisaged a relatively broad scope of activity for the Establishment. Solandt appears to have been increasingly preoccupied with the operational difficulties that confronted him at Valcartier; he considered that the ranges were inadequate, it was particularly difficult to hire physicists and mechanical engineers (he had only 16 scientific professional staff, 5 of whom were military personnel), and only the C and D Wings were housed in permanent buildings. In view of all that remained to be done, Solandt recommended a major policy shift which would limit the functions of the Valcartier establishment to research and development of explosives. First, the construction program would be reoriented towards building an explosives establishment. Second, the development work on armament equipment would be undertaken by Canadian Arsenals and, third, the ballistics research laboratory would be relocated to Ottawa to facilitate accessibility to industrial and academic contacts.[59] For reasons unknown, the proposals for re-structuring the Canadian Armament Research and Development Establishment at Valcartier were finally abandoned, but an action taken by the Inspection Board was perhaps a contributing factor.

2.4.3 Amalgamation of the Inspection Board of Canada Artillery Proof and Experimental Establishment with CARDE

At the time when Solandt raised the idea of limiting the responsibilities of CARDE, the Inspection Board of Canada was also reviewing the activities of the Artillery Proof and Experimental Establishment (APEE).[60] The situation can be better understood in the context of developments since the end of the Second World War. In August 1945, the Inspection Board of the United Kingdom and Canada found that the activities of its Valcartier establishment had been reduced considerably. But the Inspection Board was able to retain key personnel at the ranges because of the steadily increasing orders for experimental firings received from the nearby CARDE. In November 1945, Colonel E. van Steenburgh, who was responsible for liaising with CARDE, became concerned, noting that "an examination of the proposed peacetime establishment shows some duplication of functions with CARDE". In his view, the best way of resolving this problem of duplication of effort was to amalgamate APEE with the E Wing of CARDE. In a memorandum to the Master General of Ordnance, van Steenburgh suggested that the MGO approach the Inspection Board authorities to determine their position on this proposal.[61]

Apparently, no progress was made in discussing the matter since APEE remained under the direction of the Inspection Board of Canada until November 1947, at which time the lack of contracts for munitions from the Artillery obliged the Inspection Board to revise its position. At that point, the Controller General offered to hand over the ranges to the Department on a temporary basis, and work started on developing the details of the integration of range activities with those of CARDE. According to Mr. A. Ross, Deputy Minister of National Defence, the transfer of operations would take place on 15 January 1948, but because of various administrative details that had to be resolved, he envisaged that full integration of all personnel would not be completed before 1 April 1948.[62] Finally, the project was completed on 4 March 1948 when the 65 employees of this establishment were integrated with CARDE, more specifically with A, B and E Wings.[63] The fate of the ranges was sealed; they would remain henceforth under the administrative responsibility of the Defence Research Board.[64]

2.4.4 A Difficult Task: Recruiting Defence Scientists

In 1939, Canada allocated about five million dollars to research and development (R&D). With the war effort, research budgets jumped sevenfold to reach about 35 millions in 1945.[65] But the only significant increase in scientific staff occurred at NRC, where the number of scientists rose from 80 to 450 over a five-year period. As we have seen earlier, the economist Goforth affirmed in 1945 that the Army was unable to attract a steady flow of young scientists and technicians into its ranks,[66] and pointed out the need for a civilian organization that would be able to retain them. The difficulties experienced by the Army in attracting and retaining scientific minds to fill key positions are amply illustrated by the efforts expended by CARDE management at the time. This statement nevertheless needs some qualification, for several uniformed scientists continued to work in defence research after the war and some of them were located at Valcartier.

The first Director General of Defence Research, Dr. Solandt, reviewed this whole issue in 1946. In his view, it was essential to fill the scientific positions as a matter of priority. Although he proposed no concrete solution to the problem, Solandt nevertheless stressed the urgent need to create relief teams by sending selected young scientists to the United Kingdom and the United States to acquire the expertise so badly lacking in Canada.[67] Some idea of the magnitude of the task facing DRB can be gained from the fact that, in 1946, the Chiefs of Staff and the Cabinet Defence Committee made provision for 300 scientists within the fourth

Service. Despite the government's financial outlay ($14.5 million) for military research in 1946-47, there was still a desperate shortage of scientists to run Canada's establishments, since less than 100 scientists were then part of DRB. This situation, however, was common to all Canadian scientific organizations, which were greatly affected by the very small pool of Canadian scientists available for employment.

Partly for reasons of redressing this situation, the government deemed it necessary to accord DRB with a status similar to that of NRC for hiring, promoting and paying its future employees. On 28 March, the House of Commons gave formal sanction to such a status by excluding DRB from the provisions of the Civil Service Act. DRB was thus accorded authority in the manner of selection, remuneration and terms of appointment and service of its employees. As well, DRB was empowered to set up and maintain its own superannuation or pension fund. DRB immediately buckled down to the task.[68] In July 1947, the Board submitted to the government a full list of staff functions requisite to efficient operations together with salary scales and related conditions.[69] The government gave approval quickly and, on 12 December 1947, completed the process by making the provisions of the Superannuation Act applicable to DRB staff.[70] These structural changes apparently had little effect on the existing staff as "the initial recruitment of scientific, technical and administrative staff, in general, relied on ex-servicemen who already had a strong feeling for, and rapport with the Armed Services, and saw a career with the Defence Research Board as a sort of continuation of their Services link with a scientific rather than an operational input."[71]

Although these measures were taken to facilitate the recruitment of scientists, they appear to have been inadequate in meeting all DRB's expectations. In 1948, the Chairman asserted that it would take several years before the Board's objective of having 300 scientists on staff could be met. In his view, a number of factors contributed to the difficulties encountered by the Board in attaining its objective, including: the limited availability of researchers, the hesitancy of scientists to work for the government, the secret nature of defence research and the uncertainty surrounding the long-term future of DRB.[72] In short, in a labour market favouring Canadian researchers with various career opportunities, the Board had difficulty in attracting the Canadian scientists that it needed.

Group of CARDE scientists in the early 1950's. From left to right: Mr. Archie Pennie, Mr. Gordon D. Watson, Col George Donaldson, Col Tom Gemmell, Dr. Carleton Craig, third Chief Superintendent of CARDE, Col Donald Waldock, fifth Chief Superintendent of CARDE, Mr. Jean-Pierre Giroux and an unidentified individual. (Gordon D. Watson collection)

Until such time as the Board could recruit defence scientists to take over, it had to depend on experts in military research. Based on information obtained by the authors in interviews,[73] DRB recruited British scientists to fill its personnel needs. At least, such was the case for CARDE. Since detailed statistics on human resources at the Establishment for the period in question are not available, the extent to which British scientists were recruited cannot be determined with any accuracy. It appears, however, that DRB was able to attract to Canada a number of experienced scientists who were well regarded in their several fields. For CARDE, the support of these scientists was of inestimable value, for they brought with them not only their technological expertise but more importantly their long-standing tradition in the conduct of research. There were wide differences in the employment status of these individuals; some were recruited directly by DRB while others were on loan from British organizations. Dr. W.B. Littler, for example, was seconded to CARDE by the Directorate of Chemical Research, British Ministry of Supply. Dr. Littler, who had worked at the Ministry of Supply's laboratories at Waltham Abbey, England, was appointed Superintendent of the Chemistry Wing[74] and subsequently succeeded Dr. Donald C. Rose as Chief Superintendent of CARDE in October 1947, a position that he held until February 1949.[75] Following Dr. Littler's return to England in 1949, DRB was unable to find a successor from within its own organization, but secured the services of Professor Carleton Craig who came to CARDE on secondment from McGill University.

Despite all DRB's efforts to recruit scientific personnel, CARDE had only 20 defence scientists in January 1949, well below the 71 figure established as the objective in 1947. On the other hand, DRB enjoyed greater success in recruiting personnel in other categories and, in January 1949, 83 technicians and 220 administrative personnel were working at the Canadian Armament Research and Development Establishment Valcartier.[76] As pointed out earlier, the Establishment at Valcartier had always relied on military personnel since its creation. In 1949, the Army decided to form a military unit at CARDE known as the Armament Development and Experimental Establishment (ADEE), and the Air Force followed suit in 1950 by forming the RCAF Unit CARDE. In this regard, it should be noted that ADEE was directed by the Deputy Chief Superintendent - himself a military officer.[77]

2.4.5 The Establishment's Budget

Prior to 1947, when CARDE came under DRB control, the Establishment's budget was about one million dollars. As shown in Figure 3, the government almost doubled its allocation for the following fiscal year (1947-48). This implies that the Establishment budget accounted for almost half of all the Board's financial resources for defence research. It would appear that the authorities over-estimated the spending power of CARDE, since the Establishment expended roughly the same amount as in fiscal year 1946-47. This was particularly evident within the financial codings for the following items: salaries, armaments storage and bombs and munitions. Over-estimates for these three financial codings alone accounted for almost 80% of the total net surplus for that fiscal year. The surplus amounts accrued under the total payroll coding clearly indicate that the government's expectations of attracting a large number of candidates into military research through the creation of a fourth service were not, in fact, met. It should be mentioned that the total surplus amounts were also due to delays in the construction program during fiscal year 1947-48 which resulted in lower expenditures than forecast.[78]

Over the two years that followed, the government realized its mistake and progressively allocated more realistic budgets. The reduction in the net surplus over these years amply demonstrates the point. As for the total payroll, the difference between the statutory budget and actual expenditures for this item consisted of a large surplus of $246,252 in 1947-48, a slight deficit of $7,009 in 1948-49 and a slight surplus of $35,365 in 1949-50.

2.4.6 The Establishment's Construction Program

In April 1947, DRB noted that the facilities of the Canadian Armament Research and Development Establishment were far from being completed, and only C Wing and D Wing were housed in permanent buildings.[79] As we have seen, the Army had planned

Figure 3- Statutory Budget Voted by the Canadian Government, Amounts Actually Expended and Resulting Net Surplus Amounts (Total) for CARDE, Fiscal Years 1947-48 to 1949-50

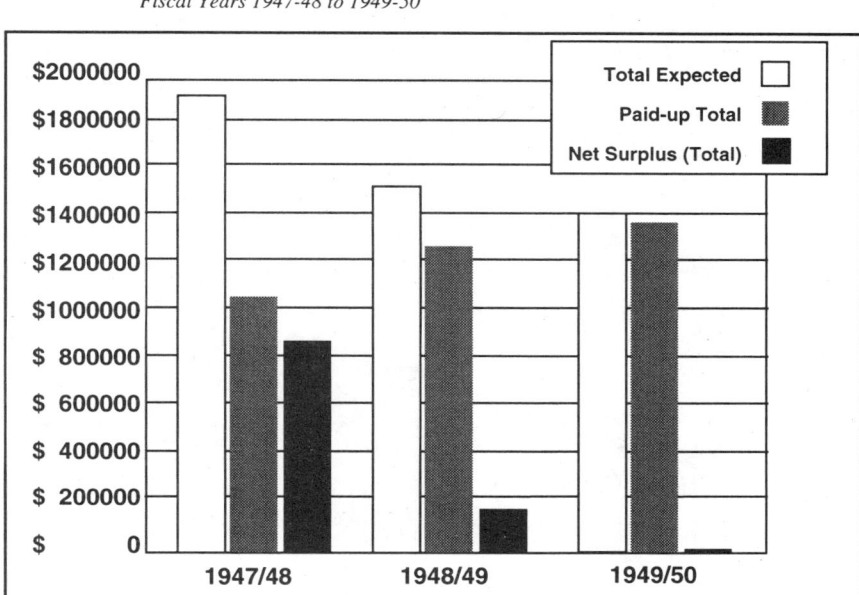

Source: CARDE Budget. DREV Document Library.

in 1945 to build the infrastructures needed to fulfil the mandate of the new establishment. In 1946, the Army had even negotiated contracts with construction companies worth $466,000.[80] For reasons unknown, the construction program fell behind schedule. It appears that DRB had no better luck, for that portion of the program which "consisted of a number of buildings to complete the explosives experimental area"[81] was still not completed in November 1947. At that point, DRB took time to re-evaluate the whole issue, particularly since the Board was playing with the idea of dividing up the Establishment and significantly reducing its activities. One month later, the Board appeared to be bent on following through with its proposed reorientation of CARDE functions by allocating the lion's share of construction funding (over half of the $878,000 budgeted) to buildings for the explosives experimental area. Subsequent DRB thinking is difficult to discern because the annual reports of DRB are somewhat less protracted on the subject. In any event, DRB committed a little over $800,000 in the following year (1948-49) to equip the Establishment with technical laboratories and buildings with the expectation of completing all the construction by 1950. But the completion date was moved up when Canada embarked on its rearmament program, and the Board shifted into high gear with its construction program at the Canadian Armament Research and Development Establishment Valcartier. It is interesting too that, in 1948, the Board thought of building a number of apartments for families of married personnel but abandoned the idea a little later when other DRB establishments argued a more pressing need.

2.5 CARDE'S FIRST SUCCESS IN CONVENTIONAL WEAPONS

Most of CARDE's efforts during the latter half of the 1940s were focused on the development of conventional weapons and related systems. The Chemistry Wing in particular pursued research on propellants and explosives of all kinds and, in 1949, obtained promising results on a new process for producing nitroguanidine. It should be mentioned that the Wing benefited greatly from the organizational talents of its Superintendent, Dr. Littler, and of a member of DRB's Board of Directors, Dr. Paul E. Gagnon of Laval University.[82] Indeed, one of the persons interviewed by the author considered Dr. Gagnon as the "father" of CARDE.

During this same period, the Design Wing undertook research on a 17-pounder anti-tank projectile (N-16), on the Heller anti-tank rocket system (N-17) and on the Light Pack Howitzer (N-18). E Wing pursued its task while integrating, in 1948, ARTY within its organization. In this context, the Board's statement, in 1950, is most significant: "the closer association of D and E Wings with the Army has stimulated the Army's interest in the work of the

Some of the buildings of the explosives pilot plant.

Establishment."[83] So much so, in fact, that military authorities negotiated with DRB to obtain technical responsibility for projects integrated and run by D and E Wings. On 1 July 1948, the Army was successful and the Weapons Development Directorate was given technical control over these two wings. On the other hand, CARDE retained its administrative prerogatives over these same wings and the civilian personnel remained in the employ of DRB.[84] Finally, the Ballistics Wing, after a period of uncertain orientation, reached a major turning point in 1950 when it embarked on preliminary studies of an air-to-air missile.

Observers who were not too familiar with defence research may have felt that CARDE's results, although promising, took a long time to achieve. This may have been the view in some Ottawa circles for, after all, CARDE was DRB's main research establishment and the wait, although normal, may have appeared unusually long. Perhaps this would explain why the DRB Chairman, Dr. Solandt, placed such emphasis in his 1950 annual report on first major successes of the Valcartier Establishment.

Although no one can be sure of this, the hypothesis has a certain appeal. Be that as it may, Dr. Solandt affirmed that 1950 was the best year in the early history of CARDE. For him, "the devoted efforts of all those who have striven to build up this Establishment since the War began for the first time to pay dividends."[85]

This first return on investment, if one might use the expression, resulted from the success of the highly improved 17-pounder projectile for anti-tank weapons which triumphantly passed the acceptance trials for manufacture in Canada and the United Kingdom. Of even greater significance for Solandt was the fact that the Canadian Army were highly interested in adopting the projectile for its special brigade within the United Nations Korean Intervention Force, and that the United States' Army planned to incorporate the projectile in its 76-millimetre anti-tank system. The Chairman of DRB considered that the 17-pounder was not only a technical success but also that it represented an important step towards achieving standardization of armaments between the three nations.[86] In 1952, the projectile was accepted as a standard inventory item by Great Britain, the United States and Canada.[87] With this projectile, CARDE recorded its first success in the field of conventional weapons.

1	Gen Charles Foulkes, *Post-War Policy for Scientific Research for Defence*, 5 October 1945, p. 1, ANC, MG 31, vol. 6.
2	Capt D.J. Goodspeed, *A History of the Defence Research Board*, Ottawa, Queen's Printer, 1958, p. 18.
3	*Ibid.*, p. 15.
4	*Ibid.*, p. 17-18.
5	*Ibid.*, p. 20.
6	*Ibid.*, p. 21.
7	Col W.W. Goforth, *The Future of Canadian Army Research and Development*, 17 September 1945, p. 16, NAC, MG 21, Vol. 6, and Wilfrid Eggleston, *National Research in Canada: The NRC 1916-1966*, Toronto, Clarke Irwin, 1978, p. 263-271.
8	Col W.W. Goforth, *op. cit.*, p. 1-2.
9	NAC, RG 24, Vol. 11,995, *Annual Report of the Chairman of DRB 1947-1948*.
10	Col W.W. Goforth, *op. cit.*, p. 19.
11	*Ibid.*
12	*Ibid.*
13	Capt D.J. Goodspeed, *op. cit.*, p. 37-39.
14	Gen. Charles Foulkes, *Post-War Policy...*, 5 October 1945, p. 5, NAC, MG 21, Vol. 6.
15	Capt D.J. Goodspeed, *op. cit.*, p. 9.
16	Gen. Charles Foulkes, *op. cit.*, p. 5.
17	NAC, RG 24, Vol. 11997, *D.G. of Defence Research: Progress Report 15 Feb 1946 - 31 Aug 1946*.
18	Brigadier M.H.S. Penhale, *Memorandum on Canadian Post-War Policy for Scientific Research for Defence*, p. 2, NAC, MG 21, Vol. 6, 22 January 1946.
19	Capt D.J. Goodspeed, *op. cit.*, Chapters III and V.
20	*House of Commons Debates*, Ottawa, King's Printer, 13 Feb 1947, p. 382.
21	Canada, *Statutes of Canada*, Chap. 5, 1947.
22	DND, *Report of the Department of National Defence for Fiscal Year ending 31 March 1947*, Ottawa, King's Printer, 1947, p. 59.
23	Canada, Statutes of Canada, *op. cit.*, and House of Commons Debates, p. 209 and *passim*.
24	Col W.W. Goforth, *op. cit.*, p. 18.
25	Ministerial Order Series 3871 HWE Cdn V/585/1: cited in NAC, Reel C-5170, HQS 8236-7-1, Vol. 1, *W.E. van Steenburgh to Dr. Laidler*, 9 January 1945.
26	NAC, Reel C-5170, HQS 8236-7-1, Vol. 1, *Steenburgh to ...*
27	NAC, Reel C-5170, HQS 8236-7-1, Vol. 1, *J.C. Murchie to Chief of*

28 *Air Staff*, 27 January 1945.
28 NAC, RG 2, Vol. 1629, PC 1/1640, 8 March 1945.
29 DRB, *Semi-Annual Report of the Chairman of DRB 1 April - 30 September 1947*, Ottawa, November 1947, p. 47.
30 Dr. O.M. Solandt, "Defence Research in Canada", *The Engineering Journal*, August 1951, p. 765.
31 Wilfrid Eggleston, *NRC...*, p. 237.
32 NAC, Reel C-5170, HQS 8236-7-1, Vol. 1, *Transfer of Personnel from I.B. of UK and Canada to CARDE*, 11 April 1945.
33 *Memorandum of Dr. Rose*.
34 NAC, RG 24, Vol. 11998, *Background Material Submitted in Support of Part III DRB*.
35 NAC, Reel C-5170, HQS 8236-7-1, Vol. 1, *Dr. D.C. Rose to Deputy MGO*, 26 May 1945.
36 *DRB Semi-Annual Report...*, p. 46.
37 CARDE, *Third Annual Meeting Administrative Staffs of the DRB...*, Valcartier, September 1952, p. 4.
38 NAC, Reel C-5170, HQS 8236-7-1, Vol. 1, *Major General Ordnance (MGO) to President Defence Industries*, 4 June 1945.
39 Col W.W. Goforth, *op. cit.*, p. 7.
40 Dr. O.M. Solandt, *op. cit.*, p. 765.
41 NAC, RG 24, Vol. 11995, File: 1-0-43-1, *Unit CARDE*, 1946.
42 NAC, MG 31 G 21, Vol. 5, *Certain Research Projects in Respect of Weapons*, 31 March 1945.
43 Dr. O.M. Solandt, *Science as it Relates to Defence*, p. 12.
44 Capt D.J. Goodspeed, *op. cit.*, p. 126.
45 *Ibid.*, p. 125.
46 NAC, RG 24, Vol. 11997, *DG of Defence Research: Progress Report...*.
47 DRB, *Semi-Annual Report...*, p. 47.
48 *Ibid.*, p. 47.
49 P.C. 101/1727 cited in NAC, RG 24, Vol. 11995, *4th Meeting of the DRB*, 16 September 1947.
50 Financial Post, "Civilian Scientist, 37, Will Direct All Canadian Military Research", *Financial Post*, 26 October 1946, p. 1.
51 NAC, RG 2, Vol. 1978, P.C. 152/2833, July 1947.
52 Capt D.J. Goodspeed, *op. cit.*, p. 120.
53 NAC, RG 24, Vol. 11995, *Chairman's Remarks to Policy and Plans of DRB*, 14 May 1947.
54 *History of Nitroguanidine Work at CARDE*, 8 March 1955; cited by Goodspeed, op. cit., p. 124.
55 NAC, RG 24, Vol. 11,995, *Chairman's Remarks ...*

56 P.C. 152/2833, *op. cit.*
57 *Ibid.*
58 Capt D.J. Goodspeed, *op. cit.*, p. 75.
59 DRB, *Semi-Annual Report..*, p. 48.
60 Previously known as the Artillery Proof and Development Establishment.
61 NAC, Reel C-5170, HQS 8236-5, Vol. 2, *Artillery Proof and Experimental Establishment - Peacetime Amalgamation*, 23 November 1945.
62 NAC, Reel C-5170, HQS 8236-5, Vol. 3, *A. Ross to J.B. Gordon*, 5 January 1948.
63 CARDE, *Survey of Organization, Facilities and Programmes of Work; September 1947 to September 1948*, p.2.
64 NAC, RG 24, Vol. 11998, *Background...*
65 Canada, *Glassco Commission*, Vol. 4, 1962, p. 200.
66 Col W.W. Goforth, *op. cit.*, p. 7.
67 NAC, RG 24, Vol. 11997, Draft.
68 Canada, *Statutes...*
69 PC 152/2833, *op. cit.*
70 Capt D.J. Goodspeed, *op. cit.*, p. 75.
71 A. Pennie, "*DRB: Quarter-Century*", Sentinel, Vol. 1, No. 4 (April 1972), p. 20-21.
72 NAC, RG 24, Vol. 11995, *Annual Report...* 1947-1948.
73 See Bibliography under Interviews.
74 DRB, *Semi-Annual Report...*, p. 49.
75 Capt D.J. Goodspeed, *op. cit.*, p. 120.
76 NAC, RG 24, Vol. 11998, *Background....*
77 CARDE, *Third Annual Meeting...* p. 3.
78 NAC, RG 24, Vol. 11995, *Annual Report...1947-1948.*
79 DRB, *Semi-Annual Report...*, p. 48.
80 NAC, RG 24, Vol. 11995, *5th Meeting of DRB*, 15 December 1957.
81 DRB, *Semi-Annual Report...*, p. 49.
82 NAC, RG 24, Vol. 11995, *14th Meeting of the DRB*, 16 March 1950, p. 5.
83 *Ibid.*
84 CARDE, *Survey of Organization, Facilities and Programmes of Work; September 1947 to September 1948*, Valcartier, 1948, p.2
85 NAC, RG 24, Vol. 11995, *Annual Report of DRB Chairman 1950*, 20 September 1950, p. 8.
86 *Ibid.*
87 DND, *Report of the DND for the Fiscal Year Ending March 31, 1952*, Ottawa, Queen's Printer, 1952, p. 71.

PART TWO
THE GOLDEN YEARS: ALMOST TWO DECADES OF GREAT PROJECTS AT DREV

> "Victory was only possible because the scientists and engineers, who supplied the weapons to our Forces, proved superior to those of the enemy."
> (Dr. O.M. Solandt)[1]

3

THE START OF A NEW ERA FOR CARDE: VELVET GLOVE AND HELLER

3.1 OVERVIEW OF CANADIAN DEFENCE POLICY AFTER THE SECOND WORLD WAR

When the Second World War ended, Canada was the fourth largest military power in the world[2] and one of the few nations on Earth possessing the expertise to manufacture an atomic bomb. It remained that Canada had never been a militaristic nation, and the Canadian Government had no wish to maintain a standing military force of almost a million personnel, particularly when the Canadian people yearned only for peace. Canada decided to demobilize its troops quickly but to respect, nevertheless, its commitment to maintain a significant occupation force in Germany until 1946.

While the nation was busily disarming, the headquarters of the three Services of the Armed Forces were bent on preserving the main assets of the Canadian war machine. The military developed post-war plans which called for the maintenance of large regular and reserve force manpower and equipment (e.g., two aircraft carriers) to conduct its proposed activities.

According to historian Desmond Morton, the "government

response [to their desiderata] was frosty. The Army's yearning for conscription, declared Mackenzie King, was perfectly outrageous."[3] In view of such a peremptory reception, the headquarters of the Army, Navy and Air Force could consider themselves fortunate that the government, in 1946, granted them almost half of the military manpower that they requested. This was the point at which the government initiated the downward spiral of defence budgets. Nevertheless, the Armed Forces remained larger and better equipped than in 1939.[4]

In parallel, Canada reviewed its defence policy to suit the international situation. The United States and the Soviet Union seemed destined to remain the dominant powers, while the European powers and Japan emerged significantly weakened from the world conflict. As the Western nations demobilized, the Soviet Union kept its imposing military potential intact. The Kremlin decision came as no surprise, for British strategists had predicted in 1944 "that Russia would emerge as the principal threat to world peace."[5]

In 1945, the United States awakened to the new strategic environment and became alarmed at the threat posed, in this new era of aviation, by the Soviet presence in the North. In view of this, the US Government deemed that Canada should henceforth be an integral part of "the strategic glacis for the defence of the United States."[6] For its part, the Canadian Government had no intention of allowing the nation to slip "back into a similar status [of colony] under another country in the 20th century";[7] there should be no return to the colonial status of the 19th Century. The government nevertheless elected to continue its military collaboration with the United States through the Canada-US Permanent Joint Board on Defence which was established in 1940.[8] Canada was "torn between two major essentials: to ensure national security through alliances and to respect the imperatives of national sovereignty."[9]

Such was the situation when, on 6 September 1945, Igor Gouzenko fled the Soviet Embassy in Ottawa and alerted the

Canadian Government to the existence of a large scale spy network in Canada. Gouzenko advised the government that the mission of this network during the war had been mainly to obtain information on the activities of the Explosives Experimental Establishment at Valcartier.[10] Canada found itself suddenly at the centre of the turmoil. The situation was delicate, particularly since the Soviet Union had been the ally of yesteryear. The Prime Minister viewed this affair as "the most serious crisis of his political career."[11] "In order not to aggravate the already strained international relations", King discussed[12] the ins and outs of the Gouzenko affair with his British and American counterparts. In February 1946, the American press disclosed the affair to the astonishment of the world. Canada reacted by forming a Royal Commission of Inquiry and proceeded with the immediate arrest of a dozen suspects.[13] Today, the Gouzenko affair is regarded as one of the incidents marking the beginning of the Cold War between the superpowers.

Despite this spy episode, scepticism prevailed in Ottawa as to the true objective of the Soviets, which was believed to be aimed more towards Europe than towards North America. Canada maintained that "the civilian population has nothing to fear, nor do the industries. It would be better not to invest too much in Western defence."[14] Prime Minister King felt a "growing fear" of Canada's association with the United States, and he became "a cautious supporter of the United Nations."[15] King even invoked the Charter of the United Nations to justify his refusal to sign the Hemisphere Defence Agreement developed by the United States in late 1945. In June 1946, the United States and Canada reached agreement on the need to defend their respective territories against aerial attack, but "the Chiefs of Staff of each nation retained the strategic direction and command of their forces."[16] By October 1946, "the Canadian Government had successfully resisted the initial rather heavy pressure for elaborate continental defence measures, but it had accepted the principle of coordinated defence efforts and in particular continental air defence."[17]

During the same period, the members of the Canada/US Permanent Joint Board on Defence had recommended increased military exchanges and had stressed the importance of standardization of weapons and equipment. The King government supported this resolution, pointing out that such an agreement would not weaken at all the control exercised by Canada over any activity undertaken on its territory. The February 1947 communiqué announcing this bilateral agreement reiterated the principle of autonomy. One year later, the new Prime Minister, Louis Saint-Laurent, sought to clarify the agreement by insisting that such "military collaboration did not really constitute a military alliance, and that the Declaration did not imply contractual obligations."[18] Furthermore, he affirmed that this collaboration involved no commitments beyond those of the agreement existing between the Commonwealth countries. But for other observers, such as historian Desmond Morton, the signing of this agreement marked the beginning of "Canadian military integration with its historic enemy"[19], the United States.

It was in February 1947 also that the Minister of National Defence, Brooke Claxton, tabled Canada's defence policy before the House of Commons. This policy embraced three major principles. First, the Canadian Forces had to be capable of defending Canada against any form of aggression. Second, the Canadian Forces had to provide aid to the civil power in maintaining law and order inside Canada. And third, the Canadian Forces had to "carry out any undertaking which by our own voluntary act we may assume in cooperation with friendly nations or under any effective plan of collective action under the United Nations."[20] This latter principle clearly illustrated that collective security through alliances would become a central pillar of Canada's own national security.

In February 1948, the Communists took power in Czechoslovakia - the country considered to be the most democratic in the socialist camp. The Western powers could not view the coup d'état in Prague as strictly an internal matter, considering instead that it bore the Soviet stamp and displayed Moscow's desire to take over Eastern Europe. The United Kingdom, France and the Benelux countries reacted to the events in Prague by signing, in March 1948, a mutual assistance treaty and forming the Western European Union Defence Organization. Despite their military power, the Western European nations could not match the might of the Soviet bear without the help of the United States. So began an extensive diplomatic campaign by Western Europe to seek the involvement of the United States in a collective defence agreement, a campaign in which Canada hastened to participate. "A few years of bilateral defence arrangements with the United States made Ottawa yearn for additional partners. 'Twelve in the bed means no rape' became an [in vogue] Ottawa slogan."[21] Canada also reasoned that partnership in this military alliance would allow the nation to assert its independence and play the full role of a middle power on the world stage.

The Americans, for their part, were reticent to join this organization and so renounce their traditional isolationist policies. They were deeply troubled by the world situation and, on 11 June, the US Senate gave the President of the United States authorization to enter into external commitments in peacetime. Despite the removal of earlier limitations, President Harry S. Truman did not sign a collective defence treaty in 1948. During this period, the Soviets used their traditional May Day parade to unveil to the world their own flying Superfortress. In doing so, they demonstrated that they would soon possess, in the form of the Tupolev TU-4, a heavy bomber capable of reaching North America.

In June 1948, tensions reached their height when the Soviets decided to test Western will through a blockade of West Berlin. The West met this challenge by establishing the Berlin airlift. Canadians were clearly concerned by the threat that hung over the world. For his part, Defence Minister Brooke Claxton judged "that in the immediate future any attack on North America would be diversionary, designed to panic the people of this continent into putting a disproportionate amount of effort into passive local defence."[22] In short, Canada would only be subjected to a diversionary attack and would be "neither the Belgium nor the Bikini of the next war." As far as the Defence Minister was concerned, Canada's prime objective was to have the capability of fielding the troops necessary to defend the country against any sudden and direct attack that might be mounted in the near future. Claxton's solution was to re-equip the Armed Forces. Since any potential attack would likely come from the air, Claxton allocated, for the first time in Canadian history, a budget to the Air Force higher than the combined budgets of the Army and the Navy.[23] This increase in Air Force funding was even more striking since the defence envelope in 1948 had been increased from the originally planned 8.9% to 12.3% of the Canadian budget following approval of the supplementary estimates. This preferential allocation to the Royal Canadian Air Force from the defence budget was to continue for many years.

In 1949, the United States became increasingly concerned with Soviet military power and, in April of that year, decided to participate with other Western nations in the formation of NATO. Four months later, the Soviet Union exploded an atomic bomb and, with great fanfare, became a member of the elite club of nuclear powers. With the United States losing its nuclear monopoly, the world gradually entered the new era of balance of terror. The threat of nuclear retaliation was no longer the sole prerogative of the Americans - it was now shared with the Soviets. This new order of things gave the Cold War a different dimension, for the two superpowers could not engage in a direct war without running the risk of engulfing the planet in nuclear flames. Admittedly, the Kremlin did not then possess the nuclear potential of the White House, but it was only a matter of time before Moscow would be able to build a nuclear arsenal of sufficient magnitude to give Washington serious cause for concern.

Such was the strategic context when the Korean War broke out in June 1950, and some observers feared that it was the prelude to general war. Six months later, the United States invited Canada to increase its contribution to collective defence. On 5 February 1951, Defence Minister Claxton announced the inception of a sweeping three-year rearmament program for the Canadian Armed Forces with the following defence objectives: "1) The immediate defence of Canada and North America from direct attack; 2) the implementation of any undertakings made by Canada under the Charter of the United Nations, or under the North Atlantic Treaty or other agreement for collective security; 3) the organization to build up our strength in a total war."[24]

3.1.1 Formulation of Policies and Programs for Defence Research

While the politicians and military strategists adjusted to geostrategic realities, and as the Cold War scenario unfolded, Canada continued its defence research activities. Colonel Goforth's appreciation, which laid the foundation for defence research policy, defined general guidelines and set in motion the process which led, in 1947, to the creation of the Defence Research Board.

Important as it was, Goforth's appreciation was only a first step. In January 1946, the Chiefs of Staff of the Canadian Armed Forces concluded that Canadian defence research policy would hinge on the fact that the Canadian Armed Forces "in any future conflict would fight either with the UK or US Forces". This being acknowledged, they considered that Canada should establish partnership agreements with these two countries to develop common weapons systems. It was no surprise, therefore, that the Chiefs of Staff recommended that Canada should negotiate an agreement with its two Anglo-Saxon allies for partitioning research work according to their respective capabilities.[25] The Canadian Government accepted their advice, and used every available platform to promote its position. The government then had to establish principles for guiding defence research and to identify real opportunities. In February 1946, Dr. Solandt assumed his duties as Director General of Defence Research for Canada. He was immediately asked to develop a policy outline and to structure a program by the end of that year. This timeframe was subsequently shortened following the announcement that an Informal Conference on Commonwealth Defence Science, attended by Commonwealth heads of defence research, would be held in London in June.[26]

Dr. Solandt rose to the challenge brilliantly and, in May 1946, set forth the principles that should guide defence research in Canada. In his view, 1) Canadian "defence research effort should be devoted to the more fundamental work that precedes engineering design", mainly in order to develop a new generation of defence scientists; 2) effort should be concentrated on a relatively small number of selected projects; 3) these projects should be chosen to make use of Canada's human and material resources; 4) and, the results of research undertaken should directly or indirectly benefit the civilian population or industry.[27] Solandt followed up by identifying 19 areas of research activity in which Canadian governmental, academic and industrial organizations could participate. These areas were selected to take account of the new geostrategic realities as well as existing and emerging technologies in fields such as atomic warfare, guided missiles, rockets, operational research, supersonic aerodynamics, electronics and conventional weapons.[28] According to Goodspeed, the essentials of Solandt's proposals were accepted by the Cabinet Committee on Defence.[29]

Although details of the substance of the London Conference are unknown, it may be safely assumed that Canada pressed for greater scientific collaboration between the various members of the Commonwealth. In any event, the participating nations considered the results of the Conference sufficiently valuable to justify the creation, in 1946, of a Commonwealth Advisory Committee on Defence Science which would meet on a regular basis thereafter. During this period, discussions continued in

Canada on the appropriateness of creating a defence research organization. Finally, in December 1946, Defence Minister Claxton decided in favour and the Defence Research Board came into existence in April 1947.

According to Goodspeed, the content of the research program was determined by the needs of the Armed Forces in undertaking the roles assigned to them by the Canadian Government[30] in conformity with its defence policy. In other words, the evolution of the government's position in response to the changing international situation was a major determinant of its policies on defence research. Because Canada's defence was linked to an alliance structure, one of the first steps taken by DRB was to establish Defence Research Liaison Offices in London[31] and Washington. In 1947 also, Canada participated in creating a Scientific Advisory Committee of the Western Union nations which was later subsumed under the aegis of NATO. As Solandt asserted, "we must never forget that our usefulness to the Canadian Services depends to a considerable extent upon the support that we get from our colleagues in the United States and Britain."[32]

According to Goodspeed, areas of research were divided into three main categories which served to define the order of priorities. First priority was accorded to areas where Canada alone could undertake the research (e.g., research related to the Arctic). Of second priority were areas in which Canada had existing scientific facilities and expertise (e.g., medicine and chemistry). Lowest priority areas were those in which Canada had no real expertise. Goodspeed observes that DRB would undertake research in the lowest priority areas only after close consultation with Canada's two Anglo-Saxon partners.[33] Priority setting was based on the a priori ideas of Solandt who considered that Canada should have a "policy of specialization because it has no aggressive intentions, and it is impossible to conceive of Canada fighting except as a member of a larger group of nations."[34] Several factors conspired to make the application of this categorization process quasi impossible, including the requirement that no field of research should be totally neglected by Canada.[35]

3.2 CARDE AND GUIDED MISSILES

3.2.1 Canada and Research on Guided Missiles

During 1946, CARDE placed primary emphasis on chemical research for explosives and propellants, and secondary emphasis on research and development in the area of conventional weapons to meet Army requirements. Under the aegis of DRB, work was being conducted on Heller, sabot shot projectiles and the Pack Howitzer. In May 1947, Solandt even considered concentrating the research efforts of the Establishment on explosives and propellants.

As we have seen, at that time Solandt seriously considered relocating the CARDE Ballistics Wing to Ottawa. If such a decision had been taken, the history of the Establishment at Valcartier would have been different. However, at that precise point in time, the Defence Research Board decided to embark on a path which, by 1951, would result in a national commitment to the development of the Velvet Glove air-to-air missile. A commitment to such a megaproject would require research in several fields and the involvement of specialists in rockets, supersonic aerodynamics, electronics and mechanical engineering.[36] As may be imagined, relocation of the Ballistics Wing would have substantially affected the course of CARDE's history and would probably have prevented the Establishment from playing a major role in the first major scientific project undertaken by DRB.[37]

Extrapolations aside, prodigious strides had occurred in missile technology with the development of the V-1 and V-2 missiles designed by the Germans during the War. Inspired by this achievement, the major powers embarked on the development of guided missiles for both defensive and offensive purposes.[38] Because of the potential of such weapons, the Canadian

Government formed a Guided Missile Advisory Committee in October 1946. During 1947, DRB examined the issue of guided missiles in the context of future requirements of the Canadian Armed Forces. It soon became clear to Solandt that "the Canadian Services could not maintain leadership unless they kept pace with developments in guided missiles and were prepared to fight both with and against these weapons."[39] DRB's Chairman considered that the question facing Canada was not whether it was appropriate for the nation to undertake work on guided missiles but rather when and how the work should be undertaken. But the enormous costs associated with the development of a guided missile prevented Canada, at the time, from launching such a venture.

Despite these negative factors, the Defence Research Board did not completely abandon this option, considering that, for reasons of national security, the nation could not allow itself to be totally isolated from this new technology. For this reason, in 1947 DRB selected a number of promising young scientists and sent them to study missile technology in the United States, at the Johns Hopkins and Michigan universities and at the USAF research and development establishment at Wright Field.[40] In DRB's first semi-annual report, Solandt stressed that general research on "liquid propellants for rockets and guided missiles is in hand". He considered that this research would be long-term, and that research conducted until then had been largely aimed at familiarizing scientific and technical staffs with the technology through a survey of the literature and the conduct of some experiments.[41] In other words, the Board was aware that Canada had few resources that could be applied immediately to this field of research, but took steps to prepare for the future by training some of its personnel in this sophisticated technology. In many respects, this approach was motivated by the defence research policy guidelines established by Solandt in 1946, specifically those concerning the training of young researchers and scientific collaboration with the allied nations.

3.2.2. Why an Air-to-Air Missile?

As the scientists were expanding their knowledge, the world situation was changing on all fronts. The Soviets consolidated their position in Eastern Europe while their Tupolev TU-4 long-range heavy bomber shattered any illusions of security held by the populations of North America. From that time on, Canada progressively set aside the scepticism that had guided, to some extent, its defence policies since 1945[42], for the threat no longer hanged only over Europe but equally over all Canadians. Defence of the Western Hemisphere began to make good sense and Ottawa came to view air defence as a priority concern.

As we have seen, air defence was the sector in which policy integration and weapons standardization between Canada and the United States had been pursued most intensely. According to Stanley, "The Royal Canadian Air Force, following the Second World War, established intimate relations with the United States Air Force and adopted not only the American managerial and control techniques but also American strategic thinking."[43]

This was the line of thinking that led the RCAF to develop a requirement for a fighter aircraft capable of operating in the extreme climatic conditions of the Arctic. Once this requirement had been formulated, it was clear that "the RCAF had drawn up a specification for a defensive fighter capable of operating by day and night, in all weather". No such aircraft existed at the time, and C.D. Howe, the all-powerful Minister, concluded that "the only alternative was to produce one!"[44] The contract was awarded to A.V. Roe, and the CF-100 Canuck began to take shape on the drawing boards of the company's engineers.

DRB, for its part, recognizing the growing importance of air superiority, decided to expand the areas of research at its Valcartier Establishment to accommodate the needs of the RCAF. In September 1949, the Chairman DRB suggested that a small working group be established to assess the needs of the Armed

Forces in the guided missile field.[45] During this period, the RCAF concluded that its future twin-jet fighter should be equipped with a guided missile, because only this type of weapon could provide it with real superiority in a combat situation. The RCAF considered the air-to-air missile "as long-term fighter armament",[46] and the Chief of the Air Staff conveyed this need to DRB.

Following receipt of this request, the Board had to decide whether Canada should develop its own missile or meet the requirement by "suitably modifying a missile under development in some other country."[47] It should be mentioned that the Americans, on the strength of their experience, were working on a missile characterized by the Financial Post as futuristic, while the British were developing a simpler missile "on a let's have-it-now-basis."[48] To have as much information as possible at its disposal, DRB consulted the Guided Missile Committee of the US Research and Development Board.

This Committee suggested to DRB that it should consult the Guided Missile Working Party 15 (WP 15) of the Air Standardization Coordinating Committee which was a tripartite group composed of the senior staffs of the British, Canadian and American air forces. The Board was not averse to this, because such an initiative was in line with one of DRB's main objectives - that of avoiding duplication of effort by coordinating Canada's military research with that of Canada's Anglo-Saxon allies. In April 1950, WP 15 deliberated on the matter. Based on American and British research programs underway at the time, the tripartite committee concluded that Canada should undertake the development of a missile that "would use a relatively simple concept, employ known technology and know-how, and incorporate the largest possible number of existing components."[49]

3.2.3 CARDE's Role in Conducting an Opportunity and Feasibility Study on an Air-to-Air Missile

Once DRB received this endorsement, the Board asked CARDE to undertake a preliminary study on some general aspects surrounding such a guided missile project. The Establishment at Valcartier completed this study promptly, and it was referenced in the Minutes of the Fifteenth Meeting of DRB, held in mid-June 1950, as the basis for asserting that development of an air-to-air missile was feasible in Canada. The authors of this study also elaborated the central objective of the project, namely to use it as a means of training scientific personnel who would be capable of developing guided missiles and of allowing the Armed Forces and industry to become familiar with the problems and technologies of this new weapons system. They also pointed out that the costs of the project would be lowered because the British and Americans would provide the information needed for the missile's development.

According to the study, the time required to develop and produce the first missile would be between four and seven years, depending on the complexity of the system. The study also estimated that the project would cost about $1 million annually, "exclusive of salaries and overhead borne by DRB to the amount of about $650,000". DRB contributions would account for some 20% of the total costs, with the Armed Forces (mainly the RCAF) accounting for the remaining 80%. The authors pointed out that 15% of these amounts would be required for the construction of adequate facilities needed to complete the project. They hastened to point out that this infrastructure would be permanent and could be used for other types of research. Based on the experience of other nations, the authors recommended that responsibility for the project be assigned to a project director. Finally, the study team expressed the belief that DRB already possessed an appreciable number of personnel and facilities needed to complete the project.⁵⁰ Based on the conclusions of this study, and the fact that the RCAF had generated an official requirement for such a missile, the Board members gave their approval to undertake the project.⁵¹

In turn, the Cabinet Defence Committee had to approve the project, but an event intervened to upset the agenda. On 25 June, North Korean troops crossed the 38th Parallel and invaded South Korea. The whole world watched as the war raged in *Chôsen*, the "Land of Morning Calm". On 7 August, Prime Minister Louis Saint-Laurent announced his intention of sending a special brigade of volunteers to Korea. In September, the news from the front was better; United Nations forces were regaining lost ground. This was the context in which the Cabinet Defence Committee, on 18 September, authorized the development of Canada's first semi-active air-to-air missile.

On 9 October 1950, the Canadian Armament Research and Development Establishment at Valcartier was tasked to undertake a technical study of the missile. A small team of researchers was formed and it immediately set about its task. Working diligently, the team completed the preliminary study barely 45 days afterwards. According to Solandt, this was a particularly intense period for the CARDE researchers due to both the demands of the work and the frequent visits that they had to make to British and American research establishments.⁵²

The Chairman DRB also recounts that the CARDE management was responsible for identifying industrial organizations capable of participating in the project. According to one person interviewed, there were no industries at the time capable "of undertaking this kind of activity as a prime contractor. We, representing the government or customer, did not have the capability to even write the proper specifications for such a contract."⁵³ Indeed, the precise aim of this project to develop an air-to-air missile was to rectify this situation by exposing industry and government establishments to this new technology. During the fall of 1950, CARDE also negotiated with the National Aeronautical Establishment and the Defence Research

Telecommunications Establishment to establish partnership arrangements and assign responsibilities in undertaking this vast project. To conclude this period of intense negotiations, CARDE succeeded in obtaining the Army's approval to conduct missile tests at the Army's anti-aircraft firing range at Point Petre, near Picton, Ontario.[54]

In March 1951, the members of the guided missile committees and the air force staffs from the three countries held an *ad hoc* meeting at CARDE in Valcartier to weigh all the factors which had emerged in the study undertaken by the scientists. At this meeting it was decided to give "unqualified approval to the CARDE technical proposal"[55], and Mr. G.D. Watson, Superintendent of the Ballistics Wing, became the project officer.[56] For administrative purposes, project number N-44 was assigned. Few people remember this number, and today the corporate memory of the Establishment at Valcartier remembers the project by the lyrical appeal of its name, Velvet Glove. The reasons why the Canadian Government chose this name are unknown, but perhaps it was inspired by the saying: "An iron hand in a velvet glove".

3.3 CARDE AND THE EVOLUTION OF THE VELVET GLOVE PROGRAM

3.3.1 Complexity of the Air-to-Air Missile

In 1951, Canada embarked on the development of a relatively small tactical missile, roughly 10 feet long and less than a foot in diameter.[57] It had a cruciform design configuration with "full wing deflection steering ..., [an] X-band pulse radar [semi-active guidance system], a microwave vacuum tube type fuze, and [a] fragmentation type warhead of 60-65 pounds."[58] The missile was complex in terms of both its intrinsic sub-systems (e.g., sophisticated electronics) and the systems integration problems associated with, *inter alia*, aerodynamic design, propulsion, guidance and control, and warhead and fuze systems (see Figure 5). As well, the development of an air-to-air missile also meant that a series of tests had to be conducted. A complex instrumentation system was used, first to check proper operation of the various missile sub-systems, and second, to ensure that the missile would function as an integrated, operational unit.[59] Despite its high level of technical complexity, Velvet Glove could not be considered as a hyper-sophisticated missile; indeed, the *ad hoc* committee selected the missile in March 1951 for the very reason that it could be used as a vehicle for training Canadian scientists and industrialists in this field of defence science.

3.3.2 Some of the Organizational Challenges posed by the Velvet Glove Program to CARDE Management

Regardless of the missile's level of complexity, the development of this air-to-air missile nevertheless represented a first achievement for Canada. It required the support and expertise of specialists from disciplines as diverse as chemistry, physics, aerodynamics, mathematics, mechanical engineering and electronics. In order to guarantee successful completion of the project, the Defence Research Board had to ensure that all the experts could work efficiently and smoothly within the framework of a vast plan. To meet this organizational challenge, the project was "organized to give effective overall system design control of the characteristics of the individual component systems and to take the maximum advantage of existing facilities and personnel. Design responsibility for the weapon system [was] assigned to CARDE."[60] Mr. G.D. Watson became the project officer as mentioned previously.

The exact manner in which Mr. Watson managed to coordinate research for the entire air-to-air missile program during 1951 and 1952 is not known. But we do know that the increased tempo of the Velvet Glove project strongly influenced the organization of work at the Canadian Armament Research and

Development Establishment in Valcartier. In 1952, it became evident that the Establishment had to create a centralized coordination service for its scientific activities. This led the Chief Superintendent to make plans for the creation of a Project Coordination Group by 1 January 1953. The mandate of this Group, which comprised three members, was to coordinate the flow of work across the various research programs in progress at Valcartier.

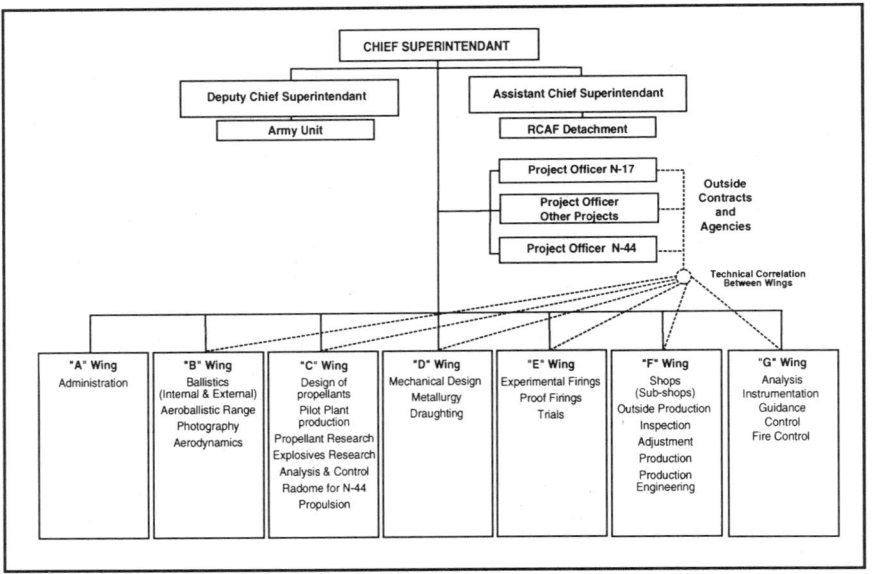

Figure 4 - *General organization Chart Showing Technical Coordination Between Various CARDE Wings on 1 January 1953.*

Source: *Annual Report of CARDE, January 1952 to December 1952. p. 40.*

Because of the size of the Velvet Glove project and the research program for the Heller anti-tank rocket, the Chief Superintendent appointed the respective project officers, Mr. G.D. Watson and Major J.M. Seldon, to this Coordination Group. The third member of the Group was Lieutenant Colonel J.S. Dunphy, who was made responsible for coordinating all of CARDE's other projects.[61] The 1953 Annual Report attests to the creation of this

Group, but does not provide sufficient detail to establish the real influence that it exerted on the conduct of research activities at CARDE.

In addition to organizing the flow of work, CARDE management also created two new wings, the F (Fabrication) Wing and the G (Guided Missile) Wing (see Figure 4). These wings were created because of the increased activities of B and D Wings and the need to split up their operations in order to refocus their responsibilities around certain well-defined functions. Thus, in January 1953, the machine shops and production engineering sections of D Wing were reorganized as F (Fabrication) Wing, while most of the guided missile research groups in B Wing were reorganized to form G Wing. As Figure 4 shows, this structural reorganization did not imply that the other scientific Wings would cease to participate in varying degrees in the air-to-air missile program.

Through this restructuring, CARDE management sought to adapt its organization to the flow of research generated by its scientists and to the management of activities on a project basis while preserving the "Wing" structure. In this sense, CARDE management was faithful to the principle that the organizational structure should remain flexible and be capable of adapting continually to the dynamic nature of research, rather than vice versa. This administrative reorganization took place under a new Chief Superintendent, Dr. H.M. Barrett, a former Wing Superintendent at Suffield, who replaced Mr. Carleton Craig. Mr. Craig, who had held the position since 1949, returned to his faculty at McGill University in September 1952.

After the air-to-air missile program started in 1951, CARDE management had to face an equally important organizational challenge, that of ensuring a continual exchange of information between the scientists (chemists, physicists, aerodynamicists and mathematicians) and engineers. The scientists would have to communicate information to the engineers and technicians, while the latter would have to bring their problems to the scientists.[62] In short, those responsible for the air-to-air missile program had to create a working environment conducive to information exchange. This was the best way of stimulating creative synergy between the various participants in the project. Undoubtedly, those responsible for the Velvet Glove project had appropriate communications mechanisms, but the Annual Reports of the Establishment are rather succinct on this matter.

3.3.3 The Participation of Industry and other Government Research Establishments in the Velvet Glove Project

In parallel with its responsibility to develop adequate internal management for the Velvet Glove project, CARDE also had to develop a solid base of guided missile expertise in the industrial sector through the award of contracts. Because there were no companies in Canada's defence industrial sector with expertise in the guided missile area, CARDE, in collaboration with the Department of National Defence and the senior military staffs, used a process of pre-selection to identify contractors with the necessary skills to manufacture the various sub-components of the missile. One person interviewed by the author stated that the following companies were selected: Canadair, for "the weapon overall systems integration, for manufacture of the body and of the test vehicles"; Computing Devices of Canada, for instrumentation and experimental models; Canadian Westinghouse Co. Ltd., "for the fire control system, fuzing and the guidance system"; and de Havilland Aircraft, for the control systems and "instrumentation help in test vehicle work".

Since Canada was breaking new ground with this project, adequately trained and experienced personnel were not always available in these companies to enable them to accomplish successfully their respective tasks. For this reason, the Canadian Armament Research and Development Establishment at Valcartier decided:

"to contract for industrial staff to come and work with us at the Establishment. These chosen industrial people from the designated prime contractors, assembled at CARDE and worked with the various divisions involved in the type of activity that eventually would be contracted out to them. When we got to a point when we knew what we were doing, when we knew what our specifications were, when we knew what our objectives were - we would then be able to write a specific contract allocated to the chosen prime contractor. The people that were trained with us were sent back to the industry to continue the contracted work."[63]

As Mr. Bobyn stressed, this customized training was not unidirectional; the CARDE scientists also benefited from the expertise of these contractor personnel to expand their knowledge in the guided missile field. Particular mention should be made of Dr. Bogdanov of Canadair who collaborated with Dr. Gerald Bull in resolving some of the aerodynamic problems associated with Velvet Glove.

At all events, the implementation of this training program for private sector professionals was surely not an easy matter from the standpoint of both human resources needed to train them and the security investigations needed to permit their presence on site. Some idea of the magnitude of CARDE's task can be gained from the fact that, in 1953, the number of private sector professionals working at the Establishment was roughly one-third of the total professional complement.[64] During the first half of the 1950s, the Establishment at Valcartier was, therefore, a true training school for contractors working on the Velvet Glove project. Because of this approach, which was aimed at maximizing technology transfer to private industry and supporting the development of a strong Canadian industry in this high technology sector, CARDE was able to achieve its ultimate objective of establishing an air-to-air missile program in Canada.

Although CARDE was fully responsible for the whole project, the Establishment nevertheless sought partnership with other government research establishments such as NRC and at

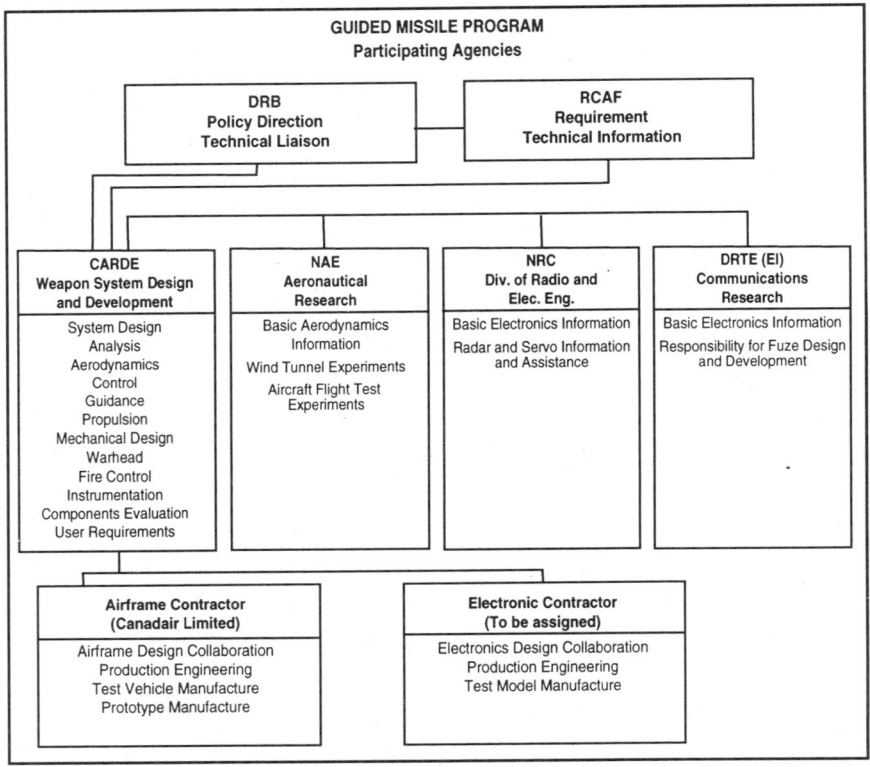

Figure 5 - *General Organizational Chart Showing Relational Structure of Guided Missile Programs in February 1952.*

Source: *Annual Report of CARDE, March 1951 to 29 February 1952.* p. 6.

least one of the other DRB establishments (see Figure 5). Two NRC divisions participated actively in the project. The National Aeronautical Establishment (NAE) worked with CARDE to solve some of the aerodynamic problems posed by the air-to-air missile,[65] while the Electronics Engineering Division assisted the Establishment at Valcartier with the integration of many electronic components for the Velvet Glove. DRB's Defence Research

Telecommunications Establishment (DRTE) collaborated mainly in the development of the guidance system. In addition, DRTE developed the proximity fuze and NAE "was responsible for the co-ordination of the design and installation of pylons and launchers for both the CF-100 and the F-86E aircraft."[66]

3.3.4 Initial Preparations

As we have seen, in 1949 the Royal Canadian Air Force generated a requirement for an air-to-air missile for its future twin-jet fighter. During the winter, DRB explored various options for meeting this requirement. At its meeting in March 1950, the Board examined the possibility of constructing an aeroballistic range at CARDE to study the trajectories of guided missiles under controlled conditions.[67] The Ballistics Wing was formally asked to look into this possibility as part of the opportunity and feasibility study for the air-to-air missile. In June 1950, the study recommendations were accepted and construction of the aeroballistic range started during the summer.[68] The staff of the Ballistics Wing did everything possible to make the range operational by the fall. This was a particularly remarkable feat since the staff was housed in temporary buildings at the time. DRB, aware of the accommodation problem, put the finishing touches to the construction plans for a permanent building to be located at the North Site of the Establishment. By the start of the new year, two events made it appear increasingly probable that the Velvet Glove project would be undertaken. The first was the decision to locate a Royal Canadian Air Force detachment at CARDE to participate in projects of interest to the RCAF. The second was the construction of a permanent building of 20,000 square feet ground floor area (Building 25) to meet the needs of the Ballistics Wing.[69] In March 1951, the tripartite committee approved the development of the air-to-air missile.

3.3.5 Evolution of the Velvet Glove Program at CARDE

From that moment, the air-to-air missile program at CARDE took off. In early 1951, the mandate of the Ballistics Wing was to conduct research to expand knowledge in the area of ballistics for application to design problems. When the Minister of National Defence announced the rearmament program for the Canadian Armed Forces, it caused a complete realignment of research at CARDE. Canada decide "while emphasis is placed on the major development projects, [Air-to-Air Guided Missile, Heller Anti-Tank Rocket, Pot Type Sabot] routine work proceeds, quietly and steadily, on general problems of research and development in the armament field."[70]

Construction of Building 25, which would become the headquarters of "G" Wing and, more recently, headquarters of the Electro-Optics Division.

But it would be wrong to consider that CARDE's share in the development of the Velvet Glove air-to-air missile - this Canadian "first" - was the work of a single individual or even of a single Wing. The success of Velvet Glove was due to all the employees of CARDE and all the public and private sector organizations involved who put their shoulders to the wheel to complete this project. It is true that, in March 1951, the Ballistics Wing of CARDE was the pivot around which the project revolved, but progressively all the Wings of the Establishment at Valcartier came to make their own contributions. This is illustrated in Figure 4, but there is little other precise information since the annual reports make only brief mention of this subject.

On the other hand, several individuals who were interviewed confirm that most defence scientists at CARDE participated in varying degrees in this research project. According to Goodspeed, the Velvet Glove project accounted for at least 50% of the Establishment's research budget in 1953.[71] But according to one person interviewed, the figure was even higher and, during a certain period, the project consumed almost 75% of the Establishment's effort. Irrespective of the actual figure, the mobilization of all the resources at the Establishment at Valcartier in support of this research project was completely consistent with DRB's policy of placing priority on research and development leading to finished products.[72]

During the first phase of the project, CARDE personnel undertook theoretical and experimental work to determine the design characteristics of all the components of the missile, except for the rocket motor, which was purchased from the United States. In support of this work, a considerable amount of electronic equipment was acquired by the Establishment at Valcartier, including "a three dimensional analogue electronic computer and the related electronic simulator equipment."[73] Electronics played a very important role in all phases of the missile's development.

The research teams responsible for the project clearly undertook their tasks swiftly because, as Solandt observes, the first CARDE studies were sufficiently advanced by the summer of

1951 to permit the first contract to be signed with a private company.[74] In a sense, it was an amazing feat, for these teams were relatively limited. The enthusiasm of the researchers in the project was clearly demonstrated by the long hours that they devoted to the work and the speed with which it was completed. We should mention too that a sense of urgency pervaded the whole country at the time due to the conviction of Canadians that a general war was imminent - a conviction that was shared by the peoples of many other nations. In such a context, CARDE staff could only respect the watchword of DRB which was to complete the project in the shortest possible time in order to equip the future RCAF fighters (CF-100 and F-86 Sabre) with air-to-air missiles.[75] Canadair, the aircraft manufacturing company, was contracted to work on "the mechanical design and construction of missile airframes for ground-launched tests. These were to be, in effect, full scale models of the missile, and were given the name 'test vehicles'."[76]

In parallel, the Velvet Glove project officer had to make sure that the site planned for testing the experimental models of the air-to-air missile was ready as soon as possible. Accordingly, he gave one of CARDE's ballistics experts the task of adapting the Army range at Point Petre to the particular needs of the project. Because this task was of the highest importance, he selected one of the few Canadian experts with guided missile training at a US university, Mr. E.J. Bobyn. In Mr. Bobyn's own words, "I was involved in designing and installing the range instrumentation at Point Petre for our firing trials. I assisted in designing the servo control systems for the Velvet Glove, that is, the aerodynamic control system". In addition, Mr. Bobyn was responsible for the design and instrumentation of all experimental models to be test-fired at this Ontario range.[77] According to a CARDE annual report, the first experimental models were fired in December 1951.[78]

By 1952, the project had reached its full level of activity. CARDE scientists had completed the preliminary systems design and, in collaboration with the contractors, had started the design of the missile structure and its electronic components.[79] The aeroballistic range, completed in 1951, was fully operational, allowing Establishment experts to conduct "guided missile scale model firings with temporary instrumentation."[80] Construction of permanent facilities for the Ballistics Wing had been completed, allowing the experts to conduct ongoing experimental studies and further development work under better conditions. In 1952, some twenty test vehicles were fired at the Point Petre range to determine the effects of acceleration and vibration. These test vehicles were ground-launched and the models were non-manoeuvring.

Figure 6- Contributions of Various Organizations Participating in the Velvet Glove Project During 1953.

RCAF/Chief of Armament	Service technical requirements and support
RCAF/Central Experimental & Proving Establishment (CEPE)	Operational control of air trials program, test facilities, personnel.
NAE	Aerodynamic testing, launcher design and development
DRTE (Electronics Laboratory)	Fuze design and development
Canadair Limited	Airframe development, pylon and launcher development, hydraulic control equipment, personnel.
Canadian Westinghouse Co. Ltd	Development of missile electronic equipment and test equipment, personnel
A.V. Roe (Canada) Limited	Launcher installation on CF-100, personnel

Source: CARDE, Annual Report for 1953, p. 27.

Once development of the various missile components was sufficiently advanced, the research team proceeded with flight-testing. This was the case for "the guidance unit, the hydraulic servo unit with control system, and a preliminary airframe". In anticipation of the flight test phase, the Royal Canadian Air Force moved half of its detachment from CARDE to the airport at Ancienne-Lorette, near Quebec City. The RCAF dispatched a contingent of 22 personnel and two B-25 aircraft in order to conduct flight testing during 1952. A four-storeyed building was constructed at the airport to accommodate research laboratories and the radar equipment needed for all the operations.[81]

The ground-launched tests at Point Petre continued through 1953. On 27 August, the first air-launch of the missile was conducted from a F-86E Sabre fighter aircraft. It was successful and, according to Goodspeed: "The first air launchings were carried out with fixed-wing models, then the program advanced to the firing of control models, and finally to models with seeker heads in them."[82] By 1954, the flight test program had advanced to the point where the performance of all missile components had been tested except for the guidance and fire control systems. Because of the restricted size of the Point Petre Range, firings at targets had to be conducted at the RCAF station at Cold Lake, Alberta. As the program continued, CARDE secured the services of two new companies, De Havilland and Computing Devices of Canada (see above). This was also the year when the project lost one of its first architects, Mr. G.D. Watson, who was transferred to DRB Headquarters in Ottawa. He was replaced by Dr. Barrett, the Chief Superintendent.

3.3.6   The Velvet Glove Missile is Abandoned

By 1955, the Velvet Glove missile was virtually fully developed. The test firings had demonstrated the capabilities of the guided missile and the Canadian Government had to decide whether or not to move the program into serial production. Originally designed for the CF-100 and F-86E fighter aircraft, the missile, if produced, would also be used as a weapon for the supersonic CF-105. At about this time, RCAF Headquarters observed that the Unites States had developed a similar, though somewhat more advanced, missile and the Canadian Government was duly informed. The government had to choose between a more effective weapon and the future of a Canadian industry that had been so meticulously created to have the capability of developing any guided missile right from preliminary design through to final production.

Canada was not swayed by the fact that some 24 million dollars had been invested in the project. It was decided "not to adopt Velvet Glove for operational use, but to modify the Velvet Glove program and go into production of one of the Sparrow series for use with the CF-100 and the CF-105."[83] The contract to build the Sparrow missile under licence was awarded to Canadair. This decision caused something of a stir within Canadian industry, as evidenced by the number of articles that were written on the matter.

In 1955, the Velvet Glove project attracted the energies of "some 400 scientists and specialists in industry and in the forces."[84] CARDE was then made responsible for ensuring that the experience acquired over the course of the former years was not wasted. For this reason, it was decided "to phase out the Velvet Glove at the same rate that Sparrow II was to be phased in."[85] The process began in March 1955 with CARDE gradually relinquishing certain responsibilities for the project. By June, most of the contractor personnel had left the Establishment in Valcartier. On 31 October 1955, the Guided Missile Project Office at CARDE closed its doors, and Chief Superintendent Barrett was transferred to DRB Headquarters. The following morning, Brigadier Waldock became the new Chief Superintendent. On the same day that he took up office, technical responsibility for the program was assigned to Canadair, but CARDE nevertheless retained design authority. Through this move, it was hoped that the Establishment could devote its efforts "to research and basic techniques to meet future service requirements."[86] In December 1955, the DRB Management Committee started to prepare for the future by planning a research program to replace the missile program that had inspired and attracted the dedicated efforts of so many. This being done, the Establishment could consider that its mission had been accomplished, for it had developed within Canadian industry the capability to undertake high-technology work in an exacting field. CARDE had thus succeeded in building up Canadian companies experienced in guided missile design and development. In April 1956, CARDE handed over its last responsibilities for the air-to-air missile to the Royal Canadian Air Force.

3.3.7 The Impact of the Velvet Glove Project on CARDE's Budget and Personnel

This transfer of responsibility marked an important step in CARDE's history, and proved that the Establishment was capable of undertaking and completing large projects. To undertake the Velvet Glove project, the Establishment had to implement an extensive plan to develop expertise amongst industrial personnel in guided missile technologies and establish an on-going partnership with industry and various government research organizations. CARDE management also had to meet the organizational and technological challenges posed by this first ever Canadian missile development venture and to maintain a climate of confidence and close collaboration with the customer, the Royal Canadian Air Force.

As one might imagine, the Canadian Armament Research and Development Establishment in Valcartier could not have accomplished this feat with the scientific staff and financial resources that were made available in 1950. Through the impetus of the project, the number of professional and other staff at CARDE was increased significantly. When the project started in March 1951, the Establishment had only 46 professionals and military officers on staff, but by December 1954 the number of professionals had reached 101.

It is not surprising there that the Establishment payroll

Figure 7 - Human Resources of CARDE and Growth by Employment Category for the Period January 1952 through December 1954.

	Jan 1952	Feb 1952	Dec 1953	Dec 1954	Increase (52-54)
CIVILIANS					
Professionals	63	76	90	101	38
Technicians	110	145	160	175	65
Draughtsmen	18	19	22	27	9
Clerical Staff	72	77	81	83	11
General Workers	129	143	141	149	20
Workshop Staff	83	107	115	117	34
Maintenance Staff	41	40	40	40	-1
Casuals (average)	75	75	75	78	3
Total	**591**	**682**	**724**	**770**	**179**
RCN (Royal Canadian Navy)			1	1	1
ADEE (Canadian Army)					
Officers	11	15	18	15	4
Servicemen	37	37	41	46	9
Total	**48**	**52**	**59**	**61**	**13**
CEPE (Air Force)					
Officers	7	5+2*	9	8	1
Servicemen	21	9+20*	24	49	28
Total	**28**	**14+22=36**	**33**	**57**	**29**
* CEPE at L'Ancienne Lorette					

Source: CARDE, Annual Reports for 1952 to 1954.

increased from almost $860,000 in 1949-1950 to $2,533,000 for fiscal year 1955-1956. The total budget of the Establishment soared from $1,351,305 to $15,654,176 in less than six years. According to available budget data, the Royal Canadian Air Force allocated the following amounts to CARDE: $250,000 in 1950-51; $500,000 in 1951-52; $1,350,000 in 1952-53; and, $1,401,000 in 1953-54. Although no precise breakdown is available, it would appear that these monies were expended mainly on the purchase of equipment. Equally, it seems most likely that these funds were allocated by the RCAF for the Velvet Glove project. In 1954-55, an amount of $3,940,000 was designated specifically for the project, and in 1955-56 the amount allocated was $10,570,000, again under the financial code for equipment. The total allocation to the Valcartier research establishment from the RCAF to undertake the air-to-air missile project was thus $18,011,000. This was a huge budget for those years and represented over 75% of the total cost of the project which was estimated at about $24 million, or 42.67% of CARDE's cumulative budget ($42,207,190) for the period.

3.4 CONVENTIONAL WEAPONS DEVELOPMENT AT CARDE, 1950 TO 1955

The main responsibility of the CARDE Design Wing since its inception was to design and develop end products (projectiles and weapons) and to conduct engineering tests on prototype equipment. It was also responsible for providing technical advice to the Armed Forces on specific weapons. In order to fulfil its mandate, the Wing had, amongst other things, a metallurgy and materials testing section together with suitable workshops, machine shops and model shops. Scientists of D Wing, many of whom were military personnel, worked on the development of the light Pack Howitzer, the 3.2-inch Heller anti-tank rocket and the 17-pounder anti-tank projectile. Under the direction of Major Donaldson, D Wing recorded its first success in 1950 when the 17-pounder pot sabot shot passed acceptance trials for manufacture in the United Kingdom and Canada.

3.4.1 Heller

In August 1950, at the height of the Korean War, the Army sought to accelerate the Heller project in order to equip its troops with an anti-tank rocket.[87] The design of this weapon was influenced by the German Hammer rocket, and Heller had been under development by the Wing for several years. The research program was not, however, considered to be of high priority and full-time engineers and technicians were not assigned to the project until 1949.[88] In August 1950, Carleton Craig, the Chief Superintendent, proposed a four-point program to the Army

Research Coordination Group for developing this weapon system: "1) design of warhead and confirmation of penetration; 2) theoretical analysis of internal ballistics in order to meet the design condition with minimum weights; 3) stability investigation; 4) final design and firing trials."[89] The proposed program was accepted and Project N-17 was initiated.

The work of CARDE scientists led to the emergence of the first complete weapon, ammunition and fire control system to have been designed, developed and manufactured in Canada. This program was conducted in collaboration with the Army Directorate of Armament Development which participated in all phases of weapon development[90] and assisted scientists in adapting the weapon to Army needs. In this way, the customer was sure that the final product would meet the operational requirements. This collaboration was greatly facilitated by the fact that one quarter of D Wing's professionals were military personnel. In terms of its military complement, D Wing was second only to E Wing which was composed exclusively of military personnel. Because of its mandate and composition, D Wing was thus able to maintain an extremely close collaboration with the Army during the whole period of project development.

In February 1951, the Minister of National Defence, Brooke Claxton, announced a major rearmament program for the Canadian Armed Forces. For Claxton, there was a real threat of general war, and it was imperative that the nation be rearmed as quickly as possible. In this climate, research priorities shifted from basic research to actual weapon development. This meant that most of the effort of CARDE's scientific Wings was focused on the Velvet Glove and Heller projects.

Despite the importance of Heller, there was little mention of the development work undertaken on this project in subsequent CARDE annual reports. For this reason, the account which follows is necessarily terse. In February 1952, Heller reached the engineering test final design stage and tests on the prototype were scheduled for the fall of that year.[91] The Army transferred

$510,000 to the Establishment during the fiscal year to pay for salaries ($100,000) and to purchase equipment needed for the Heller development project. This was an important contribution given that the Army had previously allocated only $118,000 to the Establishment for undertaking projects. It may be noted also that there was no further transfer of Army funds to the Establishment before 1956-57.

Field Marshal Viscount Montgomery of Alamein questioning Mr. Gordon D. Watson, Superintendent of "B" Wing, about the performance of the new Heller antitank weapon during his visit to CARDE on 22 April 1953.

In January 1953, Major Seldon, project officer for Heller, was assigned to the CARDE Project Coordination Group. Research work on Heller Phase B probably started during that year. In 1954, production started on Heller Phase A and the research work on Heller Phase B was sufficiently encouraging to warrant the manufacture of a few prototypes.

In April 1955, National Defence Headquarters issued a formal press release on Heller. According to Pennie, Heller was "an anti-tank missile with a unique recoilless propulsion system

75-mm pack howitzer developed at DREV between 1949 and 1954. Its range and destructive power equalled those of the 25 pounder. It was used for many years by the Indian Army.

utilizing a Canadian breakthrough in propulsion engineering and design."[92] National Defence authorities viewed it as an extremely effective weapon in terms of both accuracy and penetrating power. As well, the weapon design was highly innovative and the weapon itself was especially useful for the infantry since it could be fired by a soldier while standing, kneeling or sitting.[93] At the time, Solandt considered that Heller was the best anti-tank weapon in the world.[94] Understandably, given such favourable perceptions, the Canadian Army was to retain Heller in its arsenal for many years to come.

During the Heller development phase, D Wing staff were also working on sabot-type projectiles and the 75/24 Canadian Pack Howitzer. Because of relative priorities, it was decided that this latter work would "be wound up as rapidly as possible."[95] In 1954, the government officially cancelled the Pack Howitzer project, after only one prototype had been built, since the system no longer met the requirements of the Canadian Army. Even this cancellation could not impede the success of this system which, according to Solandt, "has since become the standard armament of the Indian Army. We gave the design but never produced anything but the prototypes ourselves."[96]

1. Dr. O.M. Solandt, "Defence Research in Canada", *Address...* CBC, January 1947.
2. Brian Cuthbertson, *Canadian Military Independence in the Age of the Superpowers*, Don Mills, Ont., Fitzhenry & Whiteside, 1977, p. 21.
3. Desmond Morton, *A Military History of Canada: 1608-1991*, Toronto, McClelland & Stewart, 1992, p. 227.
4. George F. Stanley, *Canada's Soldiers: The Military History of an Unmilitary People*, Toronto, Macmillan, 1974.
5. *Ibid.*, p. 395.
6. Brian Cuthbertson, *op. cit.*, p. 22.
7. Reginald H. Roy, "Canadian Defence Policy 1945-1976", *Parameters*, Vol. VI, 1976, p. 61.
8. DND, *Annual Report of the Department of National Defence for Fiscal Year Ending 31 March 1950*, Ottawa, King's Printer, 1950, p. 33.
9. Jocelyn Coulon, *En première ligne. Grandeurs et misères du système militaire canadien*, Montreal, Éd. du Jour, 1991, p. 109.
10. Paul Dufour, *Les "Eggheads" et l'espionnage: les réactions des scientifiques américains, canadiens et britanniques à l'affaire Gouzenko de 1946*, Master's Thesis, Université de Montréal, Montréal, 1979, p. 7.
11. J.W. Pickersgill, *The Mackenzie King Record*, p. 134; cited by Paul Dufour, *op. cit.*, p. 8.
12. *Ibid.*, p. 417-418.
13. Luc Chartrand et al., *Histoire des sciences au Québec*, Boréal, Montréal, 1987, p. 417-418.
14. Rénald Fortier, *Intervention gouvernementale et industrie aéronautique: L'exemple canadien 1920-1945*, Doctoral thesis, Université Laval, Québec, 1990, p. 408.
15. Desmond Morton, *op. cit.*, p. 327.
16. Brian Cuthbertson, *op. cit.*, p. 24.
17. *Ibid.*, p. 25.
18. George F. Stanley, *op. cit.*, p. 412.
19. Desmond Morton, *op. cit.*, p. 230.
20. Douglas Bland, *The Administration of Defence Policy: 1947 to 1985*, Kingston, Frye, 1987, p. 2.
21. Desmond Morton, *op. cit.*, p. 232.
22. *House of Commons Debates*, 24 June 1948, p. 5784.
23. *Ibid.*, p. 5786.
24. *House of Commons Debates*, 5 February 1951, p. 91.
25. Brigadier M.H.S. Penhale, *Memorandum on Canadian Post War Policy for Scientific Research for Defence*, p. 1, NAC, MG 31 G 21, Vol. 6, 22 January 1946.

26 NAC, RG 24, Vol. 11995, Dr. O.M. Solandt, *Policy and Plans for Defence Research*, 3 May 1946, p. 1.
27 *Ibid.*, p. 5-6.
28 *Ibid.*, p. 6 and Appendix A.
29 Capt D.J. Goodspeed, *A History of the Defence Research Board*, Ottawa, Queen's Printer, 1958, p. 51-52.
30 *Ibid.*, p. 80.
31 Canada, *A Brief History of the Office of the Counsellor Defence Research and Development London (CDRD(L)) 1940-1993*, Ottawa, CRAD/DND, 1994.
32 Dr. O.M. Solandt, *The Defence Research Board: The First Four Years*, Ottawa, DRB, March 1951, p. 21.
33 Capt D.J. Goodspeed, *op. cit.*, p. 80-81.
34 Dr. O.M. Solandt, "Defence Research ...", *Address...CBC*.
35 Capt D.J. Goodspeed, *op. cit.*, p. 81.
36 NAC, RG 24, Vol. 11995, *Dr. O.M. Solandt, Policy and Plans...*, p. 9.
37 NAC, RG 24, Vol. 11995, *Annual Report of DRB for 1952*, p. 7.
38 Capt D.J. Goodspeed, *op. cit.*, p. 128.
39 Dr. O.M. Solandt, *Fifth Annual Birthday Address*, 1952, p. 6.
40 *Ibid.*
41 DRB, Semiannual *Report of the Chairman of DRB, 1 April - 30 September 1947*, Ottawa, November 1947, p. 50.
42 Rénald Fortier, *op. cit.*, p. 408-409.
43 George F. Stanley, *op. cit.*, p. 413-414.
44 Robert Bradford, "*Canadian Innovation: The CF-100 Story*", AE Quarterly/Four, p. 152-153.
45 NAC, RG 24, Vol. 11995, *Annual Report of the Chairman DRB for 1949*, 1949, p. 9.
46 NAC, RG 24, Vol. 11995, *15th Meeting of DRB*, June 1950, p. 1.
47 Dr. O.M. Solandt, *Fifth Annual...*, p. 7.
48 "Science for War Means Ideas for Industry", *Financial Post*, 4 May 1957.
49 Dr. O.M. Solandt, *Fifth Annual...*, p. 8.
50 NAC, RG 24, Vol. 11995, *15th Meeting...*, p. 1-2.
51 Dr. O.M. Solandt, *Fifth Annual...*, p. 8.
52 *Ibid.*
53 *Interview with Mr. E.J. Bobyn*, p. 12.
54 Dr. O.M. Solandt, *Fifth Annual...*, p. 8.
55 *Ibid.*, p. 9.
56 Aircraft, "The Weapon that Almost was" (Velvet Glove), *Aircraft*, 19 March 1957, p. 101.
57 Dr. O.M. Solandt, *Fifth Annual...*, p. 9.

58 CARDE, *Annual Report for March 1951 to February 1952*, p. 5.
59 Dr. O.M. Solandt, *Fifth Annual...*, p. 9.
60 CARDE, *Annual Report ...* February 1952, p. 5.
61 CARDE, *Annual Report for 1953*, p. 1 and 33.
62 Dr. O.M. Solandt, "Defence Research in Canada", The Engineering Journal, August 1951, p. 766.
63 *Interview with Mr. E.J. Bobyn*, p. 13.
64 CARDE, *Annual Report...1953*, p. 27.
65 NAC, RG 24, Vol. 11995, *Annual Report of DRB for 1951*, p. 9.
66 Capt D.J. Goodspeed, *op. cit.*, p. 130.
67 NAC, RG 24, Vol. 11995, *14th Meeting of the DRB*, 16 March 1950.
68 NAC, RG 24, Vol. 11995, *Annual Report of DRB Chairman*, September 1950, p. 8.
69 CARDE, *Annual Progress Report for the Year 1950*, p. 2 and 76.
70 CARDE, *Third Annual Meeting: Administrative Staffs of the DRB...*, Valcartier, September 1952, p. 5, 6 and 9.
71 Capt D.J. Goodspeed, *op. cit.*, p. 130.
72 CARDE, *Annual Report ...* Feb. 1952, p. 4.
73 Capt D.J. Goodspeed, *op. cit.*, p. 130.
74 Dr. O.M. Solandt, *Fifth Annual...*, p. 9.
75 CARDE, *Annual Report...1953*, p. 27.
76 Dr. O.M. Solandt, *Fifth Annual...*, p. 9.
77 *Interview with Mr. E.J. Bobyn*, p. 9.
78 CARDE, *Annual Report...Feb. 1952*, p. 4.
79 CARDE, *Third Annual Meeting: Administrative Staffs of the DRB...*, p. 8.
80 CARDE, *Annual Report ...* Feb. 1952, p. 2.
81 CARDE, *Annual Report for 1952*, p. 1-5.
82 Capt D.J. Goodspeed, *op. cit.*, p. 131.
83 *House of Commons Debates 1956*, p. 5214.
84 *Ibid.*, p. 6122.
85 CARDE, *Annual Report for 1956*, p. 7.
86 CARDE, *Annual Report for 1955*, p. 1.
87 NAC, RG 24, Vol. 4238, *Memorandum, 8 August 1950*.
88 Capt D.J. Goodspeed, *op. cit.*, p. 127.
89 NAC, RG 24, Vol. 4238, DRBS-50-876-267-1 Vol. 1, *Chief Superintendent of CARDE to Chairman DRB, 17 October 1950*.
90 Canadian Army Journal, "New Anti-Tank Weapon is Developed for Canadian Army", *Canadian Army Journal*, April 1955, p. 44.
91 CARDE, *Annual Report ...* Feb. 1952, p. 1.
92 A.M. Pennie, "DRB Quarter-Century Mark", *Sentinel*, April 1972, p. 22.

93   Canadian Army Journal, *op. cit.*, p. 44.
94   Dr. O.M. Solandt, *Science as it Relates to Defence*, p. 12.
95   NAC, RG 24, Vol. 11995, *Annual Report of DRB for 1951*, p. 18.
96   Dr. O.M. Solandt, *Science as it Relates to Defence*, p. 12.

> *"The ICBM race revealed a new factor in the Cold War: The rapidly changing nature and acceleration of weapon technology had led to a technological conflict between the two superpowers. The cruciality of this conflict is evident when it is realized that any product of military technology which makes possible an advantage for one side over the other may alter the balance of power between the two nations."* B.D. Adams[1]

4

APPLIED RESEARCH PROGRAM ON ACTIVE DEFENCE AGAINST INTERCONTINENTAL BALLISTIC MISSILES, 1955-1970

4.1 DEFENCE AGAINST INTERCONTINENTAL BALLISTIC MISSILES

4.1.1 General Historical Context

The United States and the USSR emerged from the Second World War as the dominant global powers, with each acquiring part of the spheres of influence held by the pre-war powers. Soviet power derived from an impressive military-industrial complex and the rich human and material resources of the vast expanses of the USSR. American might, on the other hand, was founded on unparalleled economic power and a monopoly on the atomic bomb.

In the climate of the immediate post-war period, hope for peace was universal. American troops were extensively demobilized and the United States relied on its impressive nuclear capability to deter any potential adversary. The Americans made it clear that they would not strike first but, if attacked, they would not hesitate, if necessary and in principle, to retaliate with nuclear weapons: the concept of nuclear deterrence took shape. To implement this strategy, the United States had to develop a nuclear strike force consisting of long-range bombers equipped with an adequate number of atomic bombs. For his part, Stalin naturally had no wish to expose the Soviet Union to an open general conflict with the United States for fear of suffering a resounding defeat. In an attempt to swing the strategic balance in their favour, the Soviets mounted an immense scientific, financial and industrial effort to break the American nuclear monopoly.

Until they could close the gap in weapons technology, the Soviets strived to consolidate their position in Eastern Europe and elsewhere in the world, taking care not to clash head on with the Americans. In March 1947, President Harry S. Truman announced his policy of containment aimed at checking Moscow's strategic advances, and the West demonstrated its resolve to protect its position during the Berlin blockade of 1948. One year later, the Soviet Union altered the geostrategic balance by successfully exploding an A-bomb and completing flight tests of a long-range strategic bomber. Notwithstanding these successes, Moscow still lacked a sufficient number of delivery vehicles to counter the nuclear arsenal developed by the United States during the prior four years. The Pentagon had few concerns for the short term since it had "50 long-range bombers and 50 bombs capable of reaching Soviet territory."[2] But in the longer term, Washington's lead stood to be reduced significantly by the massive efforts expended by the Kremlin.

In Canada, the Minister of National Defence, Brooke Claxton, echoed the opinion shared by other North American leaders when he stopped using veiled language in the House of Commons to refer to the USSR and clearly identified it as the one and only potential aggressor. In the same breath, he warned that the threat could come from the sky or the sea. To counter it, North America would have to possess jet fighters, anti-aircraft weapons, a radar warning network, minesweepers and anti-submarine-warfare (ASW) ships.[3] As we have seen earlier, the Americans reacted to the Soviet threat by strengthening the continental defence system and ratifying the North Atlantic Treaty.

Harry Truman was not a man to take refuge behind a mythical impregnable fortress. At the time, American atomic scientists were working on the hydrogen bomb concept and Truman believed that such a weapon would provide the United States with a sure advantage. Truman was no procrastinator. In January 1950, he launched a new nuclear arms race by announcing that the United States would undertake the development of a thermonuclear bomb. Shortly thereafter, he declared that the United States would undertake an extensive 10-billion dollar rearmament program.[4]

With the outbreak of the Korean War in June 1950, the eyes of the world turned towards Asia. The events of this conflict were to pose a significant threat to world peace. Forces of the United Nations (UN) Organization under American command (including a Canadian special brigade) confronted Chinese ground troops who came to the aid of the North Korean army. On another plane, two antagonistic ideologies, capitalism and communism, came into violent conflict. As events unfolded in the war, General Douglas MacArthur considered carrying the conflict to Chinese soil. Had he done so, it could have broken the delicate balance established with the Soviets and plunged the planet into deadly warfare. But opposition from the British and the UN prevailed over the offensive intentions of the 1945 conqueror of Japan. A delicate ground peace was established and, on 27 July 1953, President Dwight D. Eisenhower fulfilled his electoral promise by securing an armistice between the two Korean governments.

Canada, fearing the imminent outbreak of general war with the Communist bloc, was not slow to react as the war raged in Korea. The Minister of National Defence announced that a major rearmament program would be undertaken at a cost in excess of 5 billion dollars and that the strength of the Canadian Armed Forces would be increased. In 1953, the Department's budget was over a billion dollars.

During 1951 and 1952, a Summer Study Group met in the United States to solve the technical problems of air defence. According to Brian Cuthbertson, the Study Group concluded that within two or three years the Soviets could amass a sufficient number of aircraft and atomic bombs to launch a surprise attack against the United States. Despite US efforts to protect the continent against air attack, the Study Report concluded that, under the best of circumstances, only 20% of the Soviet delivery vehicles could be destroyed. To counter the threat, the Study Report recommended the construction of a warning network in the North to give the US strategic nuclear strike force some three to six hours warning of an enemy attack. Cuthbertson recounts that the recommendations of this report stirred a lively debate within the Eisenhower Administration which centred on the fundamental premise: "the problem of early warning [is] inseparable from the cost of an effective overall air defence system."[5]

The new Republican Administration showed little interest in funding the cost of such a system, and was inclined rather to cut defence spending in the belief that the United States had regained nuclear ascendency having exploded, on 7 November 1952, a 3- to 5-megaton nuclear device using the principle of fusion of light hydrogen atoms. But this proved to be a fleeting strategic advantage following the successful detonation of an H-bomb by the Soviets some eight months later. The strategic balance of terror was restored and with it all the intensity of debate on continental defence.

Confusion reigned over the best strategy to be employed. It was not until the mid-1950s that the debate took on a new meaning with the formulation of the "first strike, second strike" concept. Under this concept, "victory, the scientists argued, was no longer a matter of who made the first strike, but how much retaliatory strength survived for the victim to strike back." This fundamental conceptual breakthrough in the conduct of nuclear war is attributed to R.J. Sutherland, a Canadian scientist with DRB.[6] The strategic objective became clearer; preservation of a retaliatory capability was primordial, for a potential enemy would hesitate to attack unless he were certain of wreaking massive destruction on all his targets.

This was the context in which three radar warning networks were installed on Canadian territory during the 1950s. In August 1951, Canada authorized the construction of the Pinetree Line near the border with the United States. Canada funded one third of the cost of this Line, at least as far as the Canadian portion was concerned. DRB was responsible for installing the Mid-Canada Line (McGill Fence) on the 55th parallel. Finally, Canada and the United States agreed, in 1954, to construct the Distant Early Warning (DEW) Line. The Mid-Canada Line and the DEW Line became operational in 1957. As George F.G. Stanley stresses, "the purpose of these three radar lines was not to protect the cities of Canada or the United States, but to protect the aircraft of the United States Strategic Air Force from destruction on the ground by a surprise air attack"[7] so as to allow them sufficient time to take off towards their targets.

To optimize the effectiveness of the three radar warning networks, the US military proposed, in 1953, that all air defence hardware on the North American continent be brought under centralized control. According to Stanley, this idea was also envisaged by the RCAF in 1954.[8] On 19 December 1956, the Military Study Group, an organization of Canadian and US officers, "had approved operational integration and the centralization of authority for operational control - the power to direct, control and coordinate operational activities"[9] and formulated recommendations to the Canadian and US Governments. The United States accorded approval in principle in April 1957.

In the pre-election climate which prevailed in Canada, the Liberal government of Louis Saint-Laurent delayed signing the agreement for fear of offending the sensitivities of Canadian nationalists. Saint-Laurent dissolved Parliament on 12 April 1957 and announced that elections would be held on 10 June. It was a vigorous campaign, with the leader of the Conservative Party, John Diefenbaker, presenting himself as a soldier of the Cold War. He won the election and assumed office on 21 June 1957.

The new prime minister appointed MGen George Pearkes as Minister of National Defence. According to J.L. Granatstein, the former Liberal government had promised a decision by June on a unified continental air defence command and the new Defence Minister was sympathetic to the plan proposed by the Military Study Group. For Granatstein, this was no surprise since, in good military tradition, the Minister deemed that the needs of defence took precedence over political considerations.[10] The position held by Pearkes was probably not too far removed from that of General Foulkes who considered that Canada and the United States were geographical siamese twins and that it was impossible to separate the defence of Canada from the defence of the United States without putting Canada's survival at risk. This was especially true in the event of nuclear war where Canada could not hope to be spared massive damage: radiation does not respect national boundaries.[11]

With the support of the Minister of National Defence, the process of finalizing the North American Aerospace Defence (NORAD) Agreement was accelerated and the Prime Minister gave Canada's approval on 24 July. General Foulkes would write *a posteriori* that this agreement constituted the logical conclusion of a process started fifteen years earlier with the decision taken by both countries to jointly defend the airspace of the North American continent.[12]

Following Canadian Government endorsement, NORAD was created *de facto* in September 1957 and officially on 12 May 1958. Since then, the air defence forces of North America have been under the command of an American Commander and a Canadian Deputy Commander. From NORAD Headquarters at Cheyenne Mountain, Colorado, Canadian or American aircraft can be assigned combat missions indifferently according to circumstances. This unique arrangement led several observers to conclude that "Diefenbaker had unwittingly signed away his country's control of when it would declare war."[13] Others, such as General Foulkes, believed that this agreement placed Canada in a privileged position because "as we are full partners in the defence of North America, we have to be consulted every time the US contemplates using force anywhere in the world." In Foulkes' view, this privileged position allowed Canada to influence American politics.[14]

4.1.2 A Major Change in Military Strategy: The Introduction of Strategic Missiles

At the end of the Second World War, several eminent American scientists seriously doubted the possibility of developing intercontinental ballistic missiles (strategic weapons) and recommended that emphasis should be placed on the design of an intercontinental strategic bomber. The US Government heeded their advice and favoured the development of an airborne nuclear strike force. Research on intercontinental missiles was consequently relegated to second priority. To be more precise, it came to a standstill. In 1947, the relative scarcity of resources for the various defence research projects led to the cancellation of the ICBM (Intercontinental Ballistic Missile) Project MX-774. This did not, however, prevent the General Dynamics Corporation from pursuing company-funded research on the ICBM and, in 1951, the US Air Force revived the ICBM project.[15]

In 1952, the test at Eniwetok confirmed the feasibility of thermonuclear fusion of hydrogen. In June 1953, the eight-engined B-52 Stratofortress entered service with the United States Air Force (USAF). US authorities were so enthusiastic about this extraordinary aircraft that they delayed the development of the forerunner of the Atlas missile and dissolved the Guided Missile Office.

In March 1954, "the 'Shrimp' shot completely revolutionized ICBM design, for it showed that the warhead could be married to the ICBM without the necessity of designing the missile and its huge propulsion system around a large unsophisticated warhead."[16] This removed the main stumbling block in developing intercontinental ballistic missiles since, from then on, they could be fitted with nuclear warheads. Other technical problems remained to be solved, but the development of ICBMs then appeared possible from both a technical and financial standpoint.

At this point in time, the Americans recognized that the Soviets had a strong lead in the ICBM field as a result of their successful experiments with long-range missiles. The technological lead of the Soviets was important and could allow them to gain a crucial strategic advantage in the development of intercontinental missiles. The Americans were deeply concerned, and felt it imperative to close the technological gap. In September 1955, President Eisenhower accorded top national priority to the research program on intercontinental missiles.[17]

In November 1955, the Bell Telephone Laboratories undertook a feasibility study on the problems of developing an effective defensive system against ballistic missiles. The study was completed during the following year under the direction of ARGMA (Army Rocket and Guided Missile Agency). Early in 1956, the US Department of Defense again created a Guided Missile Office. At this time, a major conflict arose between the US Army and the USAF concerning jurisdiction over tactical air support, continental air defence, strategic missiles and military airlift. It was a bitter battle, but a directive issued in November 1956 clarified the situation somewhat although it did not dispel all the misunderstandings.[18] The US Army was assigned responsibility "for developing, procuring and manning land-based, surface-to-air missiles for point defence [while the USAF] was assigned responsibility and control over land-based, surface-to-air missiles for area defence."[19]

Meanwhile, the Department of National Defence undertook a joint project with the USAF to study and develop components and sub-systems for defence against the ICBM. Responsibility for the

Canadian portion of the project was assigned to DRB by the Chiefs of Staff Committee. A Canadian team including six CARDE scientists made an extensive tour of US agencies participating in anti-ICBM activities under USAF direction. Following the tour, the Canadian researchers prepared a report on the visit and invited their US counterparts to make a return visit to Canada.[20] This information exchange proved to be extremely beneficial for both countries.

In 1957, the United States launched a project to develop a defensive guided missile system known as Nike-Zeus. It proved to be just in time, because the Soviet program was advancing rapidly. In August 1957, Soviet scientists successfully launched a three-stage rocket, the T-3, with a range of 10,000 kilometres. This launch demonstrated that Moscow had effectively developed an intercontinental delivery vehicle capable of carrying a thermonuclear warhead. For USAF General Earl E. Partridge, Commander-in-Chief NORAD, the situation was of deep concern: "If the aggressor's weapon is the intercontinental ballistic missile this continent stands today as naked as it did in 1946, for I have no radar to detect missiles and no defence against them."[21]

Two months later, another bolt from the blue awakened America to the power of Soviet launch vehicles when Moscow placed Sputnik, the first artificial satellite, into orbit. Following these events, the Minister of National Defence, George Pearkes, asserted before Parliament:

> "[These events] emphasize the need for the nations of the free world to collaborate in matters of defence and point up the urgency of the pooling of scientific knowledge. Officials of the Defence Research Board have for many years maintained close liaison with their opposite numbers in the United Kingdom and the United States. These fruitful discussions are now being intensified. A major research contribution in support of the defence against the ICBM can be made by Canada in

the field of radio propagation, particularly with reference to the auroral zone. [...] Other programs now being undertaken by the Defence Research Board are aimed at problems in the missile field, particularly with respect to missile detection; at means for countering submarines; at many phases of electronics in defence and at operational research studies designed to indicate the most economical means of obtaining maximum effectiveness from present and proposed weapons systems."[22]

Responding to the challenge, the Americans repeated the Soviet accomplishments step for step, by launching the 10,000-kilometre range Atlas (ICBM) in December 1957, and by placing the Explorer satellite in orbit on 1 February 1958. The United States thus closed the gap with the USSR in the area of intercontinental ballistic missiles, but remained powerless in anti-ballistic missile defence of the continent. These years truly marked the beginning of the arms and space race between the two superpowers, and it would continue without respite for either superpower for several decades to come. We turn attention now to how the Canadian Armament Research and Development Establishment in Valcartier participated in this essential research to defend the continent from any possible attack by intercontinental ballistic missiles.

4.1.3 CARDE Scientists Seek a Replacement Program for Velvet Glove

During fall 1955, with research on the Velvet Glove project inexorably winding down, CARDE defence scientists found themselves at a crossroads. As we have seen, the research program on air-to-air missiles had dominated the activities of the Establishment for many years, and the termination of this program could only instill a sense of uncertainty amongst CARDE personnel concerning the future research activities of the

Establishment.

On the instructions of the Management Committee of the Defence Research Board, planning commenced at CARDE in December 1955 on a guided missile program to replace the Velvet Glove project. Having established the policy that development of guided missile systems would henceforth be handled by industry, the future applied research program would have two main aims; first, "to keep abreast of the overall field in order to be in a position to advise on service problems" and, second, "to make worthwhile contributions to the art in selected areas dispersed across the whole field."[23]

Once the objectives had been defined, the specifics had to be determined. In reflecting on the matter, senior scientists at the Valcartier establishment drew on the lessons learned from the first major project conducted by DRB. According to one person interviewed, two major elements emerged from this exercise of retrospection which was conducted in collaboration with the DRB Management Committee. First, senior scientists recognized that the air-to-air missile project had exerted a major impact on all the activities of the Establishment, and they deemed it imprudent to repeat a project of magnitude similar to that of Velvet Glove. Second, based on this recent experience, they stressed that the selected project should involve "military research that would be relatively permanent or last many, many years rather than a few short years."[24] In short, there had to be assurance that the selected project would not become obsolescent for any reason before the planned completion date.

With these aims in mind, scientists decided that the effort absorbed by the future program should not exceed the financial and human resource levels that had previously been allocated to the Velvet Glove project. They also agreed that it was essential to establish clear long-term objectives for research in the area selected. Finally, they reported: "... to ensure that our work would not be nullified by the obsolescence factor, we decided to look some ten years ahead."[25] In short, the research area selected had to be far-reaching, with potential activities spanning over a decade.

Starting with these selection criteria, defence scientists clearly delineated the area of guided missiles as their field of endeavour. They were also persuaded to move in this direction because of the acute air defence problem existing at the time and its outstanding priority in the national defence sphere. The Director of Weapons Research visited CARDE and briefed scientists on future trends for guided missiles in the continental air defence field. It became evident that CARDE's research should be directed towards surface-to-air guided missiles. According to Establishment scientists, such a project would relate to the counter-ICBM problem as well as the "problem of countering the high altitude supersonic bomber and the Navaho-type missile."[26]

As explained in the CARDE Annual Report for 1956, this choice of program had a dual advantage: first, the problems under study had much in common from the guided missile system viewpoint and, second, most of the work would be applicable to surface-to-surface ballistic missiles also. It was also decided that the program should be supported by test vehicle firings partly to back up research activities and partly to ensure that range personnel, techniques and facilities at the Establishment were kept up-to-date.

During 1956, CARDE scientists devoted much time and effort to exploring the knowledge base in the field of ballistic missiles. According to the Annual Report, the lion's share of funding for the program was allocated to the areas of aerophysics, aerodynamics, explosives physics, infrared techniques and propellants (rocket propulsion). The depth and diversity of this program preclude detailed description, and only a few of its most important elements will be mentioned.

Aerophysics research at CARDE focused on determining the "characteristics of shock waves at hypersonic velocities in rarefied and ionized gases". In the field of aerodynamics, the aeroballistic range was used extensively by scientists to test aircraft and missile models. CARDE had an acknowledged position as a world leader in this area. In the field of explosives physics, researchers initiated a program for studying some of the more refined techniques for the shaping of detonation waves. Finally, the Chemistry Wing devoted the majority of its effort to developing a new composite propellant for rocket motors, and appropriate modifications were made to the pilot plant. Similarly, in 1956, defence scientists continued work on the infrared program which was initiated one year earlier. This program included several research projects such as a feasibility study aimed at determining the effectiveness of infrared techniques as countermeasures against targets flying at altitudes between 40,000 and 60,000 feet.[27]

Clearly, CARDE devoted immense human and material resources to this program. Officials viewed the program as an investment in the future, since the collectivity of research being conducted could only pave the way towards possible participation in a counter-ICBM project, which was a goal fervently sought.

It must be said that the CARDE scientists had good reasons to hope that the promise of such participation would be realized. Throughout 1956, while participating in the DRB Study on defence against ICBMs, they took the opportunity to develop and strengthen their contacts with various US Army and USAF agencies. The ensuing information exchange allowed CARDE to refine its research needs relative to an ICBM defensive system. It should also be mentioned that, according to one person interviewed, CARDE officials had frequently consulted the US Department of Defense during this period "to find out areas which they required for further research."[28] Again, it was important that the research areas identified could utilize to advantage both the expertise acquired by the defence scientists and the facilities constructed at Valcartier during the earlier years.

In this regard, CARDE officials were not content to rest on their laurels. They were well aware that the aeroballistic range was one of their principal assets and they had no hesitation in instituting a continuing improvement program to enhance its operational performance. This facility, aside from being the only one in Canada, was one amongst only four in the world. 1956 was also the year in which CARDE marked another "first" within the Defence Research Board of Canada by becoming the first defence research establishment to acquire a digital computer - the ALWAC III.

4.1.4 A Period of Change in CARDE's other Research Activities: 1954-1956

As one might imagine, CARDE officials were interested in orienting research towards activities which promised the greatest payoff in the future. This was particularly important since profound changes were occurring at the time in at least two of the four main areas of research conducted at the Establishment. The 1956 Annual Report of the Establishment identified these four areas as guided missiles, conventional weapons, explosives and ballistics, and weapons system studies. As we have seen, the sudden interruption of the Velvet Glove project led scientists at Valcartier to seek alternative projects.

At the very moment when CARDE sought to write a new chapter in its history, research on conventional weapons was at a standstill and several projects were nearing completion. The termination of the Pack Howitzer project, despite the initial success of the prototype, was not an isolated phenomenon. Rather, it was a precursor of the subsequent decline in procurement of new conventional weapons systems by the Canadian Armed Forces. As capital acquisition dried up, conventional weapons research wilted, and the Design Wing progressively abandoned conventional weapons research in favour of research activities related to mechanical engineering. D Wing nevertheless continued its activities on the evaluation and improvement of existing conventional weapons systems.

The underlying reasons for this situation are unknown, but one person interviewed provided an interesting insight. In his view, it was due largely to the changing policies of the main customer and the shifting market conditions. First, the Canadian Armed Forces were not inclined to undertake major development programs for new weapons which could be procured from offshore at lower cost. Second, the Canadian defence industry could not realize a profitable return on product development based solely on the requirements of the Canadian Armed Forces, its only Canadian customer. In short, industry depended on export sales to amortize non-recurring costs and hence achieve profitability. Third, the famous export control policy on armaments introduced in 1954 made weapons production less attractive for Canadian manufacturers because it limited the number of potential customers. In other words, it added one more irritant to production of armaments in Canada.

These latter observations nevertheless need some qualification. Indeed, the Export and Import Permits Act was aimed at preventing export of war materiel without prior approval from the Canadian Government, but this restriction did not apply in the case of exports to NATO nations. Other non-NATO friendly nations could, however, purchase defensive systems from Canada with the express permission of the government.[29]

Whatever the true causes of this transition, Canada witnessed at the time a shift in activities away from development towards evaluation or improvement of existing systems. Notwithstanding this policy shift, defence scientists remained conscious of the essence of CARDE's mandate, which was not only to improve existing weapons and design new ones, but to enable decision-makers from the three services of the Canadian Armed Forces to be smart buyers by providing them with full evaluations of candidate systems for procurement.

Following this policy adjustment, the conduct of weapons system studies assumed increased importance. CARDE scientists conducted a number of such evaluations. An air defence system for escort vessels of the St. Laurent Class was evaluated at the request of the Royal Canadian Navy. Under tasking from the RCAF, CARDE scientists conducted a quantitative evaluation of the combat effectiveness of the CF-105 equipped with guided missiles, and its performance for the Air Defence system of Canada. Also at the request of the RCAF, CARDE scientists participated in project SPRINT, a theoretical study on the effectiveness of the CF-100 Mk 4 equipped with the Sparrow air-to-air missile. To meet the requirements of these new projects, the CEPE (Central Experimental and Proving Establishment) Flight Detachment at CARDE refurbished its aircraft fleet by exchanging one B-25, one T-33 and one CF-100 Mk 4A for three CF-100s Mk 4B, thus giving CEPE a total aircraft complement of 4 CF-100s Mk 4B, one CF-100 Mk 4A and one Expeditor.[30]

In the context of weapons system improvement, available documents indicate that CARDE undertook leading edge research in several areas of explosives and ballistics, including advanced work on solidification of explosives and methods for filling shells of various calibre. It should be mentioned in passing that this CARDE-developed technology was adopted by Canadian Arsenals whose facilities were located in St-Paul L'Ermite now Le Gardeur. CARDE conducted other research on shaped charge parameters, shock wave propagation, the effects of detonation waves on metals, and all aspects of explosives physics. Scientists in the Chemistry Wing developed methods for producing RDX explosive and procedures for stabilizing nitrocellulose. Finally, armaments specialists focused their efforts on the internal ballistics of guns, on the terminal ballistics of new kinetic-energy and shaped-charge penetrators, and on improved materials for weapons, projectiles and armour.

4.2 AEROSPACE RESEARCH

4.2.1 The Role of Dr. Gerald Vincent Bull

Following Soviet technological advances in the strategic missile field, North-American scientists devoted a massive amount of time and effort to finding an effective means of protection against the ballistic missile threat. They first looked at possible systems using known techniques, but soon realized that the work could not be accomplished without an in-depth understanding of the physical properties of the Earth's upper atmosphere and the phenomena associated with the re-entry of ballistic missiles into the atmosphere.

Dr. Gerald V. Bull briefing the Duke of Edinburgh on the aeroballistic work being done at CARDE during his visit on 13 August 1954.

At the time, CARDE was conducting studies of the upper layers of the atmosphere using suitably-instrumented sounding balloons (see below). In addition to this work in aeronomy, scientists were conducting research on solid propellants for rockets which later led to the development of the Black Brant rocket (see below). For their part, scientists in the Ballistics Wing were intensifying work on aerodynamic performance, stability and control.

Such was the setting when Dr. Gerald Vincent Bull entered the scene. Bull became a legend, and many consider him as the von Braun of large calibre guns. A graduate of the University of Toronto Institute of Aerophysics (UTIA), Bull was recruited by CARDE to work on the Velvet Glove project. According to Fred Bosworth, UTIA Professor G.N. Patterson recommended Bull without hesitation when he learned that Dr. Gordon Watson was looking for a "young aerodynamicist with experience in supersonics."[31] Bull was hired immediately and made responsible for the aerodynamic design of the air-to-air missile.

Bull rose rapidly in the ranks of DRB and, in 1957, became the first Head of the new Aerophysics Section which was formed from the Aerodynamics Section of Ballistics Wing and augmented by staff from the Design Wing and Experimental Wing. The major activities of this new unit were divided under three basic headings: aerodynamics, aeromechanics and hypersonic physics.[32] Under the leadership of Dr. Bull, the Aerophysics Section devoted most of its effort to fundamental research in hypersonics, particularly "the physics of the flight of hypersonic missiles in rarefied and ionized atmospheres ... [which constitutes] an extension of aerodynamics to conditions of exceptionally high velocity and low air density and related electromagnetic effects."[33]

Following re-entry, the ICBM travels at speeds of about 15 times the speed of sound. "The temperatures produced by air friction in the neighbourhood of the object are sufficiently high to cause dissociation of most of the oxygen molecules (O_2) and a good fraction of the nitrogen molecules (N_2). Atoms and molecules also lose electrons to become positively-charged ions, and the free electrons form a kind of 'gas' which strongly reflects radar signals. This collection of charged particles, ions and electrons, is known as a plasma."[34] During the re-entry phase, the wake left behind the ICBM can extend for several kilometres. The temperature and degree of ionization in the wake depend on the aerodynamic characteristics of the missile and the atmospheric properties at the given altitude. The ionized wake is thus a conductive layer which reflects radar signals. These radar returns are different for different re-entry bodies, depending on the electron density in the wake. The hypersonic wake of a particular re-entry body thus has a particular so-called signature. Explanation and interpretation of this signature require a full understanding of the mechanisms which give rise to the turbulent wake structure and its physico-chemical properties, and this knowledge is essential for the design of re-entry vehicle identification and discrimination systems.[35] Through laboratory research on re-entry phenomena CARDE would later make an important contribution in the field of intercontinental ballistic missile defence.

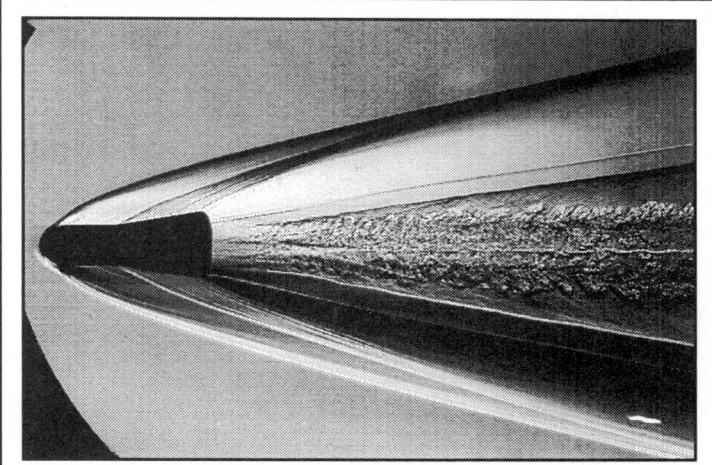

Wake produced by a 3.5-inch-long projectile shaped like an intercontinental ballistic missile launched at a speed of 6,000 feet per second (± Mach 6).

In 1957, however, little was known about the aerothermodynamic characteristics of the hypersonic wake or its radar signature, and techniques for investigating these properties were in their infancy. CARDE had only an aeroballistic range along which projectiles and models could be launched at speeds up to 5,000 feet per second by means of a conventional gun. Strategic missiles, however, could reach impressive speeds of 24,000 feet per second. The aeroballistic range had considerable limitations for studying the phenomena associated with hypersonic flight, such as "the stability, performance and control characteristics of the defensive missile and the study of radiation and radar cross-section properties for the detection and sorting of ballistic missiles."[36] In short, the Establishment had no basic tool for conducting fundamental research in hypersonic aerodynamics and physics.

For these reasons, Dr. Bull decided to develop a hypersonic range. The facility would consist of a long tank which could be partially de-pressurized to simulate upper altitude conditions and through which models could be launched using a light-gas gun. In this way it would be possible to simulate part of a re-entry trajectory in the laboratory where measurements could be made with high precision under strictly-controlled conditions.

By late 1957, CARDE had constructed a small hypersonic range, 2 feet in diameter over the first 25 feet and 3 feet in diameter over the remaining 25 feet, equipped with a light-gas gun (hydrogen/oxygen) capable of launching a 1/2-inch diameter model into the range at speeds up to 15,000 feet per second.[37] The range itself consisted of a sealed tank which could contain various gases under partial vacuum conditions. Aerodynamic and gaseous radiation phenomena exhibited by the model wake could be studied using high-speed cameras mounted in a battery of photographic stations along the tank. A light gas gun was used to launch models at high Mach numbers into the range tank. Unlike a conventional gun, the light gas gun consists of a cylinder containing a movable piston. A propulsive charge is placed in the combustion chamber behind the piston, and the cylinder ahead of the piston is filled with a light gas, usually helium. The high pressure produced when the propulsive charge is detonated accelerates the piston which, in turn, compresses the light gas ahead of the piston. The extremely high pressures produced in the light gas are applied to the base of the projectile (or the sabot which contains it) in order to accelerate the projectile in the gun barrel. Exceedingly high velocities can be achieved in this way because a gas of low molecular weight (light gas) is more efficient than a gas of high molecular weight in accelerating a projectile along a gun barrel.

A sabot is used to launch the model when it has a complex shape such as that of an aircraft, missile or other non-cylindrical configuration. The retaining sabot consists of two or four segments which are designed to separate from the model through the action of aerodynamic forces which are encountered once the sabot and model exit the gun muzzle. These forces cause the segments to peel away from the model and strike a steel impact plate at the entrance to the range while the model continues into the range through a central hole in the impact plate. With the initial thrust, the model gains "hypervelocity" within the ballistic range.

In theory, at least, the hypervelocity launch technique would enable models to travel at hypersonic speeds down the range. In practice, however, the scientists of the Aerophysics Section had to solve a number of technical problems before they were able to focus on exploring the phenomena of hypersonic physics. First of all, they had to familiarize themselves with light gas gun technology and then improve and perfect the associated techniques. The initial results, however, appear to have been assuring, for it was reported that "the gas gun technique of model launching has proved most successful and considerable advances have been made in the design of such guns and in theoretical studies of their performance."[38] Subsequently, the aerophysicists had to develop a projectile that could house the requisite electronics to permit on-board telemetry of flight data, and that could withstand the crushing launch acceleration . Finally, they had to design a sabot with petals that would detach without destroying the model. In addition to accomplishing all this, the scientists continued to improve measurement techniques, to develop all the associated instrumentation and to advance the theory of internal ballistics.

Although of scientific interest, this first hypersonic range was nevertheless experimental in nature. It soon became necessary to construct other ranges in order to expand the frontiers of knowledge in the area of hypersonic re-entry. But this required adequate funding. At the time, Canadian authorities had just given DRB approval to devote 10% of its research and development efforts to intercontinental ballistic missile defence. DRB had actually reached this limit by 1958.[39] Even though CARDE was one of the main beneficiaries of this funding, Canadian effort was, in the final analysis, limited in relation to the research program needs of an ICBM defensive system. Because of the relative scarcity of resources, CARDE officials were certainly not inclined to favour the construction of major research facilities for one component of the organization to the detriment of the other components. As well, there was a predisposition at the time for military cooperation between the Anglo-Saxon countries, as evidenced by the agreement reached between Canada, the United States and the United Kingdom to pool their resources under a Tripartite Technical Cooperation Program (TTCP).

Perhaps these factors influenced Dr. Gerald Bull in his decision to seek new sponsors to support the development of much more impressive light-gas guns for the Establishment. The question remains open. But it should be remembered that, at the time, Bull had already espoused his lifelong dream of using a gun to place a satellite in orbit.[40] Undoubtedly, CARDE officials did not share Bull's dream, but agreed that it would be timely to improve the facilities existing at Valcartier.

In any event, in view of the progress made by his team in developing light-gas gun technology and in developing expertise in internal ballistics, Dr. Gerald Bull was in a strong position to promote enthusiasm amongst US research agencies for CARDE's potential to conduct research in hypersonics. Everyone interviewed who had worked with Bull agreed that he had a great deal of charisma and displayed exceptional drive in his work. During the 1950's, numerous bilateral meetings between Bull and his US counterparts took place. In March 1958, an International Conference on Ballistic Missile Defence was held in Ottawa. Perhaps it was at this Conference or during one of his many travels that Bull succeeded in arousing the interest of General Arthur Trudeau in the research work of the Aerophysics Section at CARDE.[41] Whether Dr. Bull issued the official invitation to General Trudeau to visit the facilities of the newly-formed Aerophysics Wing at Valcartier is unknown, but Trudeau, who was Director of the US Army Rocket and Guided Missile Agency (ARGMA), accepted the invitation.

Two-stage light gas gun used to launch projectiles at hypersonic speeds in a low-pressure range to simulate the re-entry of missiles into the atmosphere.

In July 1958, General Trudeau arrived at Valcartier accompanied by the Vice-Chief of General Staff in Ottawa. Trudeau was extremely interested in all the techniques developed by the research team "for determining the aerodynamic stability of a projectile in a ballistic range"[42] and in the on-going development work on light gas guns at CARDE. In the words of Fleury, "they were the only facilities capable of accelerating objects of interesting size to speeds comparable to those attained by ballistic warheads on re-entry into the atmosphere."[43] According to one person interviewed, the existence of these novel facilities did not, by itself, explain General Trudeau's interest; at the time, other laboratories such as those at Aberdeen Proving Ground and Redstone Arsenal also possessed facilities for observing high-speed projectiles in free-flight ranges. But the CARDE team of scientists, made up of experts from around the world, was second to none in developing light gas gun technology. "The influence of Gerry Bull was [also] very important because others were impressed by his vision [of research], his intelligence and some of his more innovative accomplishments."[44] General Trudeau, the Director of ARGMA, noted, like others before him, that the unique facilities of Valcartier and its outstanding research teams were available "at lower cost than [those of] any other comparable US research establishment."[45]

In summary, General Trudeau was enthusiastic about the capabilities and research results of Aerophysics Wing, and, according to its 1958 Annual Report, ARGMA showed great interest in using CARDE's know-how in its Nike-Zeus research program. ARGMA's interest was, in fact, so great that the US agency seriously contemplated installing and operating a large diameter hypersonic range at Valcartier.[46] This expression of ARGMA interest would come to fruition in the summer of 1959 as part of a much broader project framework.

4.2.2 Prelude to the Joint Program with the United States: The Administrative Reorganization of 1958

In 1958, CARDE's primary mission was still to provide advice to the Canadian Armed Forces on the selection and utilization of weapons and weapon systems to meet the requirements of the three services. But the program of applied research and development in support of an ICBM defensive system progressively expanded to assimilate a greater proportion of the Establishment's research effort. The three major activities under this program centred on rocket propulsion, detection of infrared radiation and aerophysics. CARDE's exuberant activities in this research program could not fail to attract the interest of the US research organizations and Armed Forces. As we have seen, ARGMA expressed serious interest in the aerophysics work and only a few loose ends had to be tied before a partnership agreement could be signed. But the benefits of participation with the Americans were not solely confined to the researchers of Aerophysics Wing.

Whether due to the visit of General Trudeau or the signing of the TTCP agreement, the CARDE infrared detection team was invited to work jointly with the USAF on measuring the radiation emitted by ballistic missiles when re-entering the Earth's atmosphere. As well, the US Army asked researchers on the rocket propulsion program to conduct testing and small-scale production of a new type of rocket propellant. The interest shown by these US agencies clearly illustrates that CARDE senior scientists made a good and relevant decision when they decided to replace the Velvet Glove program with a program on ballistic missile defence.

CARDE scientists were delighted with the US interest in their research work and were extremely interested in participating in a joint aerophysics program with the United States. As one person interviewed observed, "we were ready to participate because of our experience in propellants, in hypervelocity research, with guns and rockets and in fuzes, combined with unique facilities such as the ballistic tunnel for measurements of projectiles in flight."[47] DRB gave approval and negotiations started with the Americans. Agreement was reached to the satisfaction of both parties in 1959.

Although no direct connection can be made, CARDE officials took a decision in April 1958 which greatly facilitated the implementation of joint programs with the United States. This was the decision to dispense with the administrative burden of an organizational structure which had by then become dysfunctional and to reorganize completely the Canadian Armament Research and Development Establishment at Valcartier. The Wing structure remained, but the other appurtenances were discarded in favour of a streamlined organization in tune with the new orientation towards research on ballistic missile defence. The CARDE organization chart was substantially modified. Three Wings were created to accommodate the new research activities: the Aerophysics Wing, the Systems Wing and the Electronics Wing. B and G Wings were dissolved and the functions of Ballistics Wing were redistributed within the new Systems and Aerophysics Wings. The responsibilities of the defunct Guided Missiles Wing were reassigned, with the new Systems Wing taking responsibility for computers and systems analysis and the new Electronics Wing assuming responsibility for electronics research. CARDE officials also took the opportunity to rename two Wings: the Design Wing became the Mechanics Wing, and the Chemistry Wing became the Explosives Wing. It should also be noted that the DRB Vehicle Mobility Group was integrated within the Mechanics Wing in the summer of 1958. The Establishment still comprised five scientific wings, but a large number of researchers became part of a new administrative unit (see Figure 9). A new Technical Services Wing was formed to provide the support services previously furnished by the scientific wings.[48]

In 1959, when most of the research infrastructure for the ballistic missile defence program was in place and the joint Canada/US programs had begun, CARDE authorities took the opportunity to conduct a review of all the existing research projects. This review was undertaken vis-à-vis the basic aims of the program, and the number of projects was reduced from 98 to 44. Separate projects in the same general field were combined, and some projects which were proceeding at a low level of activity were cancelled. According to CARDE officials, these changes tended to accentuate the shift in emphasis from conventional armament to ballistic missile defence.[49] In 1960, the rocket propulsion program was assigned to a different section, but the program remained essentially unchanged.

4.2.3 The Joint Canada/United States Aerophysics Program: The Physics of Projectile Re-entry into the Earth's Atmosphere

In 1958, CARDE's Aerophysics Wing planned to install five hypersonic ranges of various lengths and diameters,[50] each consisting of "a light-gas gun launcher and an observation chamber into which the model or projectile is launched."[51] One year later, the joint aerophysics program between CARDE and the United States was established. ARGMA was the main partner in this program. This US Government agency undertook to bear a good part of the costs of construction and modification of the hypersonic ranges and also to provide logistics support. As the DRB Chairman reported several years later, cooperation was excellent "and the course of information resulting from the experimentation was exchanged freely."[52] To effect this close cooperation between the two organizations, ARGMA assigned a permanent project officer to CARDE in September 1959. The name CARDE-ARGMA Range was assigned to Range 4.

ARGMA also fully funded the construction and operation of a huge hypervelocity free-flight range at CARDE. According to one person interviewed, the Americans allocated major funds to this program and, in some years, researchers could avail themselves of amounts of three-quarters of a million dollars and upwards ($850,000) in support of their research. This funding covered the cost of buildings as well as the cost of contractor personnel who were hired through Computing Devices of Canada (CDC) Limited.[53] It is difficult to determine the exact number of personnel who were engaged in this way, but CDC maintained up to 80 employees at the Valcartier site who participated mainly in the development of light gas-guns.[54]

During the early years of this program, CARDE scientists worked mostly on mastering the technology of hypersonic ranges and, to a lesser degree, on studying re-entry phenomena.

Dr. Gerald V. Bull explaining the operation of a hypersonic range to visitors.

Aerophysics Wing researchers had to scale-up the gas guns in order to obtain the desired velocity for the various sizes of model to be fired into each of the hypersonic ranges. In short, the guns had to be installed and calibrated to meet the desired parameters. Similarly, for each of the hypersonic ranges, the models and sabots had to be designed as well as the observation chambers in which the requisite altitudes had to be simulated. Finally, researchers had to improve the instrumentation and observation techniques that would ensure a reliable means of studying the wakes of hypersonic re-entry vehicles. A great deal of work was undertaken in connection with this aspect of the program. In the area of instrumentation, for example, research was conducted on the miniaturization of a high-g telemetry system which could be installed inside the models. Research in re-entry physics "involved theoretical and experimental studies of the emitted radiation and microwave interaction effects with particular emphasis on the scaling laws of the various phenomena."[55]

Figure 8- Ballistic Range Facilities Designed and Used in the 1958-1968 Period

RANGE	LAUNCHER stage diameters (in)	LAUNCHER stage lengths (ft)	DUMP TANK diameter (ft)	DUMP TANK length (ft)	FLIGHT TANK diameter (ft)	FLIGHT TANK length (ft)	Weight of projectile (lbs)	Typical velocity ((ft/s)
1	1.5/0.83/0.55	4.5/6/9	3	10	3	52	0.0044 (2g)	16000
	1.5/0.55	6./9					0.0066 (3g)	13000
2	3/0.79	13/15	6	20	6	80		
3	4/1.5	20/39	6	30	6	120	0.011 (50g)	18000
		40/50						
4	3.85				10	400	1.9	13000
5	10/4	40/60	6	64	10	400	2.3	16200
N	16/14	15/95			10	400	32 (1slug)	14500
R	14/7	25/100	6	50	N.A.*	N.A.*		

*Not applicable

Source: Gédéon Drouin, Armaments Division

In 1961, the Aerophysics Wing started to work with two private companies, Sylvania Electric Products and AVCO Research and Development Division, on specific experiments performed in the CARDE facilities. In April of that year, Dr. Gerry Bull left the Establishment and was replaced by his Assistant Wing Superintendent, Mr. George H. Tidy. Good progress was made in developing gas guns of small calibre, but progress was much slower in developing the larger calibre guns such as the 14-inch-diameter gun. Despite the earlier successes of 1959 that had been obtained with these large calibre guns, scientists appeared to have difficulty controlling the hydrogen/oxygen combustion process. Based on experience gained, scientists designed two new light gas guns of 4-inch and 7-inch diameter, respectively, using the principle of hydrogen combustion combined with the initial thrust imparted by the solid propellant.[56] 1961 was also the year when CDC constructed "a light-gas gun range and associated small aerophysics laboratories" in Stittsville, Ontario, in the expectation of finding commercial applications for this leading-edge technology.[57]

In 1962, the re-entry physics program experienced a major change when it was incorporated into a joint program between the

US Advanced Research Projects Agency (ARPA), the United Kingdom and CARDE, known as the joint ARPA/UK/CARDE program. Data gathered by CARDE were made available to the British for integration, after correlation, into the vast DAZZLE re-entry physics project. In June 1963, the Chairman of DRB, Dr. A. Hartley Zimmerman, officially opened Hypersonic Free Flight Range No. 5. The dimensions of the observation tank were impressive, and it could be partially evacuated to pressures corresponding to a 300,000-foot altitude. The range was equipped with a light-gas gun of 4-inch diameter, capable of launching model spheres and cones at speeds in excess of 15,000 feet per second. The Establishment then possessed one of the largest ranges in the Western world - a rare research facility in which wakes similar to those exhibited by bodies re-entering the Earth's atmosphere could be produced under laboratory conditions.

In 1964, the hypersonic radiation measurement program came to an end, but CARDE and ARPA continued to collaborate closely.

Range No 5 being inspected by members of the Defence Research Board at its official inauguration on 14 June 1963.

Officials of both organizations decided to reorient their joint program towards a study of the turbulent characteristics of hypersonic wakes. As we have seen, CARDE had an undeniable advantage over most other research establishments in the Western world with one of the best equipped laboratories for simulating hypersonic flight.

The hypersonic flow studies initiated by CARDE and ARPA were aimed at making point measurements of airflow velocity, temperature and density as well as electron density within the wakes of spheres and cones travelling at hypersonic speeds in free flight down the range. The purpose of the program was to obtain experimental data on the various physical properties of the wake to validate theoretical models.

The program began in 1964 and continued for several years. In 1970, the data gathering phase was completed, and most of the researchers working on the re-entry physics program turned their efforts to data processing and analysis. The analysis phase was completed in 1971. As a result of the efforts of these aerophysicists, the properties of wakes behind bodies travelling at hypersonic speeds are much better understood. Dr Lemay emphasized the link between the success of these research programmes and the major contribution of Valcartier scientists to the groundwork of knowledge upon which would be built the defence of the North American continent against ballistic missiles. It should be noted in passing that CARDE was renamed the Defence Research Establishment Valcartier (DREV) in 1969, at which time the Aerophysics Wing became the Aerophysics Division.

The North American ballistic missile defence system under development during the period of the CARDE/ARPA program was known as SAFEGUARD. It was designed to use two rockets, a short-range rocket such as Sprint, and a long-range rocket such as Spartan. The short-range rocket would be capable of reaching the upper atmosphere, while the long-range rocket would travel beyond the atmosphere to altitudes of about 400 miles. NORAD could not, however, count solely on Spartan for continental protection since ballistic missiles at the time were designed to release a series of decoys prior to re-entry in order to confuse defensive systems. It was extremely difficult, therefore, for Spartan to discriminate between real warheads and decoys, and the effectiveness of this anti-ballistic missile (ABM) was, to say the least, uncertain. But a means for resolving this dilemma was soon to be found, based on the fact that warheads are heavier than decoys.[58] During the initial phase of re-entry into the Earth's atmosphere, several physical and chemical phenomena are exhibited in the immediate vicinity of the nose of the re-entry body as well as in its wake. The characteristics of these phenomena depend, amongst other things, on the body weight and the local composition of the Earth's atmosphere. Discrimination between warheads and decoys is, therefore, possible based on observations of these characteristics and a knowledge of the composition of the Earth's atmosphere as a function of altitude.

Clearly, rapid discrimination between warheads and decoys was essential so that the largest possible number of warheads could be destroyed in the upper atmosphere where the chances of interception were greatest. The best detection and interception systems in the world would be useless if they could not discriminate between deadly warheads and damp squibs. Re-entry physics research at CARDE (later DREV) was aimed specifically at resolving this discrimination problem. The CARDE ranges were used to make observations of gaseous radiation, ablation and wake phenomena exhibited by projectiles travelling at hypersonic speeds through the controlled atmospheres of the tanks. The results of the Establishment's studies on hypersonic wakes were used to enable sophisticated radars to identify more precisely the signatures of bodies re-entering the atmosphere. This meant that the effectiveness of ABM's in destroying ballistic missiles threatening the continent was significantly enhanced because the real targets could be more easily recognized. The DREV scientists thus made an important contribution to a strategic defence posture predicated on the ability to launch a retaliatory strike with surviving missiles following a first strike.[59] This contribution was largely Canadian, since ARPA participated mainly as a sponsor and a supplier of technical support.

4.2.4 Changes Following the End of the Re-entry Physics Program

In 1971, DREV discontinued work on the phenomena exhibited by ICBM's on re-entering the Earth's atmosphere. Dr. André Lemay, the last Director of the Aerophysics Division, recalls that the impact on contractor personnel was somewhat lessened because DREV officials had earlier asked the Division to reduce progressively the human and material resources applied to the program. As for the internal research organization, termination of the re-entry physics project tolled the knell for the Aerophysics Division which then became the Data Systems Division. This change in name reflected a new program emphasis on systems for processing data obtained using various surveillance techniques and on data display systems to facilitate decision-making. The regular employees of the former Aerophysics Division were progressively assigned to work in the fields of lasers, surveillance and armaments.

4.2.5 The Study of Infrared Radiation in the Upper Atmosphere

As we have seen, during the mid-1950's CARDE researchers sought to expand their knowledge of the constitution of upper atmosphere. This was needed to gain a better understanding of the phenomena exhibited when a space vehicle re-enters the atmosphere, but more importantly to improve methods of ICBM detection and identification by evaluating parameters that limit tracking. Studies on the upper atmosphere were conducted using electromagnetic waves of low frequency, specifically radio frequencies, radar or higher frequencies and visible light frequencies. For the purposes of their research, CARDE scientists relied mainly on two frequency bands: "infrared frequencies, which are slightly lower than the frequencies of visible light, and microwave frequencies which are roughly the same as radar frequencies."[60]

In 1955, CARDE officials instituted a program on radiation in the infrared band just beyond the red end of the visible spectrum. Within this program, research projects were divided under three main headings. The first project was aimed at developing instruments and techniques. The second was concerned with determining the feasibility of employing infrared techniques in defence systems against targets flying at between 40,000 and 60,000 feet over Canada in order to obtain infrared background and radiation parameters at an altitude of 45,000 feet. The third project was aimed at making infrared background and transmission measurements between 50,000- and 100,000-foot altitudes.[61]

CARDE defence scientists directed their energies towards determining "the nature of the target emission, the background radiation and absorption characteristics of the atmosphere and, lastly, the characteristics of the detector system."[62] Attention herein will be confined to the first two aspects. According to the CARDE Annual Report for 1957, scientists considered that the nature of the target emission would be the most difficult problem to tackle because it would require observation of the radiation emitted by bodies in hypersonic flight. To resolve this problem in part, scientists intended to examine the radiation emitted from models launched at re-entry velocities in a hypersonic range. But they earnestly hoped that it would be possible to observe the re-entry of Soviet Sputnik satellites using six telescopes located across Canada. These hopes were not in vain, and scientists were able to obtain a great deal of relevant data in this way.

For investigating the radiation and absorption characteristics of the atmosphere, scientists planned to pursue three methods.

First, for the lower regions of the atmosphere between sea level and 45,000 feet, instrumentation would be carried by a CF-100 aircraft provided and operated by the Royal Canadian Air Force. This method was employed very early in the program and, by means of the on-board instrumentation, CARDE scientists made rapid progress in the measurement of atmospheric absorption of infrared radiation. Second, for altitudes between 50,000 and 100,000 feet, instrumentation would be carried by balloons and measurements would be made "of sky radiance in the near infrared and of atmospheric absorption of the solar spectra at various altitudes and solar zenith angles."[63]

Two high-altitude balloons were launched in 1958 and the data obtained was analysed to review procedures and assess personnel and materiel requirements. In the year following, balloons were launched on a more regular basis. As one person interviewed recalls, these launches generated a lot of enthusiasm amongst the CARDE staff: "It was not unusual to see thirty people from CARDE [mostly from the Electronics Wing] gathered at five o'clock in the morning at the airport [Ancienne-Lorette] where we launched the balloons - they came voluntarily, purely out of scientific interest, to participate in these launches."[64] This participation was not so much due to the fascinating sight of a soaring balloon, but rather to the common desire of employees to visibly support research useful to the defence of the nation.

Third, since balloons could not rise above 100,000 feet, instrumented rockets would be used to measure infrared emissions of the night airglow. The instrumentation would be of two types: equipment to gather data and equipment to encode and transmit the data to the ground by radio. In 1958, at the end of the International Geophysical Year, CARDE scientists were offered the use of two Nike-Cajun test vehicles at Fort Churchill. The flights produced useful data which were subsequently analysed.

4.2.6 Project Lookout

As we have seen, the United States were keenly interested in the CARDE research program on ballistic missile defence and, in 1958, the US Air Force invited the infrared research team to participate in a major joint project. In June of that year, CARDE and the Royal Canadian Air Force joined in the Interservice Radiation Measurements Program of the US Advanced Research Projects Agency (ARPA). The objective of the Canadian portion of this program, known as Project Lookout, was to measure radiation from US ICBM's launched from Cape Canaveral during their re-entry into the Earth's atmosphere. Measurements of radiation phenomena at an altitude of 40,000 feet were made by specially-equipped Canadian CF-100 aircraft based at Ascension Island in the South Atlantic. In 1961, after analysing the data, CARDE specialists concluded that "only a very small part of the re-entry emission in the infrared spectrum emanates from the high temperature gases in the stagnation region of the missile nose cap and from the missile body, and that most of the emission is from the wake."[65]

Following the completion of this phase of research, known as operation Lookout I, the United States asked Canada to participate in a new program, known as Tabstone, which the US considered an urgent matter. The program called for "measurements of the launch phase characteristics of ballistic missiles" in order to obtain information "on the radiation characteristics of ballistic missiles in the bandpass region of the Missile Infrared Decoy and Ship Engagement Model (MIDAS) system."[66] Canada accepted the invitation, and the Canadian portion of the program was known as Lookout II. The same equipment and personnel employed in Lookout I were assigned to Lookout II.

On 20 March 1961, the CARDE/RCAF team established a new home under the Florida skies at Patrick Air Force Base. In less than three months, 28 missile launches took place, 9 of which were considered as total successes in terms of the quality of data obtained. Following the data gathering phase, CARDE scientists set about analysing this impressive mass of data. The results were conclusive and demonstrated that CARDE had brilliantly completed its share of the mandate.

Following this initial success, the US Government decided to broaden the program, using the same personnel, to include

One of the Canadian pilots taking part in the study of radiation emitted when a missile re-enters the atmosphere, shown here beside his aircraft at Ascension Island (Project Lookout).

research on the characteristics "of the sustainer emission" from certain missiles such as Atlas and Titan. Operation Lookout III was thus born. The Canadian Government agreed to continue collaboration with the United States in this new program. During 1962, research work led to a "fairly good description of the 2.7-micron emission characteristics for the boost phase" of several missiles. Having obtained these first results, CARDE researchers established a new objective of "resolving detailed parameters such as aspect dependence, sustainer radiance levels, spectral variations and spatial structures."[67]

Two years later, when all the data had been gathered and analysed, CARDE scientists passed their final results to the parties concerned. The Royal Canadian Air Force (RCAF) reassessed the value of maintaining a flight detachment at Ancienne-Lorette, and decided to reassign these resources elsewhere. Thus ended a long association of over 13 years between this RCAF unit and CARDE. On 31 August 1964, the aircrews of the CEPE Flight Detachment flew a farewell flypast in the skies of Québec. But flying activities in support of the CARDE program continued at CEPE Uplands in Ottawa.[68]

4.2.7 The Cold Can Project: Atmospheric Research

In 1965, heartened by the excellent results obtained and the standing enjoyed by the Establishment scientists, ARPA and the US Air Force decided to seek CARDE's collaboration in another joint project of atmospheric research known as Cold Can. The purpose of this project was to measure certain atmospheric parameters critical to perturbing events in the ozonosphere.

During 1966, Establishment scientists developed procedures and instrumentation planned for use in the tests to be conducted in New Mexico. The studies would concentrate on measurements of the stratospheric distribution of species influencing radiative processes, such as water vapour, ozone, nitrous oxide, carbon dioxide and carbon monoxide. In 1967, during Canada's Centennial Year, quantitative measurements of the distribution of water vapour in the stratosphere were made using a solar infrared spectrometer mounted on board an RB-57F aircraft.

By late 1968, about 18,000 solar spectra had been recorded by CARDE scientists showing atmospheric absorption bands for the five above-mentioned species. The inventory of stratospheric data obtained was impressive, surpassing by far, both in number and global coverage, the sum of all other data of the Western world. These voluminous data were analysed using a digital computer to elucidate the complex processes involving oxygen, ozone and water vapour. Using spectroscopic data, scientists were able to obtain empirical results which supported existing theoretical models of the circulation of water vapour in the Earth's atmosphere. It was concluded that "water vapour formed from combustion of hydrocarbon fuel would be removed as part of the atmosphere's natural cleansing action."[69] This project was completed at the turn of the decade with a series of measurements on atmospheric composition and night airglow over the Americas.

4.2.8 Upper Atmosphere Research using Stratospheric Sounding Balloons

During this period, CARDE scientists continued to conduct theoretical and experimental laboratory studies on the composition of the upper atmosphere. The data required for these aeronomy studies were gathered by Establishment scientists using spectrometers operating in various infrared bands, specifically 3 to 5 and 8 to 12 microns (µm). Balloons, aircraft and rockets were used to carry on-board instrumentation to the altitudes of interest where measurements were made of the absorption bands of water vapour, carbon monoxide, ozone, methane, nitric oxide and other atmospheric species.

As seen earlier, in 1958, two sounding balloons were launched to evaluate measurement and telemetry systems to be used in observations of the upper atmosphere. Test results were satisfactory and the measurement program proper started in 1959. During that year, three instrumented balloons were launched to an altitude of 100,000 feet. Instrumentation included mass spectrometers and microwave spectrometers to obtain new data on radiative emission from the atmosphere. The range of interest for the scientists working in this field of aeronomy was very broad.

Radiant emission was measured both by day and night, as well as at dawn and dusk when the sun's rays within the atmosphere were longest. Measurements of the background radiation, against which missiles had to be detected, were also made.

Under this scientific program, researchers also made measurements in test flights using CF-100 aircraft and Nike-Cajun rockets. Observation equipment used on aircraft was similar to that used on balloons, and over 500 solar spectra were obtained at low altitude. Rocket-borne instrumentation was designed to measure infrared emission from OH radicals and night airglow spectra in the visible band. These measurements were obtained when the rocket reached the apogee of its trajectory in the upper atmosphere. In the early 1960's, attempts were made to determine atmospheric chemistry and the distribution of atomic oxygen by seeding the upper atmosphere with nitric oxide. The radiation produced when nitric oxide reacts with atomic oxygen is indicative of the concentration of atomic oxygen in the atmosphere. These data were gathered by instrumentation carried on-board Black Brant rockets launched from Fort Churchill in northern Manitoba and from Wallops Island, Virginia.

Experiments were also conducted in the upper atmosphere using stratospheric sounding-balloons which were launched periodically. These experiments were undertaken with the expectation that "a better understanding of atmospheric processes would lead to more accurate descriptions of the target and background characteristics" of ballistic missiles.[70] During the first half of the 1960's, researchers from the Electronics Wing made the important discovery that emission lines from the oxygen-hydrogen radical (OH) are present in the atmospheric emission spectrum. In order to improve their comprehension of OH atmospheric photochemistry, researchers directed considerable effort to understanding the excitation mechanism. The altitude of the emission and the diurnal variation of its intensity were key parameters which were investigated in a series of measurements using a grating spectrometer. Following preliminary evaluation of the data, researchers from the Establishment collaborated in a second series of experiments with Professor H. Gush of the University of British Columbia (UBC) who had developed an interferometer which promised better resolution of the solar spectrum.

In 1968, studies of the radiative properties of the atmosphere using instrumented balloons was confined to supporting the DRB-sponsored research at the Physics Department of UBC. UBC researchers used a sophisticated interferometer to make measurements of atmospheric emission, and the interferograms obtained were subjected to Fourier transformation for spectral interpretation. CARDE provided support in launching the balloons, in furnishing equipment and in recording data that was telemetered to the ground.[71]

Launch of a helium balloon with a pod containing scientific instruments for studying the composition of the upper atmosphere.

4.2.9 CRAM Collaboration in Upper Atmospheric Research

Since the time of its creation, DRB continued to support defence-related university research across Canada, and a number of scientists from Canadian universities participated either sporadically or continuously in various CARDE scientific projects. In 1967, DRB delegated responsibility to its defence research laboratories for awarding research grants and contracts to industry and academia.

Pod containing spectrometers and telemetry equipment designed to study the composition of the upper atmosphere.

This was the context in which agreement was reached between CARDE and Université Laval - the only university in the Quebec area - to establish the *Centre de recherches sur les atomes et les molécules* (CRAM). It was not until August 1968, however, that DRB and Université Laval signed the agreement officially confirming the creation of CRAM. This agreement served only to formalize and strengthen the excellent collaboration that had existed between the two organizations over the years. In the preceding years, CARDE scientists had frequently been invited to give courses at Université Laval, and university professors had often participated in CARDE scientific projects. Through this agreement, CARDE scientists were authorized to act as thesis directors at Université Laval, while university researchers could use CARDE facilities and equipment designated as forming part of CRAM.

Officially created in 1968, CRAM was particularly interested in the photochemistry of the ozonosphere. Over the following two years, a large number of CARDE scientists and "staff members from the Departments of Physics, Chemistry and Electrical Engineering, Université Laval [studied infrared luminescence and stratospheric composition. Their work produced data on] stratospheric abundance of minor gases, emission intensity of O_2 ($^1\Delta_g$) and OH, and OH rotational temperatures."[72] All this work was undertaken within the major joint CARDE/ARPA/USAF program on atmospheric radiation mechanisms.

4.3 THE DEVELOPMENT OF THE BLACK BRANT HIGH ALTITUDE RESEARCH ROCKET

4.3.1 Composite Propellants for Rocket Motors

As we have seen earlier, in 1956 CARDE officials sought to replace the Velvet Glove project with another major project. The area of guided missiles was of particular interest, specifically that of missile defence. In the context of this new program, scientists of the CARDE Chemistry Wing devoted much of their effort to developing a high-acceleration rocket propellant. Solid propellants appeared to offer promise, and emphasis was placed on the development of a composite polyurethane/ammonium perchlorate propellant. A sophisticated pilot plant facility was constructed for this purpose. After the two constituents were mixed to the desired consistency, all subsequent operations were performed electronically within a closed cylindrical vessel. Temperature and pressure conditions were controlled remotely and constantly monitored during fabrication.[73]

4.3.2   Design of the Black Brant Rocket

In order to test the performance of this new propellant, CARDE officials planned to develop and launch a test vehicle which, depending on weight, could reach an altitude of 400,000 feet. The proposed test vehicle would also serve as a prototype launch vehicle for the aeronomy and infrared projects aimed at determining the composition of the upper atmosphere.[74] With the experience gained in the Velvet Glove project, CARDE scientists structured a major work program. They immediately set about writing the specifications for the rocket motor to be tested, entered into negotiations with a private company to manufacture the airframe for an experimental model, and scheduled a series of

Black Brant rocket on its launcher.

static firings to be conducted prior to the first rocket launch. But major emphasis was placed on the stability, composition and design of solid propellant rocket motors. Tests were conducted on 8-inch and 17-inch-diameter motors. The 17-inch motor was selected for subsequent development since its characteristics met the requirements for a high altitude research rocket.[75]

Working to a CARDE design specification, Bristol Aircraft Company in the UK completed the detailed design of the Black Brant vehicle. CARDE scientists determined the exact shape and optimum chemical composition of the propellant grain for the combustion chamber. Once the rocket motors were filled, final assembly of the vehicle was completed by Bristol Aircraft (Western) Ltd., of Winnipeg, and the first Black Brant vehicles were delivered to CARDE from the Winnipeg plant in January 1959. During the following months, CARDE scientists installed the telemetry equipment and associated transducers in the nose cone in preparation for the first test flight. Static tests were completed in February and installation of the launching facilities at Fort Churchill was completed a few months later. In September 1959, four Black Brant rockets were launched and flight tested.[76]

The flight tests were an unqualified success, and it was decided to re-design certain components of the vehicle to meet the requirements of the agencies planning to conduct upper-atmosphere research using rockets. A new aircraft manufacturer, Canadair Ltd., was selected to undertake this work and the rocket was renamed Snow Goose. Through joint Canadair and CARDE efforts, "a more refined rocket was designed, with a lighter motor casing, larger fins, longer forward body and a more slender nose cone."[77] During this phase, it was decided to revert to the original name, and the re-designed high altitude research rocket became known as Black Brant II, the second in the family of Black Brant rockets. Shortly afterwards, another variant was developed, Black Brant IIA, powered by the same rocket motor used in Black Brant I, which was then being manufactured by Bristol Aero Industries Limited (BAIL), Winnipeg. In September 1959, BAIL submitted a proposal to the Department of Defence Production (DDP) seeking approval to exploit the new technology in the commercial marketplace. The resulting rockets are known as Black Brants III, IV and V. The first Black Brant III was launched in October 1960, and a new 10-inch-diameter rocket motor was developed in 1961 for Black Brant III which was also used as the second stage for Black Brant IV.

The feasibility of the design and development of this family of sounding rockets was explored by Canadian Bristol Aerojet Limited (CBA), located in Rockwood, 20 miles north of Winnipeg, in collaboration with CARDE. To assist the company, the Department of Defence Production provided 60% of the total funding for this phase of activity. Following completion of these studies, the government fully funded the construction of a solid-propellant manufacturing facility at an estimated cost of $1,375,000.[78] The Manitoban company adopted the production techniques developed by CARDE in their entirety, and built its plant as an exact replica of the Valcartier pilot-plant. CARDE also provided technical assistance by training company personnel in these new production methods. The company plant was officially opened in September 1963. In November, a decision was taken to develop Black Brant V, and additional test flights were planned to complete the development.

During 1964, CARDE terminated its Black Brant development activities, and CBA assumed full responsibility for further development and production. In 1965, the company changed its corporate name to Bristol Aerospace Limited (BAL). Black Brant proved to be a major commercial success, and the rocket was sold around the world, with NASA, in the United States, becoming one of BAL's major customers. By 1995, the company had sold 875 rockets in several variants. The programme was not limited to the building and sale of rocket engines, it included the development and production of such auxiliary systems as a recovery parachute system, a deployment system for the shell-ogive as well as payload integration and set-up services.

The majority of these goods were exported, for a total sales value of almost $140 million.[79]

Stimulated by the scientific and commercial success of Black Brant, CARDE researchers conducted further basic studies during the 1960's on rocket-motor internal combustion processes. In the mid-1960's, due largely to the expertise developed at Valcartier in novel methods of manufacturing composite propellants for rocket motors, the Establishment was invited to participate in a joint project with the United States to develop a meteorological sounding rocket (Metroc).

Experimental flight of the Black Brant IIA rocket at Wallops Island in August 1962.

1	Benson D. Adams, *Ballistic Missile Defence*, New York, American Elsevier, 1971, p. 12 (note 6).
2	Bertrand De Launay, *Le poker nucléaire*, p. 36.
3	*House of Commons Debates*, 11 November 1949, p. 1662.
4	Robert Lacourt-Gayet, *Histoire des États-Unis*, p. 255-256.
5	Brian Cuthbertson, *Canadian Military Independence in the Age of the Superpowers*, Don Mills, Ont., Fitzhenry & Whiteside, 1977, p. 38.
6	Desmond Morton, *A Military History of Canada: 1608-1991*, Toronto, McClelland & Stewart, 1992, p. 244.
7	George F.G. Stanley, *Canada's Soldiers: The Military History of an Unmilitary People*, Toronto, Macmillan, 1974, p. 414.
8	*Ibid.*
9	J.L. Granatstein, *Canada 1957-1967: The Years of Uncertainty and Innovation*, Toronto, McClelland & Stewart, 1986, p. 103.
10	*Ibid.*, p. 103.
11	Gen Charles Foulkes, *Canadian Defence Policy in a Nuclear Age*, (Behind the Headlines, Vol. XXI, No. 1), Toronto, Canadian Institute of International Affairs, 1961, p. 10.
12	*Ibid.*, p. 11.
13	Morton, *op. cit.*, p. 242.
14	Gen Charles Foulkes, *op. cit.*, p. 12.
15	Benson D. Adams, *op. cit.*, p. 9-10.
16	*Ibid.*, p. 11.
17	*Ibid.*, p. 12.
18	*Ibid.*, p. 20-22.
19	*Ibid.*, p. 22.
20	CARDE, *Annual Report for 1956*, p. 6-7.
21	Cited in *House of Commons Debates 1957-1958*, p. 1910.
22	*House of Commons Debates 1957-1958*, p. 1901.
23	CARDE, *op. cit.*, p. 9.
24	*Interview with Mr. E.J. Bobyn*, p. 10.
25	CARDE, *op. cit.*, p. 9.
26	*Ibid.*
27	*Ibid.*, p. 10-12.
28	*Interview with Mr. E.J. Bobyn*, p. 14.
29	*House of Commons Debates 1956*, p. 463-464.
30	CARDE, *op. cit.*, p. 3.
31	Fred Bodsworth, "Gerry Bull, Boy Rocket Scientist", *Maclean Magazine*, 66, 1 March 1953, p. 51.
32	CARDE, *Annual Report for 1957*, p. 12.
33	*Ibid.*, p. 2.
34	Jean-Marc Fleury, "Les canons de Valcartier", *Québec Science*, Vol. 11, No. 10, December 1973, p. 10.

35	CARDE, *Armament Research and Development*, Valcartier, Inf. 2/67, unpublished.
36	CARDE, *Annual Report for 1959*, p. 5.
37	CARDE, *Annual Report for 1957*, p. 3 and 13.
38	CARDE, *Annual Report for 1958*, p. 6.
39	Harold M. Merklinger, *Canada's Historical Involvement with Ballistic Missile Defence*, Ottawa, DND, 1994, p. 1.
40	Walter Skol, "Prepare Canadian Satellite '58 Launch", *Toronto Daily Star*, 22 April 1958.
41	For an account of this man's importance in Dr. Bull's career, and an account of the life of Gerry Bull, see Normand Lester, *L'affaire Gerald Bull: Les canons de l'Apocalypse*, Éditions Méridiens, 1991, 193 p.
42	*Interview with Dr. André Lemay*, p. 11.
43	Jean-Marc Fleury, *op. cit.*, p. 9-10.
44	*Interview with Dr. André Lemay*, p. 14.
45	*Interview with Mr. E.J. Bobyn*, p. 15.
46	CARDE, *Annual Report for 1958*, p. 6.
47	*Interview with Mr. E.J. Bobyn*, p. 14.
48	CARDE, *Annual Report for 1958*, p. 1-2.
49	CARDE, *Annual Report for 1959*, p. 1.
50	CARDE, *Annual Report for 1958*, p. 6.
51	CARDE, *Annual Report for 1959*, p. 7.
52	Dr. A.H. Zimmerman, "Defence Research Programs", *Air University Review*, March-April 1967, p. 17.
53	*Interview with Dr. André Lemay*, p. 10.
54	J.H. Chapman et al., *Upper Atmosphere and Space: Programs in Canada*, Ottawa, Science Secretariat/Privy Council Office, 1967, Special Study No. 1, p. 49.
55	CARDE, *Annual Report for 1961*, p. 6.
56	*Ibid.*, p. 6 *et passim*.
57	J.H. Chapman et al., *op. cit.*, p. 49.
58	Jean-Marc Fleury, *op. cit.*, p. 11, and Benson D. Adams, *op. cit.*
59	Jean-Marc Fleury, *Ibid.*
60	*Caméra 62,* Radio-Canada.
61	CARDE, *Annual Report for 1956*, p. 12.
62	CARDE, *Annual Report for 1957*, p. 9.
63	*Ibid.*, p. 10.
64	*Interview with Dr. Jacques Gilbert*, p. 10.
65	CARDE, *Annual Report for 1961*, p. 14.
66	*Ibid.*
67	CARDE, *Annual Report for 1962*, p. 17.

68	CARDE, *Annual Report for 1964*, p. 3.
69	DREV, *Annual Report for 1969*, p. 36.
70	CARDE, *Annual Report for 1962*, p. 21.
71	CARDE, *Annual Report for 1967*, p. 22, and *Annual Report for 1968*, p. 30-31.
72	DRB, *Review 1970*, p. 11.
73	*Caméra 62*, Radio-Canada.
74	CARDE, *Annual Report for 1956*, p. 15.
75	CARDE, *Annual Report for 1957*, p. 8-9.
76	CARDE, *Annual Report for 1959*, p. 17.
77	J.H. Chapman et al., *op. cit.*, p. 57.
78	*Ibid.*, p. 58.
79	Bristol Aerospace Limited. CRV7 and Black Brant Production History, Winnipeg, May 5, 1995. (Letter from Greg R. Ozog of BAL to Christian Carrier, DREV).

The Velvet Glove missile equipped with a booster, shortly before launching at the Point Petre, Ont., test range in 1954.

Visit to DREV by the Honourable Donald S. Macdonald, Minister of National Defence, on 19 July 1971. From left to right: Dr. J.L. L'Heureux, Chairman, DRB; the Honourable Donald S. Macdonald; Dr. C. Cumming, Director, Electronics Division; Mr. A. Lortie, Director, Experimental Division; and Dr. H.P. Tardif, Director, Armaments Division.

Automated Land Force Command and Control Headquarters.

The LUCIE underwater camera is equipped with a pulsed laser which emits green light, as well as a high-speed shutter. This system increases visibility up to six times the distance afforded by conventional means, even in murky water.

CRV7 rockets being launched by a Canadian Forces CF-105 aircraft.

PEOPLE IN THE DIVISIONS

SPRING (1995)

CHIEF'S OFFICE

left to right:

First row: C. Prince, S. King, D. Blais
Second row: LCol M. Coderre, D. Régis, J.-C. Ratté, Dr J. Gilbert,
Dr R.S. Walker, J.-F. Drolet

PLANS & PROGRAMS OFFICE

left to right:

First row: MCpl G. Boily, J. Cantin, LCol M. Coderre, D. Blais, WO R. Chevigny
Second row: P. St-Onge, Y. Noël

PERSONNEL OFFICE

left to right:

First row: C. Vaillancourt, G. Côté, M. Déry, J. Chamberland, M. Lafrance
Second row: L. Lapierre, A. Valin
Third row: J. Viens, D. Doyon, D. Ouellet
Fourth row: A. Jobidon, S.L. Boney, G. Villeneuve, D. Daigle

ADMINISTRATION DIVISION

ADMINISTRATION DIVISION
(left to right)

First row: J. Leblanc, K. Lawson, P. Deschênes, G. Turcotte, D. Morissette, J. Lavigueur, N. Lavoie, G. Lebel, M. Cabana, A. Couture, A. Dumont

Second row: G. Robert, Y. Monast, J. Tessier, M. Gélinas, A. Leblond, R. Savard, J. Gélinas, N. Genest, C. Mejia, C. Guimond, L. Légaré-Salvi, N. Péloquin, C. Potvin, C. Morneau, G. Caron, L. Juneau, D. Linteau

Third row: R. Harrisson, L. David, M. Giguère, L. Déry, M. Verreault, M. Lavoie, S. Dostie, N. Paquet, L. Chaillez, C. Therrien, L. Desrochers, S. Gagnon

Fourth row: L. Martel, D. Roy, R. Cayer, M. Thibault, D. Masse, D. Bisson, R. Drolet, L. McCoubrey, J. Germain, A. Guy, D. Bélanger

TECHNICAL SERVICES DIVISION

TECHNICAL SERVICES DIVISION

(left to right)

First row: P. Blondeau, A. Simard, G. Leclerc, J. Desmarais, R. Boivin, J. Dufour, S. Doyon, J. Desrochers, L. Fournier, N. Letarte, C. Blais, C. Ménard, D. Lortie, J.-C. Drolet, M. Porlier

Second row: N. Drouin, N. Fortin, M. Tremblay, G. Thivierge, D. Charest, R. Juneau, A. Lavoie, M. Chevalier, M. Maltais, Y. Jauvin, A. Garneau, J. Martel, E. Grenier, G. Filiault, H. Leclerc, P. Paradis, S. Wagner, P. Garon, D. Enns, M. Cardinal, M.-A. Bourgault, M. Gauvin

Third row: É. Masson, R. Lambert, B. Gendron, R. Therrien, R. Marceau, J. Cyr, G. Verreault, S. Bédard, A. Bourassa, J. Morin, W. Giasson, R. Beaupré, A. Cadoret, J-M. Dionne, M. Verreault, M. Latulippe, G. Vallières, P. Vachon, M. Boivin, B. Gravel, P. Giroux, A. Houde, R. Rouillard, D. Desharnais, M. Lavoie

Fourth row: J. Boutet, M. Racine, W. Berrouard, J.-P. Mongrain, J.-P. Bouchard, R. Larivée, A. Gagné, A. Lechasseur, J. Beaudoin, G. Boivin, Y. Beaulieu, S. Jean, J. Leblanc, D. Nadeau, B. Paradis, B. Villeneuve, G. Ménard, P. Ouellet, R. Martel, J. Lecours, J.A.D. Lemieux, R. Malouin

Fifth row: A. Roussel, A. Maheux, A. Sauvé, G. Duquet, M. Pichette, A. Jacques, P. Duchesne, D. Anctil, S. Gros-Louis, N. Viel

ARMAMENTS DIVISION

ARMAMENTS DIVISION
(left to right)

First row: A. Pépin, A. Jeffrey, M. Delage, G. Dumas, J. Laverdière, J.-P. Cayouette, C. Therrien, M. Clark, M. Drolet, G. Bérubé, K. Goulet, R. Fiset, M. Bolduc, J. Tremblay

Second row: K. Heaton, G. Couture, B. St-Jean, F. Lesage, O. Cantin, J.-P. Lavoie, R. Lévesque, C. Vallières, A. Brisson, R. Rousseau, B. Collins, M. Gingras, M. Maheux, M. Lemoine, H.-L. Parent, P. Daigle, G. Pageau, D. Fraser, D. Lefrançois, J. Bédard, R. Poulin

Third row: S. Dorval, D. Bourget, M. Szymczak, É. Fournier, L. Boutot, G. Bédard, P. Lacasse, R. Simard, J. Blais, F. Cloutier, P. Bélanger, R. Delagrave, G. Audet, C. Brousseau, G. Lortie, C. Ferland, G. Drouin, B. Girard, D. Nandlall

Fourth row: L. Ngo Phong, S. Paradis, F. Côté, M. Thibault, M. Noël, D. Brousseau, D. Lebel, M. Bonnet, C. Julien, G. Bilodeau, G. Patterson, R. Cloutier, R. Arsenault, Y. de Villers, R. Bilodeau, L. Gravel, R. Deblois, G. Abel, C. Fortier

ENERGETIC MATERIALS DIVISION

ENERGETIC MATERIALS DIVISION
(left to right)

First row: S. Thiboutot, G. Ampleman, C. Cantin, P. Twardawa, S. Villeneuve, R. Lavertu, J.-M. Garneau, C. Carrier, G. Couture, R. Stowe, D. Lepage

Second row: C. L'Heureux, S. Duncan, G. Roy, P. Harris, N. Gagnon, P. White, P. Brière, C. Bélanger, P. Brousseau, F. Perreault, M. Hébert

Third row: S. Trudel, F. Wong, J.-G. Melançon, R. Farinaccio, D. Sanschagrin, M. Lauzon, P. Carignan, S. Brochu, A. Marois, P. Lessard, G. Nadeau, M. Kervarec

Fourth row: C. Nicole, C. Bastille, G. Vallée, M. Côté, R. Durand, A. Gagnon, L.-P. Roy, C. Watters, C. Dubois

Fifth row: D. Gilbert, C. Demers, D. Dubuc, S. Giroux, H. Gagnon, J. Rapanotti, G. Richer, J. Racine, M. St-Onge, B. Gilbert, A. Roy, G. McIntosh, L. Bourret, J. Beaupré, R. Coulombe

COMMAND AND CONTROL DIVISION

COMMAND AND CONTROL DIVISION
(left to right)

First row: L. Dinel, G. Picard, S. Cardinal, D.L. Smith, G. McCoubrey, G. Otis, M. Rioux

Second row: L. Chouinard, J.-C. Paré, L. Des Groseilliers, J. Roy, F. Maheu, L.-S. Binette, M. Savard, S. Lam, P. Boucher, M. Bélanger, J. Verret, C. Rochette, M. Fortier, A. Sénécal, P.-É. Boutin

Third row: S. Lapointe, J. Berger, A. Sahi, R. Carling, B. Chalmers, M. Parenteau, P. Labbé, J. Stoern, G. Thibault, R. Côté, L. Cloutier, P. Da Ponte, D. Demers

Fourth row: R. Bégin, D. Roy, S. Roy, C. Helleur

ELECTRO-OPTICS DIVISION

ELECTRO-OPTICS DIVISION
(left to right)

First row: J. Maheux, J. Boulter, L. Forand, M. Gravel, L. Lessard, R. Corriveau, F. Da Via, C. Lahaye, P. Elliott, C. McDonald, F. Reid, Y. Han, P. Mathieu, D. Faubert

Second row: A. Fernet, R. Oermann, A. Cantin, J.-P. Morency, C. Bradette, J. Dubois, P. St-Pierre, M. Lessard, D. Dubé, C. Grenier, S. LaRochelle, C. Dumas, D. Vincent, P. Roney, R. Lambert, J.-P. Ardouin, G. Fournier

Third row: S. Dumas, J.-M. Thériault, L. Durand, M. Jean, R. Noël, B. Montminy, L. Bissonnette, G. Verreault, A. Blanchard, J. Couture, G. Tardif, G. Paré, R. Plante, V. Larochelle, M. Lévesque, L. Durand, P. Chevrette

Fourth row: C. Lejeune, M. Couture, G. Pelletier, R. Charpentier, H. Gaudry, J. Dumas, A. Deslauriers, J. Tremblay, J. Lemay, P. Pace, D. Dion, D. St-Germain, D. Bonnier, A. Morin

INFORMATICS CENTER

left to right:

First row: M. Patry, D. Ouellet, R. Bédard, L. Dinel, L. Rochon, M. Gingras, C. Therrien
Second row: J. Bélanger, J.-C. Roy, M.-J. Marcoux, J.-C.Ruelland, M. Simard, C. Roy
Third row: J. Boiteau, A. Bergeron, R. Thiffault
Fourth row: G. Rochette, D. Audet, G. Roy, A. Lapierre
Fifth row: G. Ouellet

> "In the field of fundamental research, the young researcher must be given a lot of latitude. It is important to distinguish between applied research, which can and must be planned, and fundamental research, which must give free rein to the imagination, even to fantasy.. and tolerate failure. Indeed, one must accept what might look like wasted effort because no one can know in advance which are the interesting paths. The history of the discovery of the laser has shown this to be true. While the laser today is in the domain of applied research, it would have been impossible to plan research on the laser when no one knew what a laser was and no one even considered it. The good fortune of fundamental research is the imagination of the researcher."
> (Alfred Kastler, Nobel Price for Physics, 1966)

5

RESTRUCTURING OF RESEARCH ACTIVITIES AT DEFENCE RESEARCH ESTABLISHMENT VALCARTIER

5.1 REORGANIZATION OF NATIONAL DEFENCE

5.1.1 Defence at the Centre of Political Upheaval

In the early 1960's, Canada's destiny was in the hands of the Conservative Party. The Diefenbaker government had to decide whether it would be in Canada's security interests to equip the Armed Forces with nuclear weapons. In a sense the dice were loaded, because Diefenbaker had decided in 1958 to acquire Bomarc missiles and these missiles had to be equipped with nuclear warheads to be operationally effective. It appeared that "the nuclear question was decided *de facto* if not *de jure*."[1] But the new Minister of External Affairs, Howard Green, was fiercely opposed to the nuclearization of Canada, and he worked fervently within Cabinet to win support for his viewpoint. "After his one tough decision over the Arrow, Diefenbaker seemed to have retreated into chronic indecision. [...] Only one policy line was clear: Canada would not acquire nuclear weapons."[2] The Liberal Opposition and the New Democrats were ardent advocates of this policy.

In 1962, the Cold War reached its highest peak with the Cuban missile crisis, and the world came within a hair's breadth of catastrophe. It is not possible, within the limits of this work, to review fully the position of the Canadian Government during this crisis. Suffice it to say that Diefenbaker did not appreciate the role assigned to Canada by the United States and asserted Canada's independence by refusing to submit blindly to the dictates of American leaders. But the crisis had a strong impact on the issue of nuclear disarmament. "Far more Canadians, indifferent to the complexities of defence and foreign policy, felt deep disquiet. Even before the crisis, polls found a surprising shift in favour of arming the nuclear weapons Canada had acquired."[3]

The Liberal Party took note of this shift and, in January 1963, the Leader of the Party, Lester B. Pearson, proclaimed that Canada "can only do this by accepting nuclear warheads, for those defensive tactical weapons which cannot effectively be used without them but which we have agreed to use."[4] On 25 January, Diefenbaker declared before the House of Commons that Canada's allies were satisfied. Five days later, there was a dramatic turn of events when the US State Department maintained that the Canadian Government had not "as yet proposed any arrangement sufficiently practical to contribute effectively to North American defense."[5] The Minister of National Defence, Colonel Douglas Harkness, resigned with a roar and brought the minority Conservative government down with him.

During the subsequent electoral campaign, the Liberals promised to undertake a full review of Canada's defence policy. In the wake of the economic recession, they also promised to freeze the defence budget. On 8 April 1963, the Liberals came into office. To fulfil the promise of the defence aspect of his electoral platform, Prime Minister Pearson appointed Paul Hellyer as Minister of National Defence.[6]

5.1.2 The Glassco Commission and the Department of National Defence

The report of the Glassco Commission became available when the new Minister of National Defence was appointed. The Commission was created by John Diefenbaker's Conservative government to conduct a detailed review of the organization and *modus operandi* of all components of federal administration, except for Parliament itself.

Such a review was clearly needed because the apparatus of government proliferated dramatically during the period following the Second World War due to the phenomenal growth in social services and the development of a peacetime defence organization on an unprecedented scale. In 1960, the level of federal expenditures on Canadian Government programs was twelve times that of 1939. The Royal Commission on Government Organization was created in September 1960 to address this problem. The Commissioners were charged with investigating the organization and management of the entire federal government administrative structure and with formulating recommendations "which they consider would best promote efficiency, economy and improved service in the dispatch of public business."[7]

The Glassco Commission paid particular attention to the Canadian defence establishment because of "its size, the range of and cost of its activities, and the impact of Western defence alliances."[8] The Commission observed that the composition of the Department was unique, consisting of two elements, military and civilian, differing in status, rank structure and terms of employment, although they functioned as an entity. Also of significance was "the character of the Armed Forces, whose numbers, organization and skills are predicated on wartime tasks, with the consequence that utilization in peacetime is a problem."[9] A Coordination Team was created by the Glassco Commission to scrutinize microscopically several of the Department's activities.

The work of this committee will not be described herein, particularly since it has been covered brilliantly by Douglas Bland in his book *The Administration of Defence Policy: 1947-1985*.

The Glassco Commission tabled its report in Parliament in September 1962. The report was highly critical of the manner in which the machinery of government managed its affairs and its personnel. Concerning the Department of National Defence in particular, the Commissioners wrote "it is recognized, however, that recommendations advanced to promote efficiency currently, must at the same time be evaluated in the light of their possible effect on the operational effectiveness of the Armed Forces."[10] At the same time, the Commissioners believed that the Department of National Defence, just like other government organizations, should have every interest in preparing departmental estimates on the basis of programs of activity (cost basis) rather than by standard objects of expenditure (cash basis).

The Glassco Commission also called for better coordination of the activities of the three services and more effective distribution of manpower. The Commissioners recommended that this be achieved by "consolidation [of common functions] under a single executive authority independent of the three Chiefs of Staff."[11] In the Commissioners' view, there was also a need to enhance career opportunities for civilians in the Department, and implementation of the foregoing recommendation would provide access to higher positions in the auxiliary services and facilitate cross-postings between officers and civilian executives. But the Glassco Commission had merit irrespective of the specifics of these recommendations. As Bland observes, "the Glassco Commission is important not so much because it led directly to significant changes in the administration of defence policy in Canada. It did not. What it did do was to provide authority and validity to concepts that others would champion later on."[12]

5.1.3 Reorganization of the Department of National Defence

At the time of Paul Hellyer's appointment, overhaul of the Department of National Defence was a highly topical subject in government circles. In 1963, a Special Parliamentary Committee reviewed the whole defence question. On 26 March 1964, Defence Minister Hellyer tabled his White Paper on Defence before the House of Commons. The policy had three main objectives: 1) to maintain world peace through collective defence to deter military aggression; 2) to support Canadian foreign policy, and 3) to ensure surveillance and control of Canada's territory.

Concerning the organization of defence forces, the White Paper stated: "Efforts have been concentrated on achieving coordination rather than integration of the three services. The instrument through which coordination has been sought has been the Chiefs of Staff Committee."[13] The Glassco Commission had, in fact, gone further by proposing that responsibility for common defence needs be assigned to the Chairman, Chiefs of Staff. The government's view was that "if a single command structure is not established, coordination by the committee system will remain with all of its inevitable delays and frustrations."[14]

Faced with this situation, Hellyer concluded that the best solution would be "the integration of the Armed Forces of Canada under a single Chief of Defence Staff and a single Defence Staff. [Supported by his government, the Minister of National Defence went even further, stressing that] this will be the first step toward a single unified defence force for Canada."[15] In addition to improving the organization for defence, the Minister envisaged effecting economies of scale by reducing service requirements by 10,000 personnel and by lowering general administrative costs of the Department.[16] These measures would provide significant savings at a time when the Liberal government was struggling to contain its 1964 budgetary deficit. For planning purposes, the Minister considered 1 July 1967 as an acceptable date for unification of the three services.[17]

The White Paper was received favourably by both the general public and the government. Encouraged by this support, Defence Minister Hellyer tabled Bill C-90 before the House on 13 April 1964. In Bland's view, this was "perhaps one of the most important defence bills introduced in Parliament since 1922."[18] With this first piece of legislation, the Minister could reorganize National Defence Headquarters and the command structure of the Forces. Amongst other things, reorganization of National Defence Headquarters would strengthen civil control within the Department and increase the responsibilities of the Deputy Minister of National Defence.[19]

Bill C-90 was adopted on 7 July and passed into law on 1 August. On that same day, the positions of the three Chiefs of Staff ceased to exist and Air Chief Marshal Frank R. Miller became the first Chief of the Defence Staff.[20] The difficult stage of integration of the various headquarters began, but as Stanley notes: "The new Canadian Forces Headquarters was intended to be essentially a policy-making and management body, not, strictly speaking, an operational headquarters. [...] The formation of these Commands posed a basic question: were they to be functional or regional in character?"[21] The Minister favoured the formation of functional commands, and accordingly new Commands were gradually set up, such as Force Mobile Command at Saint-Hubert. By 1967, Canadian Forces Headquarters and the various functional Commands were fully operational.[22]

Defence Minister Hellyer then decided to pass to the final stage of his unification program - that of integrating the three services of the Armed Forces into a single service. In the Minister's view, this single service would foster an *esprit de corps* throughout the whole of the Armed Forces, afford wider career opportunities, provide greater flexibility to meet changing requirements in the defence organization and, finally, increase the ability of the Armed Forces to react effectively in an emergency situation.[23] The Minister then proposed to replace the existing distinctive uniforms of the three services by a dark green common uniform.

This time the Minister ran into stiff opposition. It was a radical proposal, and many officers considered it premature, disrespectful of military tradition and of dubious effectiveness. According to Stanley, "it was the Royal Canadian Navy which opposed most strongly the changes that Hellyer proposed."[24] Holding fast to tradition, a number of high-ranking officers from the three services resigned in protest to signify their disapproval of the Minister's policies. It was of no consequence, and Hellyer tabled his bill before the House of Commons on 1 December 1966. Bill C-243 led to bitter debate and it was only at the closing of Parliament on 25 April 1967 that the bill was finally adopted. On 1 February 1968, the single unified Canadian Defence Force officially came into being. Meanwhile, Hellyer entered the race to become the new leader of the Liberal Party. At the leadership convention, he lost on the third ballot to Pierre Elliott Trudeau.

5.2 ONE CONSEQUENCE OF UNIFICATION OF THE CANADIAN FORCES: RESTRUCTURING OF RESEARCH ACTIVITIES AT CARDE

CARDE was in the process of reorienting its activities when the White Paper on Defence was tabled in 1964. Operation Lookout and the Black Brant project were winding down and members of the respective research teams were already being assigned to other projects. It was a difficult challenge. In the words of Dr. L'Heureux, Chief Superintendent of the Establishment:

> "A high powered research or development team cannot reach full effectiveness in less than four or five years; service philosophy and formal requirements can change much faster than this. Since Canadian defence research cannot possibly cover all subjects of potential military

importance, the choice of areas of specialization is extremely critical."[25]

From this perspective, the Chief Superintendent considered the integration of the Canadian Armed Forces as beneficial. As is well known, the prime responsibility of DRB was to provide scientific advice to the Armed Forces and to advance military science to meet the future needs of Canadian defence. In fulfilling this mandate, scientists had to rely on close and effective lines of communication with the whole chain of command structure for the three services. Better feedback at various levels of the Armed Forces was vital, for defence research could only flourish if its results were accepted and used. According to Dr. L'Heureux, the changes produced by integration of the Canadian Defence Forces would have a positive effect since they would allow the introduction of DRB thinking into the earliest stages of formulating Service equipment requirements. More importantly, he believed that this should substantially increase the proportion of successful research projects. Dr. L'Heureux considered that the Armed Forces would be more inclined to support the introduction into service of equipment designed at CARDE when the issue of re-equipping the Forces came up within the Department of National Defence. This was particularly important at the time given that Canada had announced a five-year re-equipment plan for the Canadian Armed Forces.

As a result of an increasing demand from the Armed Forces, CARDE officials accorded renewed emphasis to research on conventional weapons. This rearrangement proved to be important because it "made it necessary to start building up CARDE competence in areas which ... [previously] had had low priority"[26] and to reconstitute teams in areas of research that had been somewhat neglected. Weapon systems studies thus forged ahead along with a number of programs concerned with armament, detection and fire control. Increased emphasis had been placed on these research activities in 1964, and they expanded rapidly during the following year.

Despite this return to basics, so to speak, CARDE did not abandon those projects that had flourished over the prior decade. To have abandoned them would have been counter-productive, to say the least, since the scientific teams conducting research on ballistic missile defence had reached a high level of effectiveness. History shows that a good research team cannot be built up to high productivity in less than four or five years.

Despite its quality, the expertise developed by the CARDE research teams on ballistic missile defence still had to find a buyer. In 1964, the US and Canadian Governments sought to increase their knowledge in areas under study by CARDE scientists. As a result, new programs were initiated which "assured continued CARDE strength in the fields of propellant chemistry and rocket motor design, hypervelocity physics, and infrared transmission and detection". On the debit side, microwave work was terminated and CARDE's capability in missile guidance and in fusing was low and decreasing.[27] In other words, applied research on guided missiles continued, but on a lower scale.

In another vein, CARDE officials were faced with strong and increasing competition for top flight scientists and engineers in the areas of specialization selected by the Establishment. As the Chief Superintendent stressed, "reasonable program stability and a fair proportion of fundamental work are essential in attracting and retaining highly competent staff."[28] This premise was probably invoked when CARDE decided to conduct fundamental research on lasers which could have possible military application.

In summary, unification of the three Services and the five-year plan for re-equipping the Canadian Armed Forces played an important role in the reorientation of CARDE's research activities towards conventional armaments and weapon systems. This reorientation did not, however, prejudice the joint research programs with the United States. Moreover, CARDE officials were not satisfied with simply meeting existing needs, and had no hesitation in initiating research activities in totally new fields, such as lasers, in anticipation of future requirements. In the remainder of this Chapter, we shall deal with the evolution of research conducted at CARDE on conventional armaments and weapon systems, as well as the circumstances surrounding the invention of the Transversely Excited Atmospheric Carbon Dioxide (TEA-CO_2) laser.

5.3 RENEWED EMPHASIS ON WEAPON SYSTEMS STUDIES AND RESEARCH ON CONVENTIONAL ARMAMENTS

5.3.1 Weapon Systems Studies

Since the time of its creation in 1958, Systems Wing devoted major effort to determining how the components of a complex system could be integrated to achieve maximum efficiency. Generally, the research was aimed at assessing system potential and behaviour. Because of the mass of data obtained, researchers at the Establishment had to design new methodologies for analyzing data and develop efficient data processing and analysis programs. This involved the use of analog and digital computers, and a data processing section had to be established at CARDE.

During the early years, the research team focused on guided missile projects, such as Sprint and Green Light. As we have seen, a considerable portion of the CARDE research effort was devoted to collecting data on the characteristics of the ballistic missile target and the phenomena associated with its re-entry. This was the context in which Systems Wing was charged with the responsibility of ensuring coordination of this activity and providing a consolidated picture of the ballistic missile as a threat. The Systems Wing was also required "to maintain sufficient working knowledge of the existing and future development in the field to advise on the effectiveness of systems for Canadian and Continental defence". In partial fulfilment of this mandate, the Wing undertook a program in 1958 with the RCA Victor Company on radar capabilities. The purpose of the study was "to review the statistical aspects of signal detection and parameter determination in the presence of noise."[29]

The Periscopter design team, consisting of an unidentified Westinghouse engineer, Mr. Jean Baillot, Mr. Chris Wilson, Project Leader, Maj L. MacIntosh, Mr. Laval Pelletier and Mr. Pierre Lemay, shown behind the flying vehicle that can observe the enemy behind their own lines.

Researchers of Systems Wing also undertook a detailed study on enhancing battlefield surveillance for the Army, with particular emphasis on interactions between small combat units. The study focused on improving methods for collection, transmission, processing and distribution of data obtained in a combat situation. In the area of data collection, researchers examined the military potential of passive infrared systems and "imaging detectors". Research was also conducted on techniques for detecting tanks in conditions of restricted vision. In this latter context, a feasibility study was undertaken in 1960 on a novel aerial surveillance device for data collection known as the Periscopter.

The Combat Intelligence Research (CIR) Project initiated in 1958 accounted for an ever-increasing portion of the activities of Systems Wing. The project was originally funded by the Canadian Army, but by 1960 financial support was provided entirely by DRB. Following a review of the CIR project in 1960, three priority programs were identified: "the Periscopter Program, the Intervisibility Program and the Thirty-Element Scanner Program". Of these three programs, the Periscopter project accounted for the majority of the research effort of Systems Wing; the Canadian Westinghouse Company also worked under contract to CARDE in this area. The Periscopter was a "short-range surveillance, fire control and missile guidance system" which consisted of a small tethered helicopter equipped with a television camera.[30] The efforts of the scientists were totally successful and the system was finally perfected in 1964.

5.3.2 The Creation of the Armament Engineering Wing

For several years, CARDE's main research efforts were directed towards ballistic missile defence. In parallel, there had been a decline in Armed Forces demand for conventional armaments. Although CARDE still conducted research in this area, for example development work on the 105- and 155-mm Howitzers and the Heller-Stage B for BUSRAT (Battle Unit Short Range Anti-Tank), conventional armaments no longer had the importance of earlier years.

In 1963, CARDE officials were of the view that this situation could change. In Parliament, National Defence was the issue of the day, and everything indicated that there would be significant changes in the defence sector. As well, CARDE officials were aware that Western strategists were beginning to question certain pre-conceived ideas on the ability of complex defence systems to function effectively in any circumstance. It was clear that in limited warfare, for instance, sophisticated defence systems were not able to displace conventional weapons as rapidly as had been anticipated.[31] As the cost and complexity of weapon systems increased, systems analysis came to play an ever-increasing role in military technology, and analytical studies became key elements in the process of selecting and developing military hardware.

CARDE officials thus considered it important to increase the effort expended on systems studies. As reported at the time, "armament and systems studies must be closely coordinated to ensure, on the one hand, that a proposed technical improvement or innovation in a weapon will effectively improve the ability of the system to deal with its designated targets and, on the other hand, that the elements of a proposed new or improved weapon system are technically feasible."[32] To achieve this close coordination, CARDE officials opted for a vertical restructuring of the relevant research by integrating specialists in both armaments and systems studies within the same Wing.

In August 1963, Systems Wing was disbanded and the Armament Engineering Wing created. The new Wing included all the personnel from the former Mechanics Wing and some of the personnel from the Systems Wing. Another group of personnel from the Systems Wing was attached to the Electronics Wing to form the nucleus of the Military Applications Section. Finally, because of the increasing importance of data processing in all spheres of research, CARDE officials expanded the responsibilities of the Data Processing Section to serve the whole Establishment and decided to attach this Section to the Technical Services Wing (see Figure 9, Chapter 7).

5.3.3 The Main Activities of the Armament Engineering Wing

Armaments research and weapon systems studies were pursued in parallel by scientists in the Armament Engineering Wing. Activities in these two areas will be described separately. When the Wing was created, the weapon systems research team was just completing its work on the Periscopter surveillance system, and the device was flight-tested in 1964. During the following year, a study was conducted on the Rapidaim concept which would employ a laser-computer device (laser rangefinder) to increase the effective range of an anti-tank direct-fire weapon. The study employed "a simplified version of a mathematical model of a tank engagement developed by CAORE (Canadian Army Operation Research Establishment), now DLAOR (Director Land/Air Operations Research)."[33] In 1967, the Wing reoriented its research work towards studies of artillery systems and anti-tank weapons in collaboration with the Canadian Armed Forces. Aside from these projects in support of land operations, the Wing also worked with naval personnel on systems studies of a hydrofoil craft conceived to facilitate the detection and destruction of submarines. These studies accounted for a major part of the research efforts of the Armament Engineering Wing's Systems Section during the 1960's.

For its part, the Armaments Section continued to collaborate with the Canadian Armed Forces, with primary emphasis on the design and development of conventional armaments. Basic and applied research was conducted in the areas of internal, external and terminal ballistics, and in related areas such as metallurgy and applied mechanics. During the 1960's, research activities encompassed areas as diverse as the physics of armour penetration, uranium alloys and the mechanical properties of materials, development of smoke bombs and canisters, internal and external ballistics, and dynamic tests of penetrating and other special-use warheads. From 1967 onwards, the Canadian Armed Forces increasingly sought the support of the armament specialists to demonstrate the feasibility of prototypes and to undertake trouble-shooting in respect of in-service equipment.

5.3.4 The Canadian Forces Special Projects Laboratory

CARDE established the Canadian Forces Special Projects Laboratory (CFSPL) in 1967 to promote even closer collaboration between CARDE and the Armed Forces in light of the growing number of projects undertaken in direct response to Service needs.[34] The CFSPL did not, of course, duplicate the research infrastructures already existing at CARDE. Its mandate was to develop new concepts to improve the effectiveness of soldiers in combat situations. The concepts selected were those identified as the most promising by the National Defence Operational Techniques Study Coordinator (OTSC). The Laboratory consisted of a nucleus of officers, and technical assistance was provided by researchers from all the scientific Wings of CARDE.

The creation of this research unit evidently met a real need, for no less than 25 studies were undertaken during its first year of operation. The field of investigation was extremely broad, encompassing the development of warning, navigation, observation and training devices, and metal detectors for searching personnel. The Laboratory's research team progressively appears to have been transformed into a technical assessment team concerned with evaluating commercial equipment used by the Armed Forces. In 1973, DREV undertook a major reorganization of the scientific and technical components of the Establishment, and CFSPL personnel were integrated into the Canadian Forces Projects Office which was responsible for assigning projects and tasks to DREV.

5.4 DREV BECOMES A WORLD LEADER IN LASER RESEARCH: THE DEVELOPMENT OF THE TEA-CO_2 LASER

5.4.1 CARDE Research on Military Applications of Lasers

The development of the first laser by Maiman[35] in 1960 fired the world's imagination, and new types of laser were invented in rapid succession.[36] Many people at the time considered the invention of the laser as one of the most sensational of the modern age, second only to the invention of the atomic bomb. Lasers appeared to have unlimited application to fields as diverse as medicine, manufacturing, photography and communications. For many, the appearance of the laser foreshadowed the early development of weapons such as the laser cannon or the hand-held ray-gun. The idea of concentrating radiant energy in a beam that could inflict damage on a target at a distance had left the world of legend[37] - or the science-fictional world of H.G. Wells and Buck Rogers - and had entered the world of reality.

But as Hecht observed, the majority of these "science-fictional weapons bear little relationship to the concepts being considered by the deadly serious planners in the Pentagon and the Kremlin".[38] Military establishments across the world explored more modest and immediate military applications of lasers in fields such as imagery, optical radar, communications, target tracking and target designation. In Canada, some visionaries considered that this technology would revolutionize certain aspects of optical warfare.[39] In Valcartier, CARDE scientists seemed to be particularly suited to explore the potential of the laser, having acquired recognized competence in the microwave field and having developed expertise in optical and infrared spectroscopy through projects such as Lookout. CARDE scientists envisaged the development of a laser rangefinder as the first military application of the laser. This device, which measures the distance to a target, is also called an optical radar (or "ladar") since the light impulses emitted by a laser are used to fulfil the same functions as the microwaves of a conventional radar."[40]

In early 1962, Dr. Guy Giroux and John Higgins of CARDE built a laser prototype based on the design of Dr. Javan of Bell Telephone Laboratories in the United States. The active medium was a mixture of helium and neon, and although the laser was bulky and of low power output, it nevertheless allowed the researchers to study the propagation of laser beams in the atmosphere. But the appearance of commercial units of superior quality and performance tolled the knell for this prototype.[41]

CARDE researchers then turned their attention to solid-state lasers, particularly ruby lasers. When these units were operated in the pulse mode, "the high peak powers achievable [...] coupled with the sensitivity of detectors in the visible spectrum, readily suggested their utilization as rangefinders."[42] On the other hand, ruby lasers had some disadvantages when used in optical radars. Because they emitted light in the visible spectrum, they were extremely dangerous for the eyes. In addition, the ruby rods (crystals) needed to obtain lasing action could not be made "without specialist knowledge, installations and extremely expensive techniques."[43] At the time, the use of ruby lasers was very much in vogue, and on many occasions CARDE researchers encountered difficulties in procuring quality laser rods. These difficulties were compounded by the fact that not all suppliers were able to provide suitable material within a reasonable time frame.

Despite the often poor quality of their ruby rods, CARDE researchers continued to experiment with this type of laser. This work "matured into a working laser prototype that was used as a rangefinder in the Rapidaim system developed to increase the hit probability of guns against moving targets."[44] The Rapidaim concept was successfully demonstrated to the military during a series of field trials in 1965, but "never went into production because the electronics technology of computers at the time was not sufficiently advanced to enable the device to be manufactured as a compact instrument."[45] Despite this disappointment, the main objective of the CARDE experimental work with lasers had been attained, specifically that of acquiring a basic knowledge of laser techniques and their application to military systems.

5.4.2 A Shift in Research Emphasis: From Solid-State Lasers to Electrically-Excited CO_2 Lasers

In 1964, the American Townes and two Soviets, Basov and Prokhorov, shared the Nobel Prize in Physics for fundamental research on the laser. Also in 1964, researcher C. Kumar N. Patel of the Bell Telephone Laboratories unveiled the most powerful electrically-excited molecular gas laser of the decade, the CO_2 laser. This device provided the first indication that a laser could achieve high efficiency and operate at high average power.

In 1965, the Chief Superintendent of CARDE, Dr. Léon L'Heureux, grouped all the laser researchers together within the same section - the new Electro-Optics Section attached to Aerophysics Wing - and appointed Dr. Jacques A. Beaulieu to the position of Section Head. Dr. Beaulieu, a physicist who had joined the Establishment in 1954, had just returned from educational leave in England where he had obtained a doctoral degree in solid-state physics from London University.

The creation of the Electro-Optics Section allowed scientists to re-evaluate their programs in the field of lasers. The impossibility of growing crystals at the Establishment in Valcartier made it increasingly difficult for scientists to pursue original research on solid-state lasers. At that time, "solid-state specialists at DRTE [Defence Research Telecommunications Establishment] in Ottawa were responsible for growing crystals and evaluating them as lasing media. CARDE did not have the necessary resources to undertake that kind of research."[46] After Patel announced his spectacular results, the research effort on solid-state lasers was phased out and effort was applied instead to the carbon dioxide molecular gas laser. The CO_2 laser promised a number of potential advantages in military applications. First, the laser emitted infrared light at a wavelength of 10.6 microns, within the atmospheric transmission band, which meant that the laser beam would propagate over large distances. Second, the CO_2 laser could operate at high average power with an efficiency ten times that of the solid-state laser. Since the lasing medium was a gas, the costs of fabrication and operation were relatively low. Finally, the infrared radiation posed no danger for the eyes, and this was an advantage for both the scientist and the soldier.

5.4.3 Invention of the Transversely-Excited Atmospheric Carbon Dioxide (TEA-CO$_2$) Laser

Following the reorientation of activities in 1965, scientists of the Electro-Optics Section quickly constructed a continuous wave CO$_2$ laser of moderate size in order to develop a fundamental understanding of this type of laser device. "One year later, feasibility studies led to the construction of a 1.25-metre prototype CO$_2$ laser having an average power of 55 watts at a 20% efficiency [...]. This unit was later scaled to a 10-metre laser capable of delivering an average power of 500 watts."[47] For both prototypes, lasing action was stimulated by the standard technique of passing an electric current through a long glass tube which contained the lasing medium (a mixture of nitrogen, helium and carbon dioxide). The current induced an electric discharge along the axis of the tube, whence the term longitudinal excitation. The extremities of the tube were sealed by mirrors which faced each other to form an optical resonator, and the laser beam output was thus in the axial direction.

Encouraged by the potential of this type of laser, CARDE scientists considered ways of increasing the power output. Two options were apparent: lengthen the tube, or increase the number of molecules producing the lasing action, i.e., increase the pressure of the gas mixture. In the prototypes already built, "the maximum output power was obtained when the total gas pressure was about one-fiftieth of an atmosphere. Since an increase in gas pressure also produced an increase in temperature which reduced the laser efficiency, the only way of increasing the output power was to increase the length of the laser."[48] At the time, the solution envisaged for obtaining higher output was to use laser modules in cascade. CARDE scientists thus concentrated on "the design of bigger units to achieve higher energy while maintaining or improving the overall efficiency and beam quality."[49] The powers obtained in the continuous wave (CW) mode were of interest, but the physical dimensions of the device were too large for military application. Moreover, "these long conventional lasers could not be operated in the giant pulse mode and had not produced peak powers higher than 250 kW."[50] This constituted an upper limit for the envisaged application, that of a laser radar. CARDE researchers, like others in the scientific community, had reached a dead end. A new approach was required to circumvent this impasse in developing a sufficiently high-powered CO_2 laser of acceptable physical dimensions.

CARDE researchers had the original idea of exciting the laser medium transversely instead of longitudinally, i.e., at right angles to, rather than along, the optical axis of the resonator formed by the two end mirrors. In late 1967, Dr. Jacques Beaulieu undertook fundamental work on the transverse excitation technique using many parallel pin electrodes distributed along the tube. This fundamental work allowed scientists "to gain new knowledge on the physics of electrical stimulation in gas lasers."[51] With this configuration, the length of the excitation discharge was no longer dependent on the physical length of the laser. In addition, the laser could be operated in pulse mode at much higher pressures and produce very short laser pulses at very high peak pulse power. Since the new transversely excited CO_2 lasers operated at atmospheric pressure, they were called TEA (**T**ransversely-**E**xcited **A**tmospheric) lasers. According to the 1975 DREV Annual Report:

> "Some close observations revealed that gas heating was responsible for the poor performance. To alleviate this problem, the technique of pulsing rather than continuously exciting the medium was tried. The use of short pulses at low repetition rate did, in fact, eliminate the difficulty. It also indicated that population inversion could be established rapidly enough to achieve gain switching, which allows the formation of a giant pulse without the assistance of external elements, such as

spinning mirrors or bleachable absorber cells. Moreover, this technique showed a very important point: by resistively loading the numerous discharge electrodes, it was possible to increase the operating pressure while maintaining a fairly uniform discharge distribution along the laser chamber. Since the average power available per unit volume of laser gas [...] is proportional to the square of the pressure in the system one can appreciate the significance of this discovery."[52]

The impact of this discovery can be better appreciated when it is remembered that a conventional CO_2 laser operates at a maximum of one-fiftieth of an atmosphere. With the TEA laser configuration, a minimum gain of 2,500 in average power per unit volume of laser gas can be achieved. The TEA laser technique thus represented a major technological breakthrough in the development of pulsed CO_2 lasers.

CARDE researchers were the first in the world to use CO_2 lasers at atmospheric pressure to "simultaneously produce high peak power and repetition rates [...] unparalleled in the field of lasers."[53] It thus became possible to design modules of small physical dimensions that would produce laser peak pulse powers of several megawatts, ideal for laser radar applications. Another advantage of operating the laser at atmospheric pressure was that the laser cavity could be made with inexpensive materials such as plastic. In fact, personnel of the Electro-Optics Section even made one with plywood! According to Dr. Beaulieu, "the electrical power source presently accounts for the major portion of the cost."[54]

5.4.4 Project LOTION

The feasibility of the $TEA-CO_2$ laser was demonstrated in initial experiments conducted in early 1968. Realizing that CARDE scientists had just paved the way to a new generation of high power lasers with significant military application, the Chairman of DRB, Dr. R.J. Uffen, decided to release substantial funds in order to build a laser laboratory at CARDE.[55] The Director General of CARDE, Mr. E.J. Bobyn, grouped into one highly secret project all research effort directed to the refinement of the novel excitation technique for CO_2 lasers. This project was known under the code name Project LOTION. The project team consisted of about ten scientists under the direction of Dr. Beaulieu, and its activities centred around "the development of mathematical and experimental models to be used in the design of electrode configuration and distribution to realize more effective transverse-excitation mechanisms."[56] The team built over a hundred prototypes using various types of material and electrical excitation techniques "to determine the effects of electrode shape, composition and distribution across the cavity on the beam quality, output energy and overall efficiency."[57] Researchers made strenuous efforts to achieve uniform excitation of the lasing medium over a large section of the cavity, which was the main problem encountered in developing this laser. In 1970, Dr. Albert Laflamme found a solution to the problem by developing a new type of electrode and a new two-stage electrical excitation mechanism. The cathode was a metallic grid, behind which a low-energy discharge was initiated to pre-ionize the gas prior to application of the main excitation discharge which produced the laser pulse.

Two years of intensive research conducted by this group of highly-skilled researchers led to 25 inventions, and sixty patent applications were filed in fifteen countries.

5.4.5 World-Wide Renown for the Invention of the TEA-CO_2 Laser

In the late 1960's, CARDE officials became aware that other laboratories across the world were nearing the solution found by the Electro-Optics team. The issue they faced was whether to retain the secret as long as possible with the attendant risk of losing all the prestige that would accompany the announcement of this invention, or to disclose it and thus receive all the credit. For the scientists, the choice was clear: it was essential that they receive the credit.[58] Consequently, in October 1969, the scientists took the precaution of filing patent applications in several countries.[59]

Some of the members of the Project LOTION team that was awarded the gold medal of the Professional Institute of the Public Service of Canada for discovering the TEA-CO_2 laser. From left to right: Dr. Jacques Beaulieu, Mr. Martin Hale and Dr. Maurice Gravel. In the background: Mr. Gilles Boily.

On 13 January 1970, Dr. Beaulieu revealed this important technological breakthrough. Instantly, the potential of the TEA-CO_2 laser fired the imagination of journalists and the invention received tremendous media coverage. For a good while, DREV scientists were recognized as leaders in laser research. They were invited to participate in symposia and scientific conferences across the world, and their articles were accepted for publication in the most prestigious scientific journals. Their patent applications for the various inventions based on the new excitation mechanism for gas lasers were accepted. In its year-end review of 1970, the Canadian press described the invention of the TEA laser as a major event in Canadian science. Perhaps more importantly, the efforts of the DREV laser specialists won recognition from their colleagues when the TEA laser was featured on two occasions on the cover of *Laser Focus*, the most authoritative international periodical of the laser industry.

The disclosure in 1970 of the discovery of the TEA laser gave new impetus to the race to design high-power lasers among laserists the world over and particularly in the United States, France, United Kingdom and the USSR. In fact, an amusing anecdote is told about this. In response to the Canadian TEA laser, American scientists of the Westinghouse Electric Co. introduced another type of laser in 1972 that could operate at atmospheric pressure which they called COFFEE (Continuously Operated Fast-Flow Electrically-Excited)! The COFFEE laser could generate 6 kW of power in continuous operation, but required a mammoth CO_2 recirculation system that circulated the gas inside at a velocity in excess of 200 km/h.s."[60]. Much too cumbersome, the COFFEE laser quickly became obsolete and, unlike the TEA laser, is never mentioned today.

For a while, due to the efforts of DREV scientists, Canada ranked first amongst world nations in laser research. This was remarkable given that Canadian researchers lacked the immense resources which were made available to researchers of other major nations.

5.4.6 Spin-off from the Invention of the TEA-CO_2 Laser

The invention of the TEA-CO_2 laser in 1970 not only spurred the imagination of the public, it also generated enormous interest amongst specialists in scientific and industrial circles. Canada was inundated with requests from scientists in allied nations for authorization to visit the Establishment at Valcartier and study the new laser. Industry also showed marked interest, and over 60 industrial organizations, including 14 Canadian companies, applied to DRB for licences to develop and market this new invention. According to press reports at the time, DRB considered that 14 firms were prime candidates.

The selection process was not lengthy. In June 1970, scarcely six months after the invention of the TEA laser was announced, two Canadian firms were awarded licences: Gentec Inc., Québec, and Lumonics Research Ltd., an Ottawa firm that was created especially to exploit this invention. Each company, armed with its government licence, developed special applications to secure a specific niche in the marketplace. Gentec, which pulled off a masterstroke by securing the services of Dr. Beaulieu in 1971, focused its efforts on devices of high repetition rate and average peak power (~1 MW) Gentec first targeted the education market with demonstration lasers before moving into micro-machining applications, specifically dynamic balancing of gyroscopes. Later, Gentec specialized in accessories for TEA lasers, such as high tension probes and laser energy detectors. For its part, Lumonics developed lasers of high peak power and low repetition rate for use in research applications in the fields of spectroscopy and plasma physics. In the mid-1970's, Lumonics produced a new type of TEA laser which was used for the marking of goods (electronic components, ordinary consumer products, etc). Because of its vitality, Lumonics succeeded so well that, in the late 1970's, it became the third largest producer of lasers in the world. Through their considerable efforts, DREV defence scientists successfully transferred the technology of their invention to the private sector and contributed to the creation and development of an important laser industry in Canada.

1	J.L. Granatstein, *Canada 1957-1967: The Years of Uncertainty and Innovation*, Toronto, McClelland & Stewart, 1986, p. 116-117.
2	Desmond Morton, *A'Military History of Canada: 1608-1991*, Toronto, McClelland & Stewart, 1992, p. 246.
3	*Ibid.*, p. 248.
4	J.L. Granatstein, *op. cit.*, p. 126.
5	*Ibid.*, p. 129.
6	Desmond Morton, *op. cit.*, p. 246 *et passim*.
7	Glassco Commission, "Special Areas of Administration", *Royal Commission on Government Organization (Glassco Commission)*, Vol. 4, Ottawa, Queen's Printer, p. 1.
8	*Ibid.*, p. 61.
9	*Ibid.*, p. 61.
10	*Ibid.*, p. 64.
11	*Ibid.*, p. 71.
12	Douglas Bland, *The Administration of Defence Policy: 1947-1985*, Kingston, Frye, 1987, p. 30.
13	Canada, *White Paper on Defence*, Ottawa, DND, March 1964, p. 17.
14	*Ibid.*, p. 18.
15	*Ibid.*, p. 19.
16	*House of Commons Debates 1964*, p. 3066.
17	*Ibid.*, p. 1941.
18	Douglas Bland, *op. cit.*, p. 41.
19	*House of Commons Debates 1964*, p. 3068 and 3188.
20	George F.G. Stanley, *Canada's Soldiers: The Military History of an Unmilitary People*, Toronto, Macmillan, 1974, p. 425.
21	*Ibid.*, p. 426.
22	*Ibid.*, p. 428.
23	*House of Commons Debates 1966*, p. 10828 and 10829.
24	George F.G. Stanley, *op. cit.*, p. 429.
25	CARDE, *Annual Report for 1965*, p. 1.
26	*Ibid.*, p. 1.
27	*Ibid.*, p. 1 and 2.
28	*Ibid.*, p. 1.
29	CARDE, *Annual Report for 1959*, p. 20.
30	CARDE, *Annual Report for 1961*, p. 34.
31	CARDE, *Annual Report for 1963*, p. 1.
32	CARDE, *Annual Report for 1965*, p. 8.
33	*Ibid.*, p. 6.
34	CARDE, *Annual Report for 1967*, p. 1.
35	T.H. Maiman, "Stimulated Emission in Ruby", *Nature*, **187**, 493 (1960); cited by Jeff Hecht, *Beam Weapons: The Next Arms Race*, New York and London, Plenum Press, 1984, p. 23-25.

36 Jeff Hecht, *op. cit.*, p. 22 *et passim*.
37 For example, Jeff Hecht recounts the legend surrounding the defence of Syracuse by Archimedes, who was one of the most eminent scientists of antiquity. An outstanding mathematician and physicist, Archimedes was recognized by his contemporaries mostly for his inventive genius. A native of Syracuse in Sicily, this Greek scientist invented war machines to prevent his city from being sacked by the Romans throughout a three-year siege. Legend has it that Archimedes used large, hexagonal, polished mirrors to focus sunlight on to Roman galleys in the harbour in 212 B.C. Jeff Hecht, *op. cit.*, p. 16-18.
38 Jeff Hecht, *op. cit.*, p. 40.
39 *Interview with Dr. Jacques Gilbert*, p. 11 and 12.
40 Jean-Marc Fleury, "Laser québécois; un succès éblouissant", *Québec Science*, Vol. 12, No. 3, December 1973, p. 34.
41 DREV, *Annual Report for 1975*, p. 10.
42 DREV, *Annual Report for 1975*, p. 11.
43 *Comments of Dr. Jacques Beaulieu.*
44 DREV, *Annual Report for 1975*, p. 11.
45 *Comments of Dr. Jacques Beaulieu.*
46 *Ibid.*
47 DREV, *Annual Report for 1975*, p. 12.
48 *Comments of Dr. Jacques Beaulieu.*
49 DREV, *Annual Report for 1975*, p. 12.
50 *Ibid.*, p. 12.
51 *Comments of Dr. Jacques Beaulieu.*
52 DREV, *Annual Report for 1975*, p. 13.
53 Québec Industriel. "Un laser à gaz accessible aux petites industries", *Québec Industriel*, February 1970, p. 35.
54 *Ibid.*
55 *Interview with Dr. Jacques Gilbert*, p. 18.
56 DREV, *Annual Report for 1975*, p. 15.
57 *Ibid.*, p. 15.
58 *Interview with Dr. Jacques Gilbert*, p. 16-17.
59 *Comments of Dr. Jacques Beaulieu.*
60 R. Conally, "Laser seek wider markets", *Electronics*, June 21, 1973, p. 71.

PART THREE

AN ERA OF CHANGE: DREV ON THE EVE OF THE THIRD MILLENIUM

> *No organization in the fifty years since World War II has changed more than the military, even though uniforms and titles of rank have remained the same. Weapons have changed completely, as the Gulf war of 1991 dramatically demonstrated. Military doctrines and concepts have changed even more drastically. And so have organization structures, command structures, relationships, and responsabilities. (Peter Drucker)[1]*
>
> *With this White Paper, the government has fulfilled its obligation to provide Canadians with an effective, realistic and affordable defence policy. (1994 Defence White Paper, p. 49)*

6

CANADA'S DEFENCE POLICY DURING THE PAST 25 YEARS

Since the early 1970s, the state of Canada's public finance has progressively deteriorated to a degree unprecedented in the annals of Canadian history. The current federal deficit and the total national debt have now reached staggering proportions. A problem of such magnitude clearly has a significant impact on the machinery of government and on the formulation and evaluation of Canadian Government policy. Not a single individual nor, *a fortiori*, a single government service could escape the consequences. For this reason, it is important to review the state of the country's public finance before assessing the impact of fiscal policy on Canada's defence policy.

6.1   STATE OF CANADA'S PUBLIC FINANCE

When Canada entered the Second World War, the Canadian Government tightened its control over the economy and started to set in place the first significant social programs, such as the unemployment insurance program. Canada then experienced an unprecedented economic boom and the public could only wait and see, with some apprehension, what would happen at the end of this period of prosperity. The government was aware of the public's concern and, as early as 1943, developed plans to avoid a return to the depressed economic situation which existed prior to the war: "The government had unequivocally converted to Keynesianism during the war and henceforth there would be constant government intervention to regulate economic activity."[2] This vision of the State won support from everyone. The Canadian Government gradually built up the welfare state and with it the machinery of government. The major element of this Keynesian policy was the use of fiscal and monetary policy to speed up or slow down the economy. Even so, neither the Liberal nor Conservative governments were tempted to take economic development out of the hands of private enterprise in order to establish a controlled economy. Rather, they viewed their interventions as stimulants or incentives to adjust the various phases of the economic cycle.

Canada enjoyed a phase of remarkable prosperity following the war, and federal intervention in the economy seemed to be working rather well. But Canadian-style interventionism met with its first setback in 1957 when the country experienced its biggest post-war recession: "The Liberal administration did not initiate countercyclical measures, while the Diefenbaker administration dealt with the recession in piecemeal and *ad hoc* fashion."[3] At this point, federal public spending accounted for 17.6% of GDP. In 1962, there was an upturn in the Canadian economy and the average rate of growth of the GNP was over 6% until 1967. As the economy began to revive, the government increased taxes, and "policy in the late 1960's was concerned more with inflation than unemployment".[4] In 1970, the government became preoccupied with rising unemployment, and Canadian fiscal policy became "expansionary partly in response to the persistently high unemployment rates as measured against 1960's standards and also because expansion was made more acceptable by rather low inflation rates arising from the 1969-70 slowdown."[5] For this reason, Finance Minister Benson announced a projected deficit of

$145 million in the 1971 federal budget. Also in 1971, the United States decided to allow its currency to float and announced a 10% surtax on imports which negated, for all practical purposes, the stabilizing influence of the Bretton Woods Agreement on the world economy. Given that Canada was the main trading partner of the United States and was considered a major trading nation, this US decision could hardly fail to affect Canada's long-term economy. In the short-term, however, the Trudeau government proceeded with its 1972 fiscal policy.

In 1973, the world was faced with its first oil crisis. Because of Canada's position as a net energy exporter, the oil crisis had a favourable terms-of-trade effect on the Canadian economy, but this advantage was counterbalanced by the fact that Canada was also the OECD's largest energy user per capita. In short, gains in the energy sector were largely offset by income losses in the non-energy sector which had to absorb the higher price of oil. In 1974-1975, the Canadian economy experienced a period of stagflation, characterized by stagnation of economic activity and supply together with a price explosion. The Liberal government decided that priority had to be given to fighting inflation. The mini-budget tabled by the Liberals in October 1975 introduced a policy of wage and price controls together with a policy of reduced government expenditures, one effect of which was to limit the growth of the public service to 1.5% for the following fiscal year. As Campbell observes, "governments concluded, however, that the Keynesian tools were incapable of dealing with inflation. The authority of Keynesianism had disappeared."[6]

Although the 1976-79 period witnessed a slow recovery, the unemployment rate reached an alarming level: "One of the features of fiscal policy during this period was that tax cuts, rather than expenditure increases, were employed wherever possible."[7] According to Purvis, this was partly to stimulate the economy on the supply-side and exert a downward impact on prices, and partly to limit public expenditures. Despite these measures, the deficit continued to grow. In 1979, the Conservatives regained power and made deficit reduction one of their top priorities. But it was a minority government that was soon to be defeated on the issue of excise tax on gasoline.

The Liberals returned to power in 1980. During their mandate, they had to contend with a second oil crisis as well as extreme fluctuations in interest rates in the United States and, *de facto*, in Canada. The Liberals were also faced with an economic slowdown in the late 1970s which, by 1982, had degenerated into the worst economic recession since 1929. During this period, the Liberals introduced the National Energy Program, a tax reform budget designed to increase federal revenues significantly[8] and a "6 & 5 Program" which limited indexation of a number of government programs, as well as salary increases of federal government employees to 6% in 1983 and 5% in 1984.[9] Despite these initiatives, Canada was unable to control the rising deficits, which climbed from $3.8 billion in 1975 to $21.1 billion in 1982. During the four-year Liberal administration, the public debt grew at an annual rate of 23.5%.[10]

As Donald Savoie notes, "some observers suggest that the deficit problem coincided with the oil crisis of the mid-1970's and the resulting downward shift in growth trends in Canada and other Western industrialized nations."[11] Savoie also notes that the Department of Finance pointed to the severe recession of the early 1980s as the principal reason for the deficit problem, adding that "tax expenditures - or spending by not taxing - became very popular soon after the government implemented a series of expenditure restraint measures in 1976. [...] There is no doubt that the various new tax expenditures introduced since the mid-1970's have entailed a significant revenue loss for the federal government."[12]

The 1980's witnessed a growing awareness by the political leaders of the need to control government expenditures and contain the deficit. This imperative to set public finance on firm foundations became solidly entrenched in the political agenda, and was one of the major issues in the 1984 election when the national debt was approaching $200 billion. The Conservative Party won the election and the Mulroney government immediately announced a series of new taxes "and new revenue-generating measures" to increase federal tax revenues. New measures were added annually during the Conservative government's first term in office. As Savoie observed in 1990, "it is clear that an expanding economy, new taxes, and tax increases explain in large part the recent reduction in the annual growth in the deficit."[13]

When the Conservatives first came into office in 1984, "the federal government was spending $16 billion more on programs - everything except our interest costs - than it collected in revenues."[14] During this first term, the Mulroney government tried to transform this operating deficit into a surplus by reducing expenditures on all federal programs and services, including downsizing of the public service, to match predicted economic growth. This objective was achieved towards the end of the first term. By 1989, "interest payments on the debt [had] become the single largest component of expenditures"[15] and the growth rate in the national debt had been reduced to 12.7% annually, roughly half of the growth rate under the previous Liberal government. In the final analysis, despite the policies of sound financial management and debt reduction pursued by the Conservatives, the national debt grew to $300 billion by 1988, and the annual deficit stood at about $30 billion. Prime Minister Mulroney called an election in 1988 and throughout the campaign defended the need to retain tight control over public finance. Mulroney was re-elected.

At the start of its second term, the Mulroney government implemented further budget cuts that were spread over all government departments and programs. But "there were no major program cuts in any one area and taken together they [were] not as extensive as the 1984 or the 1985 cuts."[16] In 1990, Finance Minister Wilson confirmed that the deficit would exceed $30 billion, but stated that he would take the necessary steps to reduce the deficit to $10 billion by 1995. He would accomplish this by introducing a new five-year program to cut public spending by almost $19 billion. To increase government revenue, Wilson introduced the goods and services tax (GST), despite its unpopularity, to replace the federal sales tax on manufactured goods.

This tax reform was introduced in January 1991 when the first signs of the biggest economic recession since 1929 were beginning to make their appearance. As a result, the anticipated fiscal benefits were substantially reduced. The government then introduced new budget cuts through the Public Sector Compensation Act which limited salary increases to 0% and then 3%. But it was to no avail, for the government found that it was increasingly constrained by the weight of the national debt and the resulting fiscal burden carried by the public. In 1993, the popularity of the Mulroney government hit an unprecedented low. Prime Minister Mulroney resigned, and was replaced by Kim Campbell who quickly called an election. Jean Chrétien's Liberals won, and inherited this public finance crisis.

This crisis strongly affected the overall activities of the machinery of government and hence the basic reasons for the existence of several of its elements. Although the gravity of the situation is obvious to everyone in 1995, it was not so evident when the first annual deficits appeared and governments looked to expansionary policies to boost the economy. Various finance ministers during the 1980's tried to increase the tax yield while containing public spending. The solutions advocated by the present government have been no more convincing, and the budget cuts which have now been adopted can only lead to considerable changes in the role and mission of the Canadian Government.

6.2   THE IMPACT OF BUDGETARY POLICY ON CANADA'S DEFENCE POLICY SINCE 1969

During the past two decades, the Canadian Government has formulated the objectives of its defence policy in three successive White Papers published in 1971, 1987 and 1994. The budgetary issue received only marginal attention in the first of these, but has become a central theme in the latest one.

6.2.1 Defence Policy in the Early 1970's and the 1971 Defence White Paper

In 1968, the newly-elected leader of the Liberal Party, Pierre Elliott Trudeau, enjoyed unprecedented popularity with the Canadian public. Trudeaumania was born. On 25 June, Trudeau won the election and embarked on a full review of Canada's foreign policy to address the realities of the new international context. The Prime Minister's statement in the House of Commons: "We feel of necessity that defence policy must flow from foreign policy, and not the contrary", was to have significant implications for national defence. Trudeau went even further by asserting that, until then, Canada's defence policy had been conditioned by NATO policy, and that the government was "trying to put this pyramid on its base" by first enunciating Canada's foreign policy.[17]

On 3 April 1969, Trudeau affirmed that the four objectives of Canada's defence policy should be: 1) protection of Canadian sovereignty; 2) defence of North America; 3) support for NATO; and 4) peacekeeping operations. On 12 April 1969, Trudeau delivered an important address in Calgary in which he stated "the primary purpose of Canada's defence policy is to serve the national interest and, by extension, to contribute to world peace."[18] On 23 April 1969, he stated before the House of Commons that nations would have to recognize five conditions if world security were to be ensured: preservation of nuclear stability, prompt and peaceful resolution of conflicts, participation in peacekeeping operations, support for negotiation of arms limitations and disarmament agreements, and support to relieve such causes of unrest as economic insecurity.[19]

For the Prime Minister, Canada's NATO relationship was not a military decision but a political decision. Trudeau observed that the European members of NATO had developed a strong economic union and had "increased considerably their capability of defending their own region", and argued that "this increased capability in turn reduces the present need for a sustained Canadian military contribution [in Europe]."[20] In September 1969, the Minister of National Defence, Léo Cadieux, froze the defence budget for a period of three years. The strength of the Canadian Forces in Europe was reduced, and equipment was not upgraded. In the long-term, this could only lead to a disparity in conventional equipment between the Canadian Forces and their allies who were rapidly upgrading their equipment.

The freeze on the defence budget was essentially a plan to reduce military costs, since the defence budget was not indexed to the rate of inflation. But this was not perceived as an outcome of the defence policy review because Canada had announced at the time that it would pursue an expansionary budgetary policy. In any event, this budgetary freeze reduced the purchasing power of the Department of National Defence by 15% per annum over the three-year period.[21] The 1971 White Paper on Defence more or less included these main elements.

In addition, the Department of National Defence had to contend with an increased payroll starting in 1972 following "the alignment of military salaries with those of the public service."[22] It should be added, however, that pay equity for the military was part of the Trudeau government's inclination to allocate "funds for the defence budget [...] mainly to personnel, operations and maintenance" rather than to capital acquisition.[23] This was not inconsequential, given that "expenditures for capital acquisition fell from 16% in 1967 to 9% in 1972 (the lowest level since the end of the war)."[24]

6.2.2 The Mid-1970's: A Change in Course Dictated by *Realpolitik*

The international situation changed in 1973. The world experienced its first oil crisis, the United Kingdom joined the European Economic Community, and the United States launched the Year of Europe which would provide US support to the EEC in exchange for increased European defence effort. According to Fortmann, there was a high risk that Canada would be excluded from this emerging agreement, since it was considered in international circles that Canada was destined to gravitate more and more into the American orbit: "Canada thus changed course, progressively reconsidering the decisions of 1969."[25] Participation in NATO was again seen as essential. As Desmond Morton observes, members of the government discovered that a military withdrawal from Europe would not be without consequence for Canada's trade relations. In short, "belatedly, the experts discovered that defence, diplomacy, and commerce might be linked."[26]

Following the realignment of Canada's defence policy, the defence budget was brought into step with fiscal policy; the defence budget would increase by 7% annually for the following five years. One year later, however, the effects of this increase were wiped out by inflation. In 1975, the Defence Structure Review Group tabled its report and the government took the opportunity to announce a new five-year defence modernization plan which provided for equipment acquisition valued at $8.5 billion spread over ten years. The overall defence budget would increase by 12% per annum. Once again, this increase was insufficient to overcome inflation during this period of stagflation. In 1976, Canada announced the acquisition of the CP-140 Aurora long-range patrol aircraft from the United States, and the purchase of Leopard tanks from West Germany to replace the ageing Centurions in Europe. This according to Byers, "reflected the extent to which the government has upgraded its NATO commitment. In effect, this constituted a major shift in the order of priorities outlined in *Defence in the 70's*."[27]

On 1 January 1977, Canada established an exclusive economic zone extending 200 miles out to sea from its shores over which it would have full jurisdiction for exploitation of all resources. At the time, because of the deplorable state of its fleet, the Navy was incapable of exercising surveillance and control of Canadian coastal waters. As two admirals observed, "the Navy of 1978 is closer to the wrecking yards than most people realize."[28] Later, the federal government would undertake the frigate construction program to provide Maritime Command with the requisite means of protecting Canadian sovereignty.

But we should not look too far ahead. In 1977, Defence Minister Danson announced that the government would undertake a review of the Defence White Paper to better define the links between the several objectives of Canadian defence policy. Despite this announcement, the Department of National Defence did not produce another White Paper until 1987. In the interim, many shared the view of a certain staff general who declared that "defence policy in this country [between 1971 and 1987] amounts to a single statement on the purchase of equipment."[29] Be that as it may, in 1978 the Canadian Government experienced financial difficulties which slowed the growth of the defence budget and "it became quickly apparent that Canada could not respect its commitment to maintain a real growth rate of 3%."[30]

During the 1979 election, both the Liberals and the Conservatives promised to increase military strength and "to raise capital spending to a fifth of the defence budget."[31] The Conservatives won the election. In October 1979, the Clark government affirmed that it would maintain the course and continue to increase the budget of the Department of National Defence by 3% per annum in real terms until 1984, despite the difficult economic circumstances facing the country.[32] It was high time, since the defence share of the federal budget dropped from

14% in 1970 to 8.7% in 1980. The defence budget increased from $1.8 billion to $4 billion during this period, while the federal budget increased from $10 billion in 1969 to $45 billion in 1980. In terms of gross national product (GNP), the defence budget was 2.6% of GNP in 1968, but only 1.6% of GNP in 1980.[33]

As we have seen, the minority Conservative government was defeated in the House on the issue of excise tax on gasoline. In the election which followed, the Liberals were re-elected under Pierre Elliott Trudeau. Trudeau's return to power occurred during a period when détente, which had characterized the 1970's, was weakening. Americans were outraged at the inability of the US Government to resolve the Iran hostage crisis, and were eager to elect a President who would restore US military power. The new President, Ronald Reagan, was good to his promise and engaged in the arms race with the Soviet Union as soon as he came into office.

Even though "Canada clung longer to détente",[34] the Trudeau government nevertheless instituted a broad military re-equipment program to contribute to international stability, general disarmament and world peace. At the end of the Liberal mandate, the Minister of National Defence, Jean-Jacques Blais, stated "we still consider it prudent to contribute as best we can to collective strength with our allies, and to hold ourselves ready to help the United Nations in its efforts to foster and maintain global peace. This calls for sea, land and air forces which are highly professional and well equipped with the modern weapons of defence."[35] To this end, the Liberals placed greater emphasis on the capital portion of the defence budget, which grew from $363 million (11.4% of the defence budget) to $2.3 billion in 1984-85 (26.4% of the defence budget), an increase which greatly exceeded the objective of their 1979 electoral promises.

The growth in this budget item is even more striking when one remembers that the defence budget increased by $1 billion per annum during this period. These increases constituted "the most significant increases since the Korean War."[36] In terms of constant dollars, the 1984-85 defence budget represented "the highest level of defence spending [...] achieved since the early 50's."[37] As Paul Mann observed, "the ousted Liberal Party consistently met and by some calculations exceeded NATO's 3% target in the early 1980's."[38] Finally, it should be mentioned that although equipment acquisition accounted for 89% of the capital portion of the 1984-85 defence budget, 5% was still allocated to R&D.

Despite Canada's obvious effort under the Liberal government to modernize and re-equip the military, particularly through the purchase of the CF-18's and the frigates, the Liberals were unable to derive any political advantage from honouring their electoral commitments. In other words, armaments upgrading only counted in the long-term, whereas politics centred more on the short-term. According to Coulon, "the Liberal government derived no political benefit [while] the opposition continued to denounce the pitiful state of the Armed Forces"[39] and charged that the Trudeau government, during its first mandate, had "neglected defense and cut forces, without proportionately reducing commitments."[40]

6.2.3   The 1987 White Paper: *Challenge and Commitment*

The Progressive Conservative Party, led by Brian Mulroney, won the 1984 election. During the campaign, Mulroney made a commitment to maintain Canada's military alliances, to increase the strength of the Canadian Forces and to develop a new White Paper on defence. In addition, he promised "to increase military spending by 6% after inflation"[41] as a matter of priority. But the Mulroney government had great difficulty reconciling this objective with that of battling the deficit, and successive Ministers of National Defence had to argue fiercely with a determined Minister of Finance on the need to meet this 6% objective. Although they failed to convince the Finance Minister, the various Defence Ministers nevertheless succeeded in obtaining a real growth rate in defence spending (2.75% in 1986-87, for example).

During the Conservatives' term in office, the Department of National Defence pursued its equipment acquisition program in order to honour Canada's many defence commitments, including territorial defence (continental, maritime and arctic), participation in NATO and support for UN peacekeeping missions.

The incursion of a US icebreaker into Canadian Arctic waters in 1985, and Canada's inability to fulfil adequately its NATO commitment to send reinforcements to Norway, were two of the factors which led to the tabling of the 1987 Defence White Paper, *Challenge and Commitment*. This document reflected the concerns of the Cold War in terms of potential threats, requisite reactions and Canada's responsibilities. Thus, the deployment of a Canadian Mechanized Brigade Group in Europe remained the cornerstone of security policy and defence policy, together with the maintenance of a relief group in Canada and another group to ensure the security of Canadian territory. The Minister of National Defence, Perrin Beatty, advocated a policy based on collective defence and reaffirmed the need to maintain a strong Canadian presence within the various military alliances of which Canada was a member.

In 1987, the Canadian Forces lacked the necessary equipment to fulfil their many missions. In the Minister's view, "the results of decades of neglect can be overcome, but it will require a long-term solution: a steady, predictable and honest funding program based on coherent and consistent political leadership [...] A rolling five-year plan will be introduced within a fifteen-year planning framework."[42] In particular, Beatty's proposals included the acquisition of Aurora aircraft, frigates and additional CF-18 fighter aircraft, and the modernization of the North Warning Network. But the proposal which struck the public most was, without question, the decision to reinforce Maritime Command through the purchase of 8 to 12 nuclear-powered submarines at an estimated cost of $8 billion. This last initiative was no doubt aimed at affirming Canadian sovereignty in the North which had been challenged by the American venture into the Canadian waters of the Arctic Ocean in 1985. When the Defence Minister tabled his White Paper, he estimated that the defence budget would be $154 billion spread over fifteen years, with an additional $29 billion for new acquisition programs.

According to a senior executive in External Affairs, "the White Paper was stillborn when it went to press, simply because the funding implications made no sense."[43] As well, the White Paper assumed that the Cold War would continue until the year 2000, even though Soviet President Mikhail Gorbachev was pursuing his vast reform of Soviet society. With the thaw in the Cold War and the problem of containing the national debt, military expenditures became one of the hot issues in the election of November 1988. But as early as April 1988, the Finance Minister showed his colours by "unveiling a plan to reduce the defence budget for the following five years."[44]

Although the Conservatives won the election on the issue of free trade with the United States, the Mulroney government had to reckon with the unpopularity of military expenditures amongst the public and the scarcity of available budgetary funds in Canada. The post Cold War context and the attendant succession of questions on the relevance of the White Paper's geostrategic premises did not serve the cause of the military either. In this climate, the new Minister of National Defence, Bill McKnight, tried to save the essentials of the acquisition program by deciding to close seven military bases and to reduce the level of military activity elsewhere in the country. But this concession did not prevent Finance Minister Wilson from announcing, in April 1989, that he would make deep cuts in the equipment modernization program by cancelling, for example, the purchase of nuclear submarines. For Coulon, these events signalled that "the modernization program was going down with all hands."[45] Nevertheless, the defence budget increased slightly from $11.2 billion in 1988 to $11.3 billion in 1989.

6.2.4 The 1994 Defence White Paper: The Impact of Fiscal Policy and the End of the Cold War on Defence Policy in the 1990's

In 1990, Canada participated in the Gulf War. US President George Bush argued the need for a new world order in which the UN would play an integral part. Canada has always been one of the main pivots of UN peacekeeping missions, and this type of mission became more frequent in the 1990's. Canada participated in most of these missions, including the one in ex-Yugoslavia. In 1990, the Canadian Army applied the experience gained in peacekeeping to its successful intervention in the Oka Crisis in Quebec. But this series of interventions imposed unforseen demands on the defence budget.

In developing its 1991-92 budget, the Conservative government allocated an additional $600 million to allow the Department of National Defence to fulfil its increased responsibilities. In 1991 also, in light of the end of the Cold War and certain pressing national priorities, the federal government again reviewed the defence program. The government concluded that Canada could accelerate the withdrawal of its troops from Europe while retaining its NATO commitments. In presenting his 1992 budget, the Minister of Finance announced that "defence spending is being cut by $2.2 billion over the next five years."[46] "These cuts are in addition to reductions of $3.4 billion announced through the 1989 and 1990 federal budgets, so that the Department of National Defence, given other fiscal adjustments, has contributed nearly $6 billion to deficit reduction since 1989."[47]

In April 1992, Defence Minister Marcel Masse published a Statement entitled *Canadian Defence Policy* to elaborate the defence policy formulated by the government in September 1991. In this publication, the Department outlined the transformations occurring on the international scene and the political and financial challenges that Canada had to face. The Statement continued:

"Canada remains, therefore, committed to defence and collective security, arms control and disarmament, and the peaceful resolution of disputes",[48] thereby confirming Canada's intention to respect its alliances. The Minister also used this document to update the Department's strategy against the backdrop of international change, fiscal restraint and the capital acquisition program.

In this context, the Mulroney government attempted, throughout its second mandate, to adhere to the policy of allocating three-quarters of the defence budget to personnel, operations and maintenance, and one-quarter to capital acquisition. Equipment procurement programs are, of course, necessarily long-term, requiring extensive planning, since requirements generation, design, development, contracting and production activities span several years.

Despite the extremely high cost of some acquisitions, they rarely give rise to public controversy. A notable exception was the acquisition of the EH-101 helicopters at a cost of almost $6 billion, which a good number of Canadians considered too expensive. In the House of Commons, the official opposition echoed public disapproval. During the fall 1993 election campaign, the leader of the Liberal Party, Jean Chrétien, promised to cancel the program if elected. Following the Liberal victory, the new Prime Minister was good to his word and swiftly cancelled the helicopter procurement contract.

In 1993, responding to a fundamental reordering of international affairs and the need to confront economic difficulties at home, Prime Minister Chrétien announced a comprehensive review of Canadian defence policy which resulted in the 1994 Defence White Paper. The document observes that, with the end of the Cold War, "Canada faces an unpredictable and fragmented world, one in which conflict, repression and upheaval exist alongside peace, democracy and relative prosperity."[49] In this new world order, Canada would continue, within the context of international alliances, to defend freedom and democracy. In the words of the White Paper, "Canada continues to have a vital interest in doing its part to ensure global security, especially since Canada's economic future depends on its ability to trade freely with other nations."[50]

Having outlined the international environment and the potential threats looming on the horizon, the White Paper reviews the traditional roles of the Department of National Defence against the backdrop of public finance and the post Cold War world. These traditional roles concern the protection of Canada, Canada-United States defence cooperation, contributing to international security particularly through Canadian participation in NATO and in many multilateral peacekeeping operations throughout the world. The document also affirms the need to maintain Canadian Forces' capabilities to defend national territory and to provide aid to the civil power in various related tasks: assisting the civil power in controlling riots or disturbances which occur or are likely to occur; securing Canada's borders against illegal activities; conducting surveillance of fisheries to prevent the devastating effects of overfishing; providing humanitarian relief in cases of natural or man-made diasters; conducting environmental surveillance; and, conducting search and rescue operations in Canada.[51]

With the end of the Cold War, the authors of the White Paper observed: "Given that the direct military threat to the continent is greatly diminished, Canada will reduce the level of resources devoted to traditional missions in North America. It will, however, remain actively engaged in the United Nations, NATO, and the Conference on Security and Cooperation in Europe (CSCE)."[52] Mainly because of the Chrétien government's intention to continue Canada's participation in UN peacekeeping operations, the strength of the Army would be increased while the number of Air Force and Navy personnel would be reduced.

The White Paper, while stressing the need to maintain certain core capabilities, emphasizes the important contribution that the Department of National Defence and the Canadian Forces must make in fighting the deficit. The following conclusion had, therefore, to be expected:

> "To achieve these goals, the Regular and Reserve Forces will both be reduced and refocused, the command and control system will be reorganized, and affordable equipment will be purchased so our troops will have the means to carry our their missions. [...] This policy recognizes that the defence budget will be under continuing pressure as the government strives to bring the deficit under control. More reductions can and will be accommodated, including the military reductions outlined in this Paper and cuts in the Department's civilian workforce arising from a number of additional facilities closures and consolidations."[53]

In short, national security and collective security remain omnipresent in Canada's new defence policy, but the role and mission of the Department of National Defence has sharply changed because of the new Canadian fiscal reality. Thus, in 1994, Finance Minister Paul Martin announced that military expenditures would be 60% lower than estimated in the 1987 White Paper, and that further budget cuts would be needed in the defence sector. The recent 1995 budget shows that the Minister intends to adhere to this approach.

Finally, the Department of National Defence has developed a strategic framework over the past years, known as Defence 2000, aimed at improving the cost effectiveness of the Canadian Forces and retaining their military capability while reducing operational costs. Within this framework, accountability and control of expenditures have been passed to command bases, and personnel must now provide competitive services on a par with those of the private sector, and be innovative in managing their budgets. Through Defence 2000, Canadian Forces personnel are steadily acquiring a more business-like approach to management, similar to that of private enterprise. Nevertheless, the results so far are uneven, because the principles involved in this management reform are not all applied, for instance the principle of eliminating red tape and bureaucratic inertia.

1   Peter Drucker, *Post-Capitalist Society*, New York, Harper Business, 1993, p. 59.
2   Paul-André Linteau *et al.*, *Quebec Since 1930*, Toronto, Lorrimer, 1991, p. 29.
3   Robert Malcolm Campbell, *Grand Illusions: The Politics of the Keynesian Experience in Canada, 1945-1975*, Peterborough, Broadview Press Ltd., 1987, p. 191.
4   *Ibid.*, p. 191.
5   Douglas Purvis and Constance Smith, "Canada's Fiscal Policy, 1963-1984", in John Sergent (ed.), *Fiscal and Monetary Policy*, University of Toronto in cooperation with the Royal Commission on the Economic Union and Development Prospects for Canada, and the Canadian Government Publishing Centre, Ottawa, Supply and Services Canada, 1986, p. 18-19.
6   Campbell, *op. cit.*, p. 216.
7   Douglas Purvis and Constance Smith, *op. cit.*, p. 23.
8   *Ibid.*, p. 27-29.
9   *Ibid.*, p. 29-30.
10 *House of Commons Debates*, 08 May 1989, p. 1446.
11 Donald J. Savoie, *The Politics of Public Spending in Canada*, Toronto, University of Toronto Press, 1990, p. 321.
12 *Ibid.*, p. 322.
13 *Ibid.*, p. 325.
14 *House of Commons Debates*, 20 February 1990, p. 8594.
15 *Ibid.*, 28 April 1989. p. 1078.
16 Donald Savoie, *op. cit.*, p. 353.
17 *House of Commons Debates*, 14 April 1969, p. 7465.
18 Michel Fortmann, "La politique de défense canadienne", in Paul Painchaud *et al.*, *From Mackenzie King to Pierre Trudeau: Forty Years of Canadian Diplomacy, 1945-1985*, Québec, Presses de l'Université Laval, 1989, p. 507.
19 *House of Commons Debates*, 23 April 1969, p. 7868 and 7869.
20 *Ibid.*, p. 7868.
21 Michel Fortmann, *op. cit.*, p. 510.

22 *Ibid*, p. 510.
23 Jocelyn Coulon, *En première ligne: Grandeurs et misères du système militaire canadien*, Montreal, Éd. Le Jour, 1991, p. 149.
24 Michel Fortmann, *op. cit.*, p. 510.
25 *Ibid.*, p. 513.
26 Desmond Morton, *A Military History of Canada: 1608-1991*, Toronto, McClelland & Stewart, 1992, p. 260.
27 R.B. Byers, "Defence for the Next Decade: The Forthcoming White Paper", *Canadian Defence Quarterly*, Vol. 7, No. 2, Autumn 1977, p. 20.
28 Cited by Fortmann, *op. cit.*, p. 511.
29 Coulon, *op. cit.*, p. 155.
30 Michel Fortmann, *op. cit.*, p. 514.
31 Desmond Morton, *op. cit.*, p. 264.
32 *Le Soleil*, 27 October 1979.
33 Michel Fortmann, *op. cit.*, p. 510.
34 Desmond Morton, *op. cit.*, p. 264.
35 Jean-Jacques Blais, "The 1984 Defence Budget: Goals, Priorities and the Allotment of Funds", *Canadian Defence Quarterly*, Vol. 4, No. 1, Summer 1984, p. 8.
36 Jocelyn Coulon, *op. cit.*, p. 149.
37 Jean-Jacques Blais, *op. cit.*, p. 8.
38 Paul Mann, "Budget Deficits Constrain Canadian Defense Efforts", *Aviation Week and Space Technology*, 30 June 1986, p. 46.
39 Jocelyn Coulon, *op. cit.*, p. 149.
40 Paul Mann, *op. cit.*, p. 46.
41 *Ibid.*, p. 46.
42 Cited by Jocelyn Coulon, *op. cit.*, p. 150.
43 Jocelyn Coulon, *op. cit.*, p. 152.
44 *Ibid.*, p. 151.
45 *Ibid.*, p. 151.
46 *House of Commons Debates*, 28 February 1992, p. 7752.
47 *Canadian Defence Policy*, Ottawa, Department of National Defence, April 1992, p. 14.
48 *Ibid.*, p. 4-5.
49 *1994 Defence White Paper*, Ottawa, Department of National Defence, 1994, p. 3.
50 *Ibid.*, p. 3.
51 *Ibid.*, Chapter 4.
52 *Ibid.*, p. 49.
53 *Ibid.*, p. 49-50.

> *"Intellectuals see the organization as a tool: it enables them to practise their tekhnè, their specialized knowledge. Managers see knowledge as a means to the end of organizational performances. Both are right. They are opposites; but they relate to each other as poles rather than as contradictions. They surely need each other: the research scientist needs the research manager just as much as the research manager needs the research scientist. If one overbalances the other, there is only non-performance and all-round frustration."* (Peter Drucker[1])

7

REORGANIZATION OF DEFENCE RESEARCH IN CANADA

Despite its importance, defence policy was not the only factor which strongly influenced defence research policy in Canada. The development of national science policy and, more importantly, the reorganization of defence research in 1974, were key factors in the realignment of defence research policy as outlined below.

7.1 DEVELOPMENT OF NATIONAL SCIENCE POLICY

7.1.1 The Glassco Commission and Scientific Activities within Government

In 1960, the federal government established the Glassco Commission with the mandate to examine the activities of all departments and agencies. Part of the Commission's mandate was to study scientific activities conducted in-house or contracted out by the government. These activities were of significant proportion since, in 1959, they accounted for some 75% of all Canadian research and development effort. Equally, the Commission was charged with examining the organization and management of government research, and with advising the government on a national science policy.

The Commissioners first assessed science policies existing at the time. They noted that, aside from the creation of the National Research Council of Canada in 1916, government research had its origins in the scientific front that was formed during the Second World War. At the end of the war, the government retained the most promising research groups in the area of physical and biological sciences and formed a multitude of government organizations such as DRB. According to the Commissioners, federal research since then embraced three broad groups of activity, each having its own organizational form, with a total budget in 1959 of $220 million. Government research consisted of 1) research conducted by the departments themselves, in most cases for the furtherance of resource development; 2) defence research conducted by the Armed Forces and DRB within the Department of National Defence, and by the Department of Defence Production; and 3) research and development, mostly non-military, conducted by organizations independent of any department of government, such as NRC.[2]

Following this examination, the Commission concluded, somewhat ironically: "It is not unfair to say that the scientific policy of Canada today is the result rather than the cause of growth in the many scientific activities undertaken by government."[3] In part to rectify this situation, the Commissioners recommended that a Central Science Bureau be established, to maintain an overview of government-funded research "which had been lacking for a long time."[4] The Bureau, which would be administratively attached to the Treasury Board, would be responsible for gathering all the data needed to develop a national science policy, and would also serve as the Secretariat for a National Science Council constituted from the scientific community.

The recommendations of the Glassco Commission provoked a general outcry from the Canadian scientific community, particularly over the proposal to attach the Bureau to Treasury Board. Many considered it dangerous to place such an organization under the supervision of a department whose main role was the parsimonious management of Crown funds. Indeed, it was essential that the Central Science Bureau be autonomous.

7.1.2 The Development of Organizational Mechanisms for Managing

The debate was initiated by the Conservatives, but continued to rage after the Liberals took power in 1963. Faced with an explosive situation, the Pearson government felt the need to seek the enlightened advice of a respected leader in the Canadian scientific community. The choice was Dr. Chalmers Jack MacKenzie, former President of NRC, who was asked to study the situation. In his report of January 1964, MacKenzie endorsed the proposal to establish a Central Science Bureau, but recommended that it report organizationally to the Prime Minister's Office. MacKenzie also recommended that a scientific advisory body be established to review existing scientific programs and recommend government priorities. In short, the report generally endorsed the conclusions of the Glassco Commission on the need to establish organizations to oversee all scientific activities in Canada, but sided with the scientific community in recommending flexible administrative linkages to preserve the autonomy of the Bureau.[5]

The Pearson government responded quickly. In July 1964, the Science Secretariat was established, which corresponded more or less to the Bureau proposed by the Glassco Commission. As part of the Privy Council Office, the Science Secretariat was responsible for providing information or advice on scientific matters on request by the Prime Minister, and for participating "in the determination of government priorities to the extent that scientific and technical input is relevant."[6] According to its Director, "as a purely advisory body, with neither operational nor granting funds in the scientific area, it is well constituted to act as a neutral arbiter in science questions and to act as a focus for interdepartmental and interagency discussion and cooperation."[7] In 1966, the Science Secretariat advised on the constitution of the Science Council of Canada. "Under the Act of 12th May 1966, which set it up, the Council's functions cover a very wide field and they illustrate the need for clarification felt by those responsible for science policy in Canada."[8] Amongst other things, the Science Council was responsible for submitting recommendations to the Prime Minister on the priorities that should be assigned to specific areas of scientific and technical research, and for long-term planning in these areas. The Science Council undertook a number of sectoral studies, one of which was on the upper atmosphere, in order to draw a general picture of the national scientific effort.[9] At the time, the Science Council was still not segregated from the Science Secretariat, and the Secretariat played an important role in the development of these studies.

In the late 1960's, significant thought was given to Canada's science policy by a number of national and international organizations. The Senate established a Special Committee on Science Policy and another committee (Senate Committee on Science - Lamontagne Committee) which later produced the well-known Lamontagne Report. In November 1968, the Science Council of Canada was segregated administratively from the Science Secretariat and granted similar status to that of the Economic Council of Canada. Immediately, the Science Council set about formulating a national science policy. Finally, in 1969, the Organization for Economic Cooperation and Development (OECD) produced an exhaustive report on national science policy in Canada. This was the context in which the Governor General, in the Speech from the Throne on 8 October 1970, announced the introduction of a program "to gather and focus these sometimes divergent and competitive scientific resources."[10] In 1970, having clearly established its intentions, the Trudeau government passed the Government Organization Act (1970) authorizing the creation of Ministries of State. In 1971, Parliament ratified a proclamation authorizing the creation of the Ministry of State for Science and Technology.

By so doing, Parliament reinforced the measures taken in 1964 aimed at injecting science, as an important aspect of national policy, into official government structures. For Alastair Gillespie, the first Minister of State for Science and Technology, the essential thrust of science policy could be summarized in a few words: "Maximum exploitation of scientific opportunities requires programs that combine concern for the growth of science itself and provision for the rapid, deliberate application of its fruits to human welfare."[11] In addition, the Minister clearly showed his colours by endorsing the observation that science was too important to be left to the scientists, an observation that caused concern for more than one of the leaders of the various government scientific organizations, particularly since the Minister was empowered to coordinate scientific and technological programs and activities with other federal programs. As one person interviewed recalls, "from the start, this Ministry had grand designs on controlling research, [and] the separate employers [such as DRB and NRC, were] something of an obstacle to the centralization of research"[12] being pursued at the time. It would seem more than likely that the Minister of State for Science and Technology supported the proposals to incorporate DRB personnel into the federal public service and to transfer responsibility for the activities of the defence research establishments from DRB to the DND Assistant Deputy Minister (Materiel).

7.2 TRANSFORMATION OF CANADA'S DEFENCE ESTABLISHMENT AND THE DEFENCE RESEARCH BOARD

7.2.1 The Glassco Commission and the Defence Research Board

The Royal Commission on Government Organization, as is evident from its name, had a very broad mandate to review the whole apparatus of government. When the Commission reviewed Canada's defence establishment, its members did not confine their review simply to an examination of the central administrative structure of the Department of National Defence. Their examination probed deeper into the activities of DRB and the future conduct of defence research.

In general terms, the Commissioners noted that defence research accounted for only five percent of the defence budget in Canada compared with about 20% in the United States. Another major disparity between the two nations was that the United States devoted 80% of its defence R&D budget to development with the balance devoted to basic and applied research, while Canadian expenditures were divided approximately equally between research and development.[13] Further, Canadian defence research programs covered almost the entire range of the scientific disciplines and, as a result, "the research and development effort as a whole [was] spread rather thinly."[14] The Commissioners nevertheless acknowledged the exceptional contributions of Canadian researchers in fields such as hypersonic physics and upper atmospheric research.

The Commissioners went on to point out that the establishments of the Defence Research Board conducted mostly research and only limited development of military equipment. The aggregate output of the research work was considered impressive, while the development work was judged promising. The members of the Glassco Commission considered that the research program at CARDE was particularly well-balanced even though the emphasis was mainly on applied research. By way of example, they cited "the close collaboration between the Establishment and the Canadian Army" and suggested that the "future evolution of Canadian defence programs may perhaps be patterned on the CARDE model, which has proved that joint development programs can be effectively coordinated and executed."[15] Finally, the Commissioners reviewed the development programs of the three Services and concluded that the participation of Canadian industry in defence research was very low.

In order to optimize the efficiency and effectiveness of defence research programs, the Commissioners recommended that applied research and development programs be coordinated within a new agency, to be called the Defence Research and Development Board. This new agency would replace DRB and be responsible for all research and development activities undertaken by the Department of National Defence. CARDE would be renamed the National Defence Laboratory Valcartier and, although it would retain some degree of autonomy, it would operate on behalf of the three Services under the general direction of DRB's successor.[16]

7.2.2 Impact of the Integration of the Armed Forces on the Defence Research Board

The views of the Glassco Commission on responsibility for defence research and development seemingly were not shared by Defence Minister Hellyer. In his 1964 Defence White Paper, Hellyer reviewed the general situation in these areas but stopped short of formulating recommendations aimed at changing the basic roles of the several responsible organizations.[17] In other words, DRB would retain its mandate to conduct defence research and coordinate equipment development programs. More significantly, the status of the Board would not be challenged; DRB would remain, along with Canadian Forces Headquarters and the Office of the Deputy Minister, as one of the constituent entities of

National Defence Headquarters in Ottawa.

Even so, this did not imply that the administrative panorama of defence research and development would be totally spared in the reorganization of the Department of National Defence. Indeed, with the unification of the headquarters of the three Services, all development programs were centralized under the authority of the Chief of Technical Services of DND. In order to retain its advisory role, DRB responded to this change through a slight adjustment of its administrative links with the Canadian Forces. Some DRB scientists were appointed as Scientific Advisors to the Vice-Chief of Defence Staff and Chief of Technical Services. Perhaps more significantly, DRB scientists were also appointed to a number of senior positions within Canadian Forces' Headquarters, including those of Director General of Operational Research, Director of Scientific and Technical Intelligence, and Director of Project Formulation.[18] In the final analysis, DRB suffered little from the reorganization of National Defence Headquarters.

In April 1967, Parliament passed the bill authorizing integration of the Canadian Armed Forces. At about that time, DRB availed itself of the reorganization of Headquarters to justify a major decentralization of its activities. The members of the Board, one of whom was Dr. L'Heureux, former Chief of CARDE and newly-appointed Vice-Chairman DRB, decided to focus the activities of DRB Headquarters in Ottawa in two general directions, namely policy formulation and overall planning. In keeping with this decision, they disbanded the Scientific Services Division and assigned responsibility for program coordination and provision of advice to the Canadian Forces to the research establishments. The research establishments were also accorded responsibility for technical cooperation and for awarding grants and contracts for university and industrial research.[19]

7.3 NEW DISTRIBUTION OF RESPONSIBILITIES FOR DEFENCE RESEARCH ACTIVITIES WITHIN DND, OR THE END OF THE FOURTH SERVICE CONCEPT

In the early 1970's, Canada redefined its defence policy in the *White Paper on Defence* and reduced the strength of the Canadian Forces. It was in this context that the Minister of National Defence, Donald S. MacDonald, perceived the need to review the organization and management of his Department. To undertake this review, the Minister created a committee of experts, the Management Review Group (MRG), responsible for improving coordination between the military, civilian and research staffs of the Department, and for rationalizing the management of all its components. In 1971, National Defence Headquarters was characterized by two sub-structures, one civilian and one military, which, although connected by a few formal communications links, operated in relative isolation. The result, it was maintained, "was duplication, poor lateral communication, and inefficiency."[20]

In the course of their full review of the Department's activities, the members of the MRG recognized the independence of the DRB and disagreed with it. In their opinion, "the Board was unresponsive to defence needs of the 1970's and lacked proper administrative controls."[21] It was no surprise, therefore, that the report of the MRG, which was sent to the Minister in June 1972, contained a recommendation to disband DRB and distribute its personnel throughout the various components of the Department. The members of the DRB succeeded, however, in convincing the new Minister of National Defence, Edgar Benson, of the importance of maintaining DRB in operation. They obviously had great persuasive powers, because the only significant recommendation of the MRG that Benson did not act upon was the one directed at dismembering the Defence Research Board.[22]

Following presentation of the MRG report, the Minister acted swiftly and directed that restructuring be implemented by the end of 1972 at the latest. The reorganization of Headquarters was well underway by the time that James A. Richardson was appointed Minister of National Defence. With this new structure, "the administration of defence policy became defined as a managerial problem *alone*, with the expectation that better management practices could make the 'sharp end sharper'".[23]

From all appearances, DRB had a sufficient number of powerful allies in 1972 to avoid the impact of the restructuring in progress within the Department of National Defence. Apparently, this was no longer the case in 1974 for, on 29 March, DRB staff learned with surprise that:

> "a) the present research and administrative activities and staff of the DRB are to be integrated within the framework of DND;
>
> b) research activities under the control of DRB and development activities under the control of the military will be restructured into a single program under the Chief Research and Development (CRAD), a new Branch in the Assistant Deputy Minister (Materiel) Group;
>
> c) the staff of the DRB will be brought under the Public Service Employment Act."[24]

In other words, the Defence Research Board would lose all administrative and executive responsibilities for the defence research program as well as responsibility for personnel in the various research establishments across Canada and in the Operations Research and Analysis Establishment in Ottawa. The Chairman DRB, Dr. L'Heureux, "and a small staff were, at the same time, regrouped into a special unit to advise the Minister of National Defence on all matters pertaining to the role of science in defence work."[25] But the Defence Research Board was unable to survive following the subsequent resignation of its Chairman, Dr. L'Heureux.

This commotion provoked a number of comments from former DRB officials. In an article on this issue, former Chief of Plans, Gordon D. Watson, made no attempt to mince his words. He spoke out against the secret nature of the whole decisional process which led to the announcement of the loss of DRB's executive and decision-making functions and their transfer to other groups within DND. In his view, the desire of public administrators to centralize government research activities had strongly influenced the decision taken by Defence Minister Richardson to restructure the whole defence research sector. According to Watson, who was a former CARDE official, "the decision to reorganize was also influenced by the unpopularity of military activities, the increasing disillusionment with science, and acceptance by some of the greatly oversimplified 'customer-contractor' relationship that assumes that the customer, as the user of research results, should know better than the scientists what research will be needed in ten or fifteen years by the customer."[26]

For Watson, "perhaps the most important factor leading to the reorganization of DRB was the decision of the Public Service Commission to upgrade the administrative role of the public service". The effect of this decision, according to Watson, was to shift the allegiance of senior managers away from the particular departments to which they were attached towards the federal bureaucracy as a whole. The absence of any feeling of belonging to a particular organization promotes a tendency on the part of managers "to place emphasis on reorganization and administration rather than on the primary functions and decisions of the departments to which they are assigned."[27] In short, there was a move towards increased bureaucratization of the public service which in turn challenged the autonomy of some organizations such as DRB.

Douglas Bland, in his analysis of the administration of defence policy, shares this viewpoint, asserting that the restructuring which led to the demise of DRB "was a reflection of the growth of influence and power of administrators and their ability to control the policy process."[28] As for Solandt, he was even less sympathetic to this administrative reorganization, which he perceived as "an act of mayhem committed in the name of administrative tidiness."[29]

7.3.1 Restructuring Provides for Better Coordination of Research and Development Programs within DND

Irrespective of the real reasons for reorganizing defence research, DRB no longer had control, and Minister Richardson divided the responsibilities and duties originally assigned to DRB between three organizations: DRB itself, the Assistant Deputy Minister (Materiel) (ADM(Mat)) and the Assistant Deputy Minister (Policy) (ADM(Pol)). From then on, DREV reported to ADM(Mat) through the Chief Research and Development (CRAD). The CRAD Branch was made responsible for the overall direction of the DND's research and development program and also "for ensuring that knowledge of actual and anticipated advances in science and technology are available to support DND decisions concerning engineering, design, procurement, installation, maintenance and operation of equipment and systems."[30]

As can be seen, the area of jurisdiction of CRAD differed somewhat from that of DRB. When the Defence Research Board was founded it was assigned responsibility for undertaking and coordinating research and development or improvement of military equipment and materiel[31] of interest to National Defence. Under DRB, the development program, despite fluctuations in its relative importance, remained a limited activity while basic defence research grew noticeably. This was due to several factors, in particular the research-oriented mentality which pervaded DRB and the fact that other organizations shared the responsibility for development of defence materiel in Canada. Thus, "the three

Armed Services, each with its own development programs [had a sufficiently large budget to] enjoy a greater measure of autonomy [in the development of military materiel. In addition, Canadian Arsenals Limited, a Crown corporation, was] engaged in munitions production [and conducted] development programs initiated in the Defence Research Board and by the Armed Services."[32] The activity of the Department of Defence Production in this field related specifically to the development-sharing program initiated with the United States in 1959.

In 1962, the members of the Glassco Commission considered that "applied research and development merge one with the other so intimately in practice that, to maintain a balanced and realistic program, it is most unwise to separate them"[33], and recommended that a new organization be formed to coordinate all these activities. As we have seen, the complete reorganization of National Defence Headquarters gave DRB the opportunity to appoint a scientific advisor to the Chief of Technical Services. In 1972, DRB increased its efforts to better control the development budget by seconding one of its senior managers to the Office of ADM(Mat) in National Defence Headquarters.

Two years later, DND senior management dismantled DRB and consolidated the budgets for research and development under CRAD. For the first time, defence scientists became part of a single organization with budgetary authority to control and coordinate all their research and development efforts. This facilitated planning of R&D within the Department of National Defence, since program objectives and results could be better aligned with the current and future needs of the Canadian Forces. In the view of the first Chief Research and Development, Mr. E.J. Bobyn, this was one positive aspect of integration.[34]

7.4   SCIENTIFIC ACTIVITIES OF DREV FROM 1970 TO 1974

Before further examination of the impact of these structural changes on DREV's research activities and personnel, some account should be given of the Establishment's research activities between 1970 and 1974. During this period, the Establishment's scientific divisions were again reorganized so that their activities could be better adapted to meet Canada's new defence needs and the evolving imperatives of defence research. Flexibility of operation was key, from the standpoint of both administrative procedures and personnel in each of the research programs. In short, the general framework had to be flexible enough to allow management to increase research effectiveness quickly without need of a major reorganization. The divisional structure offered this advantage, in that Establishment officials could create, dismantle or combine scientific divisions without changing the overall structure. Despite the impression that one might gain of perpetual organizational change within DREV, there was a certain rationality in the process as shown in Figure 9. Basic modifications were only made when there were major reorientations of research at the Establishment, and this certainly contributed towards easing the problems inherent in organizational change.

The situation in the early 1970's was no exception. At this time, the Aerophysics, Armaments, Electronics and Propulsion divisions essentially participated in the Establishment's scientific program and, *de facto*, reported to the Director General. The Assistant Director General managed Administrative and Support services as well as the Experimental Division which engaged in the Establishment's scientific activities by conducting experiments and firings at the request of DREV researchers.

When the hypersonic wake program was terminated, the activities of Aerophysics Division were reoriented towards "investigations of systems involving computer processing of sensor data and presentation of information for human decisions."[35] The Division was renamed the Data Systems Division in December 1971 to better reflect the content of its scientific program, and the Computer Centre was integrated with this new Division. The ballistics and aerodynamics programs that had been conducted by the Aerophysics Division for decades, were transferred in 1972 to the Experimental Division which once again became a full scientific division. Since DREV was organized into two principal branches, one concerning scientific programs and the other dealing with support functions, responsibility for the Experimental Division was, therefore, transferred from the Assistant Director General to the Deputy Director General.

In 1973, DREV undertook a major reorganization aimed at creating a much greater synergy between related scientific programs and disciplines. Research activities that were dispersed throughout various scientific sections were regrouped along divisional lines. Thus, pyrotechnics research was integrated into the activities of Propulsion Division and weapon systems studies were assigned to the Data Systems Division.

Senior management personnel in October 1970. From left to right: Dr. H.P. Tardif, Director, Armaments Division; Dr. W.G. Brownlee, Director, Propulsion Division; Mr. E.S. Guy, Assistant Chief; Mr. A. Lortie, Director, Experimental Division; Mr. E.J. Bobyn, Director General of DREV; Mr. W.G. Mylett, Director, Administration Division; Dr. A. Lemay, Director, Aerophysics Division; Mr. C. Cumming, Director, Electronics Division; Col J.C. Boughton, Military Assistant; and Dr. H.H. Waterman, Director, Plans and Programs Office.

Most of the laser-related activities were regrouped within the Electronics Division which assumed responsibility for the high-energy-pulse and high-repetition-rate laser laboratories previously attached to the Experimental Division. DREV management also decided to regroup researchers conducting work in the areas of military materiel and aeromechanics within a single division by integrating the Experimental Division within the Armaments Division. The new Armaments Division became solely responsible for military materiel following the dissolution of the Canadian Armament Development and Experimental Establishment (CADEE) in 1973. Most of the personnel of CADEE, which was a Canadian Forces unit, were integrated within the divisions of DREV. Finally, in 1974, DREV management decided to change the name of the Electronics Division since most of its activities were related to electro-optics, an area of increasing importance to the military. This division thus became the Electro-Optics Division. The divisions themselves were "subdivided into sections and groups to ensure viable specialist teams while maintaining enough flexibility to enable effective cooperation in multidisciplinary studies."[36]

Structural changes aside, the mission of the Establishment was to acquire and expand scientific knowledge for the defence of Canada and to provide technical assistance and advice to the Canadian Forces. DREV's program combined both short- and long-term research and included the development of new and improved equipment, techniques and systems for the Canadian Forces. Throughout this period of change, the Establishment did not deviate from its mission of advancing the frontiers of defence science and of providing advice and technical support to the Department of National Defence. Between 1970 and 1974, with the aim of contributing effectively to Canadian defence, DREV accorded increased importance to a broad program of scientific analysis, evaluation, and research and development in several different areas such as lasers, armaments and surveillance.

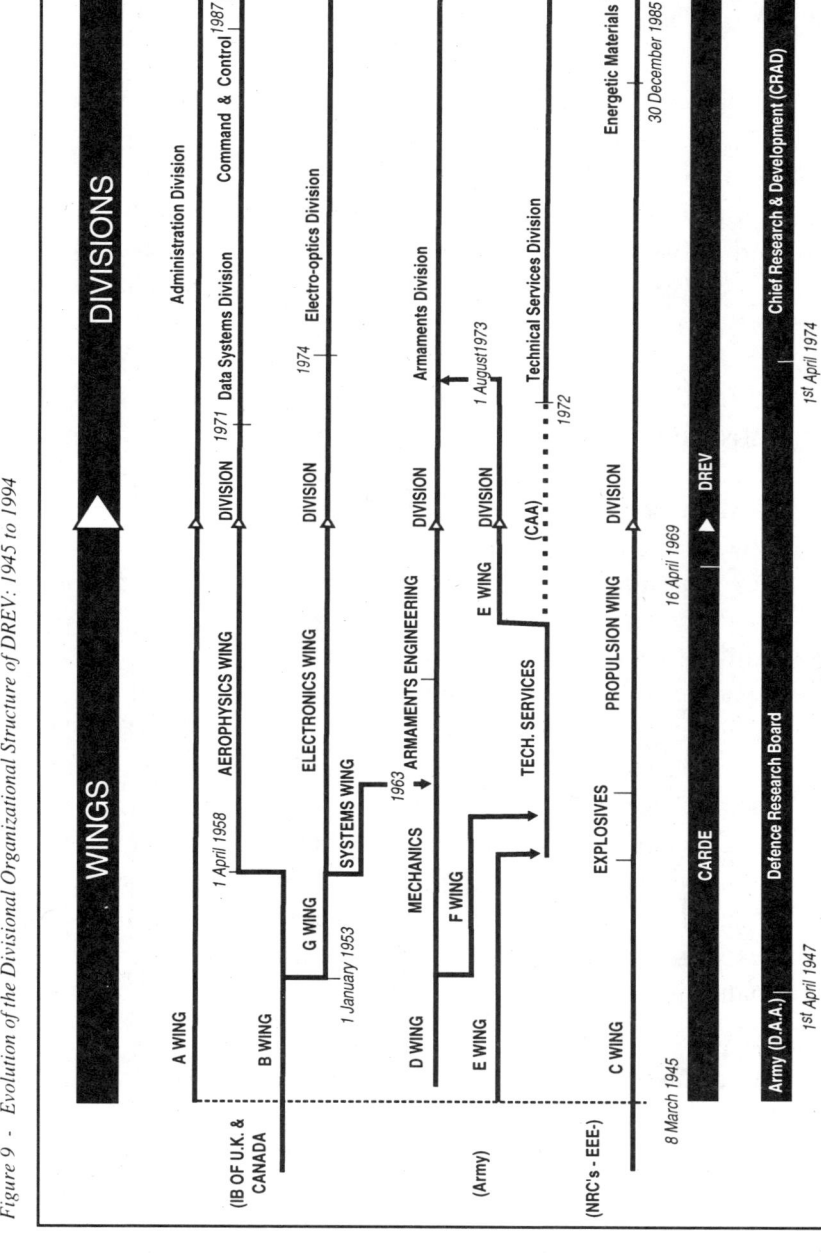

Figure 9 - Evolution of the Divisional Organizational Structure of DREV: 1945 to 1994

7.4.1 Research in the Field of Lasers

7.4.1.1 The TEA-CO_2 Laser

The discovery of the TEA-CO_2 laser, and its public disclosure in 1970, received wide attention from the general public, the scientific community and the press. DREV gained a world-wide reputation, and licences to develop and market this invention were awarded to two Canadian companies. At that point, the objectives of the program were reviewed to ensure maximum exploitation of the TEA-CO_2 laser. The new objectives were:

> "first, the conduct of fundamental and applied research into the phenomena that control the amplification and the energy extraction properties of the CO_2 laser medium, principally with a view to enhancing the peak power and energy capabilities at 10.6 µm; second, the development of prototype laser sources and amplifier modules for the construction of an experimental laser facility; third, the research of new technologies for the design of more reliable and more efficient pulsed lasers at higher repetition rates and higher peak powers; fourth, a search for military applications; fifth, the transfer of the laser technology to Canadian industry, and assistance to governmental agencies and Canadian universities; and, finally, pending the successful realization of the experimental high-peak-power laser facility, limited research in the fields of laser propagation and laser-matter interaction."[37]

While awaiting the development of commercially-available lasers to meet their needs, Establishment scientists had to develop their own lasers with a view to improving reliability and increasing peak-power outputs. In addition to studying physical phenomena and various techniques for improving laser efficiencies, scientists focused their research on two types of laser: the High-Energy-Pulse Laser (HEPL) and the High-Repetition-Rate Laser (HRRL). Work on the HEPL led to the development of amplifier-chain lasers of extremely high peak power (1 GW) or of extremely high energy per pulse. These various laser configurations were later used to generate and study plasmas. The knowledge and technology generated by this research was later used by the National Research Council of Canada and by Lumonics Research Limited in the Fusion Canada program. Work on the HRRL led to the development of a TEA-CO_2 laser capable of operating at 1,000 pulses per second, which required an impressive gas refrigeration and recirculation system. This laser was used subsequently in studies of laser-target interaction. In parallel with these developments, other members of the electro-optics team succeeded in developing military applications of TEA-CO_2 lasers, by building and testing various prototypes, in the fields of laser radar (rangefinders), surveillance and target identification .

7.4.1.2 Chemically-Excited Lasers

As we have seen earlier, the first conclusive experiments on the feasibility of the TEA-CO_2 laser led to the creation, in 1968, of a team of researchers to work on Project Lotion. At the time when DREV scientists were developing a new generation of molecular lasers, there was great excitement amongst researchers in the field of chemical lasers with the discovery that the products of several chemical reactions could sustain laser action at atmospheric pressure. For DREV scientists, this discovery extended "the simplicity of operation of the TEA-type CO_2 laser developed previously at DREV to new wavelengths."[38] Scientists then undertook "preliminary studies aimed at obtaining true chemical laser action in a combustion mixture. This was intended to serve as the basis for more advanced work."[39] DREV management thus demonstrated that no avenue of research would be left unexplored in the study of lasers and the search for new military applications.

In this regard, it should be noted that chemically-excited lasers offer an unquestionable advantage over electrically-excited lasers, "the laser energy being stored in chemical bonds, rather than in huge power supplies."[40] This advantage is of considerable importance in military applications. Dr. Jean-Louis Boivin, a highly-skilled chemist and Deputy Chief of the Establishment, immediately recognized this advantage, and his support played a large part in initiating activities to develop chemically-excited lasers within the Propulsion Division. The crucial role played by Dr. George Kimbell in this scientific project should also be noted.[41]

Despite the potential of chemical lasers in military applications, it was first necessary for the researchers of Propulsion Division "to acquire a fundamental understanding of the chemistry necessary to achieve laser action with a variety of chemical systems. [Initial studies were conducted on] a variety of experimental laser prototypes for both the CW and pulsed modes and led to a few inventions for which patent applications [were] made."[42]

The world's first continuously-operating chemically-driven laser was developed in 1969 at Cornell University. In 1970, inspired by the success of the Cornell researchers, DREV scientists succeeded in achieving CW operation using a second chemical system consisting of carbon disulphide and oxygen (the CS_2/O_2 combustion laser). Continuing research on chemical lasers between 1976 and 1986 led to the development of "the world's first purely chemical hydrogen chloride laser based on the reaction of atomic chlorine with hydrogen iodide"[43] which offered "the distinct advantage of compact energy storage and high efficiency."[44] Other major achievements included the development of a free-burning flame laser based on carbon monoxide, and an efficient, pulsed deuterium fluoride (DF) laser.

Following these early breakthroughs with hybrid and purely chemical lasers, DREV efforts began in 1974 to identify military applications of hybrid, pulsed and experimental hydrogen fluoride/

deuterium fluoride (HF/DF) lasers. As in the case of TEA-CO_2 lasers, these efforts uncovered military applications in the areas of rangefinders, trackers and designators.[45] A greater proportion of scientific effort was then progressively devoted to those projects which had shown significant promise.[46]

7.4.2   Armaments Research

Most of the armaments research conducted at DREV has been in response to requests from the Canadian Forces, and emphasis has been placed on developing an appropriate technology base. The scientific effort in the area of armaments has been mainly devoted to applied research on ballistics, pyrotechnics, the physics of shaped charges and materials, and to the development of weapon systems such as the CRV7 air-to-ground rocket and the spinning tubular projectile (STUP). Because of the variety of research work conducted in the area of armaments, it would be futile to attempt any detailed account herein. Only the major thrusts will be discussed, including a description of two significant achievements in the weapons field, namely the development of STUP and the CRV7.

Research in the area of ballistics was focused on improving the accuracy, range and effectiveness of conventional weapons. It was also aimed at developing a mathematical model to permit solutions to the equations describing the internal ballistics of guns. By late 1973, this work resulted in an internal ballistics numerical prediction method. Research on the physics of shaped charges included, amongst other things, a study of the performance of various types of shaped charge in penetrating targets.

During the 1960s, DREV chemists and chemical engineers with expertise in propellants and explosives worked on the development of pyrotechnic devices. Their efforts were originally directed towards developing smoke-producing signalling devices which would pose no fire hazard for the Canadian Forces. This work was extended in 1971 to include pourable formulas. Three years later, research on pourable smoke compositions was sufficiently advanced to allow the development of devices for specific military purposes.

Materials research was aimed essentially at developing the best materials for use in weapons and munitions, and at increasing the reliability and service life of military equipment. In the early 1970's, research was conducted on heavy materials such as tungsten and uranium alloys for kinetic energy rounds, metallic foam for attenuating the blast of explosives by energy absorption, ceramic armour with high penetration resistance, and high-speed compaction of metallic powders for fabricating munitions' components. Long-term research focused on crack propagation and measurement of end stress, the dynamic properties of materials and mechanisms for penetrating ice.

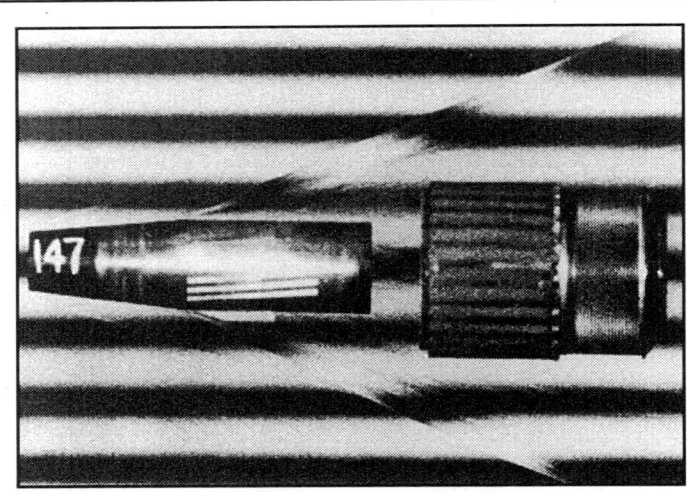

Invented at DREV, the spinning tubular projectile has unusual aerodynamic properties that make it an ideal training projectile for use in restricted training areas.

Technological advances and changing military strategy were the driving forces underlying continual requests from the Canadian

Forces for improved weapons or totally new designs. In the early 1960's, DREV researchers were tasked by the Armed Forces to design a practice round for the 105-mm tank gun. In 1970, DREV researchers "considered a new armaments concept after more than a century of conventional projectile designs."[47] The new design was the spinning tubular projectile (STUP).

Initial test firings confirmed that STUP combined "low drag, good stability and low dispersion."[48] Analytical studies and further test firings revealed that STUP had several unique features which made it a highly effective round that could be used over a wide range of calibres. It possessed all the qualities that nations required of a high-speed practice round, and was particularly useful in the European context where the ranges were of limited dimensions.

In order to ensure that Canadian industry would derive economic benefit from this major technological breakthrough in the field of armaments, DREV quickly established linkages with Space Research Corporation - Quebec (SRC-Q), a firm founded by Dr. Gerald Bull. Once again, through this technology transfer to the private sector, DREV contributed to the industrial development of Canada. Both parties concentrated their efforts on developing a viable product. DREV engaged in work aimed at improving the prototype, while SRC worked on refining the manufacturing techniques for STUP.[49]

7.4.2.1 The CRV7 Rocket

In conformity with Canadian policy, the role of the Air Group in Europe "was changed from that of nuclear strike to conventional ground attack."[50] As a result, it was decided that the CF-104 fighter aircraft based in Europe would be rearmed with a conventional air-to-ground weapon. In June 1971, DND selected the 2.75-inch diameter Folding Fin Aerial Rocket (FFAR) for this purpose. Shortly afterwards, orders were placed with Canadian industry for the manufacture of the Mk4 motor for the FFAR. But problems arose when the rocket was subsequently tested. "At the time, the US Mk4 rocket motor, used to propel the FFAR, provided neither the range nor the accuracy required by the air force; as well it had the disconcerting habit of blowing up in front of the launch aircraft."[51]

In light of these deficiencies, DND sought the advice of DREV specialists. It was proposed that DREV examine the feasibility of developing an improved motor for the 2.75-inch rocket based on technologies developed under the Metroc Project. These leading-edge technologies included, amongst others, hydroxyl-terminated polybutadiene (HTPB) rubber binders, compression-moulded phenolic-resin or fibreglass exhaust nozzles, and calendered asbestos insulators. Through the use of these technologies and novel wrap-around fins, DREV scientists were able to build a rocket with twice the delivered kinetic energy of the existing version, capable of penetrating the reinforced concrete hangars of the Warsaw Pact.

During the 1970's, DREV developed a series of rocket launchers and warheads. Canadian industry, as is usual in defence research efforts, was very closely associated with the development of the CRV7. In 1970, Bristol Aerospace Limited (BAL) had gained considerable expertise in solid-propellant motor technology through the company's extensive experience with Black Brant and Metroc. It is not surprising, therefore, that the company was awarded contracts in 1974 to produce the first rocket motors. For the next few years "the process cycled through analysis, design, fabrication, test, evaluation and re-design, and it was not until 1980 that a complete rocket and launcher system was certified to the appropriate military standards and declared fully operational on Canada's CF-104 and CF-5 aircraft."[52]

After the first CRV7 rocket motor entered full operational service in 1980, "DREV continued propellant research to address launcher erosion, excessive smoke and combustion instability problems."[53] An improved, reduced-smoke motor entered service in 1984. It is important to recognize that this achievement was due largely to very close cooperation between DREV scientists, BAL engineers and the air force officers of the operational and engineering directorates of National Defence Headquarters and the Aerospace Engineering and Test Establishment (AETE). This commendable collaboration between the various participants was probably one of the major reasons why Canada was able "to develop the most advanced air-to-ground ballistic rocket in the world."[54] This view of the CRV7 appears to have been shared by the air forces of NATO and other friendly nations who placed a large number of orders with BAL for the CRV7. The CRV7 has become the mainstay of the rocket motor industry in Canada. Over 560,000 rocket motors have been manufactured by BAL and under licence in Norway, and the worldwide sales figure to date is approaching $300 million. The CRV7, developed by Canada's defence industry, is internationally renowned.

The CRV7 upheld its reputation during its baptism of fire in the 1991 Gulf War, when it was successfully used by RAF Jaguars against Iraqi patrol boats. Unquestionably, the CRV7 is one of DREV's major accomplishments, for it provided a real military advantage to the Canadian Forces and enabled Canadian industry to enjoy commercial success.

7.4.3 Surveillance

During the 1960's, research in the field of electro-optics was focused mainly on electrically-excited molecular gas lasers which led to the development of the TEA-CO_2 laser. DREV scientists nevertheless recognized that infrared and visible spectrum technologies had enormous potential for various military applications, especially surveillance, detection, tracking and identification of targets. For this reason, scientists in the Electronics Division maintained some research effort on optical and infrared surveillance techniques.

During the first half of the 1970's, the interest of the Canadian Forces in military surveillance continued to increase with the advent of new technologies and countermeasures around the world. As Dr. Gravel recalls, the availability of increasingly sophisticated infrared sensors made it possible for DREV scientists to build unobtrusive detection and tracking systems that were highly accurate and which could operate equally well by night and by day. The same was true of laser technology which promised superiority over radar technology in weapon fire-control and guidance applications. It thus became increasingly evident that electro-optics technologies could revolutionize the art of warfare.[55]

Between 1970 and 1974, DREV management attempted to maintain a delicate balance between research activities requested by the Canadian Forces and research initiated to evaluate new concepts proposed by DREV research teams. In other words, managers of the Establishment's scientific program sought to avoid too large an imbalance between tasking from NDHQ and fundamental research to meet future defence needs. Equal emphasis was thus accorded to technology applications work and technology base work on optical and infrared systems. As well, DREV tried to manage its activities so that the time spent by scientists would be "almost equally distributed among basic technology, such as development of evaluation techniques, equipment calibration, investigation of the effect of noise, and choice of optical bandwidth on target detection; applied work directed toward innovations for improving surveillance; and field trial activities to evaluate equipment under operational conditions."[56]

The surveillance and countermeasures programs were concerned mainly with analysis and evaluation of detection and imaging systems in the visible and infrared, basic research in visionics, study of problems caused by whiteout in Arctic surveillance, thermal imaging, radiation properties and processes, advanced remote sensing techniques, etc. A major breakthrough in optical surveillance occurred in 1971 when DREV researchers "suggested that sea and air capabilities could be incorporated into the same optical head."[57] This idea met both Canadian maritime and US air requirements and marked the beginning of a joint US/Canada project to develop an Infrared Search and Target Designation (IRSTD) system. The system consists of an on-board passive infrared (IR) surveillance system for the detection of aircraft and missiles, including sea-skimming missiles, and for the observation of surface features such as ships, coastlines and icebergs.

7.5 CHANGES IN ORIENTATION OF DREV RESEARCH FOLLOWING THE DEMISE OF DRB AND THE RESTRUCTURING OF DEFENCE RESEARCH UNDER CRAD

Before the demise of DRB, much of the Board's research work was conceived and conducted by scientists in areas they considered the most promising, based on their vision of scientific advances that could occur in the technological areas of existing major projects. The early 1970's witnessed the progressive termination of these extensive projects which had marshalled the majority of DREV scientists around a common research objective and core activity, but which had also spawned a wider diversification of research. Defence scientists still devoted a large part of their effort to technology base activities, although work on specific short-term applications appeared to assume increasing importance for some researchers.

With the integration of research and development activities within the Chief Research and Development Branch, defence research gradually acquired another dimension which gave greater importance to small application projects. Generally, projects were of narrower scope and oriented more towards the solution of military problems.

Integration forced defence scientists to work closer with the military, for their new mission was to develop technologies for the Canadian Forces and to provide advice and expertise to enable the Department to be a smart buyer. Since its creation, the Defence Research Establishment Valcartier had always worked closely with the Armed Forces, and this fact was noted by the Glassco Commission. All things considered, the integration of DREV within DND gave the technical directorates of the Canadian Forces more direct access to the Establishment's expertise, and DREV participated with these directorates to a greater degree in designing new projects and in undertaking projects of primary interest to the Canadian Forces. According to Dr. Gravel, restructuring "brought researchers closer to the military and enabled them to better fulfil their mandates. Over time, this led to a better DREV perception of military needs and a better military understanding of DREV's research potential. Research became more relevant, and the proportion of effort applied to 'military tasks' increased to the point where 'military tasking' became one of the criteria used in selecting scientific research projects at DREV."[58]

One should not conclude from this, however, that research aimed at meeting military requirements 15 to 25 years into the future was abandoned in favour of direct technical assistance to the various elements of the Canadian Forces. According to Ken Peebles, presently CRAD and formerly Chief of DREV, direct technical assistance to the military in 1992 constituted only 35% of the scientific activities of the Establishment.[59] DREV thus continued to devote a significant amount of research effort towards developing the technology base to meet the long-term requirements of the Canadian Forces.

Closer collaboration between military and scientific staffs also resulted in a greater number of studies and projects to meet Canadian Forces' needs in the areas of energetic materials, rockets and missiles, munitions and weapons systems. A great deal of work was also undertaken in electro-optics to exploit the advances made in laser and infrared technologies. During the 1980's, part of DREV's research was focused on the application of computer techniques to weapons and military tactics. The rapid progress made recently in the field of high-speed microcomputers and programming has led to many new applications which have until now been considered impossible because of the volume of equipment and the complex software involved.[60] In a very proactive way, electronic data processing, data fusion and artificial intelligence were applied to command and control, combat systems integration, tracking, fire control, threat evaluation, weapon designation and battle management in its broadest sense.

During this period, DREV diversified its program by initiating a number of research projects in highly specialized and advanced areas of defence science, while maintaining several activities of average scope relative to the major projects of the golden era of the Establishment. Over the past twenty years, a large number of projects have been undertaken and significant achievements realized in the DREV's four major defence technology areas. These are outlined below.

Most of the projects mentioned below were conceived by scientists, but always after consultation and agreement with the military; the customer-oriented approach predominated. The majority of these projects focused on the most promising emerging technologies for military applications.

Common denominators can be found within the various defence technologies at DREV in such a way that particular groupings can be regarded as major projects. Surveillance, including night vision, is one of these major projects which has received considerable funding over the past twenty years. Optical and infrared countermeasures can also be regarded as a major project, encompassing activities related to obscurants, decoys, signature reduction, camouflage and laser countermeasures.

In the final analysis, although DREV no longer undertook major projects, but rather a stream of smaller projects to meet current or anticipated military needs, there were nevertheless major basic orientations in each of its four defence technology areas. Over the years, defence scientists sought to meet military needs and continued to maintain a customer-oriented approach. This was exemplified in 1986 by the change in format of the DREV annual reports which subsequently structured research projects by force group within the four Force Elements: Air; Land; Maritime; Space and Terrestrial Communications and Electronics. This change reflected the fact that CRAD was tuned in to the needs of its customers.

This whole reorientation necessarily affected the structure of scientific activities at the Establishment. During the period 1974-1994, these activities stabilized around four defence technologies: energetic materials, armaments, information technology and electro-optics. But stabilization did not mean stagnation; new scientific developments and budgetary restrictions forced DREV to make choices. Some traditional programs were de-emphasized in favour of more promising technologies. While funds for electro-optics research remained relatively stable, those for armaments and energetic materials research were reduced in order to increase funding for information technology which found application in all aspects of command and control and information management systems.

7.6 SCIENTIFIC ACTIVITIES AT DREV SINCE 1974

As a result of the above-mentioned stabilization of research activities, the names of the DREV scientific divisions have remained relatively unchanged through to 1995. The only notable changes were the renaming of the Propulsion Division as the Energetic Materials Division in 1985, and of the Data Systems Division as the Command and Control Division in 1987. When the latter change was made, DREV management took the opportunity to withdraw the Computer Centre from the new Command and Control Division and create the Informatics Centre, so as to integrate administrative and scientific data processing within a single unit. Through this reorganization, DREV management gave recognition to the increased importance of information technology in all aspects of science and management.

Although no major reorganizations have occurred at the divisional level, adjustments were made within the organizational structures of each of the scientific divisions. As technologies evolved, the various divisional managers adapted their organizations to the situation by creating, regrouping and disbanding their units (groups, sections, *ad hoc* committees) as necessary. In early 1995, DREV's organization chart showed four scientific divisions: Electro-Optics, Command and Control, Armaments, and Energetic Materials.

As we shall see later, DREV is currently overhauling its scientific program under a new organizational structure composed of three scientific divisions, the Weapons Systems Division, the Electro-Optics and Surveillance Division, and the Information Systems and Command and Control Division.

7.6.1 Energetic Materials

There have been numerous activities in this field over the past twenty years:

- development of a family of plastic-bonded and other energetic material explosives to meet the criteria of low-risk munitions;
- development of high-performance, low-signature rocket motor and propellant technologies;
- development of pyrophoric decoy flares for aircraft protection;
- development of Trigran, a pourable granular explosive;
- development of a family of smoke-producing signal grenades using pourable compounds;
- chemistry of energetic polymers;

- CRV7 (development of minimum-smoke propellant and methods for predicting the useful life of rockets);
- bio-degradation of soil contaminated with energetic materials;
- demonstration of advanced propulsion technologies;
- development of smoke screens effective at visible, infrared and sub-millimetre wavelengths.

Energetic materials, such as high-performance, minimum-smoke, reduced-sensitivity powders, propellants and explosives, provided the common factor in all research. About 80 scientists and technicians participated in this research over the past twenty years.

The development and introduction into service of pyrophoric decoy flares was a project of rather major proportions. In 1982, "the Energetic Materials Physical Chemistry Group [started] studying the possible use of pyrophoric liquids for flares."[61] A pyrophoric material is a compound which, in the presence of oxygen, ignites spontaneously. The project was of great interest and was pursued jointly by three divisions, involving about ten scientists, chemists, spectroscopists and mechanical engineers over the past ten years. The process of technology transfer to industry for the manufacture of products for the Canadian Forces is now well underway. This is true also for another major research project on the use of energetic polymers, in particular the use of glycidyl azide polymer (GAP) as a binder in explosives or other energetic materials. This work quickly produced significant results and a large number of patent applications were filed. Canadian Patents and Development Limited (CPDL) awarded a licence to ICI Explosives Canada for commercial exploitation of these inventions. Another innovative product, the Trigran cratering explosive, was patented in 1976 and licensed to Canadian Arsenals Limited (CAL) in 1980. Trigran is a free-flowing, water-resistant granular explosive which can be poured easily into any cavity. It is in service with the Canadian Forces and has been subjected to trials in other countries.

Evidently, all these projects evolved and changed in concert with scientific advances, government and environmental policies and the emergence of new military requirements. Although DREV research focused on conventional explosives, new explosive materials were developed and employed (polymers, new molecular compounds, etc.). Studies were also conducted on toxicological and environmental aspects during manufacture, use and disposal. For example, studies were conducted on the possibility of replacing perchlorates with nitrates in the manufacture of propellants. Finally, pyrophoric materials and multispectral grenades were also developed to meet the newly-emerging requirements of electronic warfare, such as the need to prevent detection of aircraft and other vehicles by enemy seekers employing infrared or sub-millimetre waves.

7.6.2 Armaments

Armaments research is an essential step in the acquisition of weapons systems. DREV is the only Canadian organization capable of testing advanced weapons and of developing new test and evaluation procedures in many areas.

During the past twenty years, the Armaments Division has distinguished itself in the following areas:

- assessment of the vulnerability of armoured combat vehicles;
- vulnerability and survivability methodologies for aircraft and ships;
- new acoustical, seismic and electrostatic techniques for target detection and tracking;

- characterization of missiles using millimetre-wave radar;

- intelligent fuzes for penetrating warheads;

- development of various warheads for the CRV7;

- development of an 84-mm recoilless light gun;

- improvement of accuracy of Leopard C-1 tank gun;

- light roof protection system for trenches;

- behind-armour effectiveness of munitions;

- penetration of hypervelocity projectiles;

- training munitions;

- spinning tubular projectiles (STUP);

- joint Canada/France evaluation of the Eryx guided weapon system.

One of the major successes of DREV was the development of computer programs for simulating the effectiveness of weapons. This work involved methodologies for determining hit probabilities, ship survival and the effectiveness of minefields. The expertise was transferred to Navtech Inc., of Quebec, and used by its division Navware Canada Inc. NATO has adopted this technique as a standard for ship vulnerability.

Another significant success was the development of the spinning tubular projectile (STUP) during the 1970's. STUP is an excellent ballistic equivalent for high-velocity combat ammunition, and its drag-control short-range feature makes it an ideal training round on practice ranges of limited dimensions. Developed under a shared-cost agreement between DND and Canadian Arsenals Limited, STUP is selling well on the world market. The Armaments Division also undertook a study to identify the strengths and weaknesses of commercially-available protective helmets. Based on this evaluation, Division researchers selected the best designs and established a collaborative program with the manufacturers to promote production in Canada.

7.6.3 Information Technologies

The use of data processing and information technologies in support of the Canadian Forces increased considerably during this period. Although data processing was employed initially in a variety of projects, it gradually became an essential tool in the area of command and control for the Air, Land and Maritime elements of the Canadian Forces. Some examples of work undertaken since the 1970's are given below:

- image processing for surveillance and intelligence gathering;
- guidance and control of missiles;
- effectiveness of underwater weapons systems;
- integration of ship combat systems;
- complementarity of sensors, in support of the NATO air defence system;
- threat evaluation and target designation;
- automatic tactical data processing system for the land forces.

The key ingredient for most of these studies was, without doubt, the enhancement of decision-making through the use of leading-edge data processing technologies. "Over the last decade, the Tactical Information Systems (TIS) Section [participated in] a major research program to design and develop a test bench for evaluating automated command and control concepts sponsored by PMO TCCCS."[62] This program spawned a number of projects on geographical information systems, tactical data fusion, expert systems, multiprocessors, etc., and facilitated the definition of requirements for an automated combat information system. Most importantly, this program led to the development of a prototype data fusion system which integrated data from all possible sources and provided officers responsible for decision-making with a complete picture of the disposition of friendly and enemy troops on the battlefield.

7.6.4 Electro-Optics

During the past twenty years, work in the field of electro-optics at DREV has continued to evolve towards addressing the current and future needs of the Canadian Forces. Three main fields of research exist at the present time: surveillance (observation, detection and identification of various platforms), target acquisition (acquisition, fire control and guidance) and electro-optical warfare (threat detection, sensor protection, camouflage, dazzling and jamming).

Scientists of the Electro-Optics Division have conducted research and have made significant progress in many areas, as indicated below:

- high-resolution spectral imagery;

- signal processing for detection and tracking of targets;

- eye protection against laser radiation (filters and optical limiters);

- new concept of multi-angle lidar;

- transmission and propagation of waves in the atmosphere and under water;

- surveillance and target acquisition systems, both passive (infrared, image intensifiers) and active (lasers);

- detection systems for laser and missile threats;
- space applications of electro-optics;
- military applications of laser systems: automated detection and identification of targets, missile guidance, telemetry, fire-control, ocean optoelectronics and countermeasures;
- eye-safe lasers.

Since the development of the now famous TEA-CO_2 laser, DREV has recorded a number of other successes in both the defence and commercial fields, including, amongst others, the development of: pyroelectric joulemeters (Gentec) for measuring laser beam energy; alignment and control systems for artillery pieces (Bendix Avelex); image processing circuit boards (manufactured by ICS Limited and sold to several countries) for improving image quality; Stark cells for stabilization of CO_2 lasers (MPB Technologies); Gaussian mirrors (NOI) for increasing laser performance; optical isolators (Seastar Optics) for increasing by the Faraday effect, the injection of a laser ray in a fiber optic; video tracking systems (Image Tracking Research) for tracking points in movement on an image; high angular resolution laser irradiation detectors (EG&G) for warning pilots that they are being tracked by a guidance laser; and gallium arsenide (GaAs) emitter/receiver pairs (EG&G) for use as a source and a detector in laser rangefinders.

In collaboration with Leitz Canada, DREV also developed a muzzle-mounted reference system which uses laser telemetry to improve the accuracy of the Leopard C-1 tank gun. This system has attracted wide foreign interest, particularly in countries using the Leopard tank. Belgium alone has purchased 300 units. Finally, in collaboration with Bomem, DREV has developed a high resolution Fourier-transform IR spectrometer of short integration time. This system has been sold as a laboratory instrument in over 30 countries, and improvements continue to be made in response to numerous requests.

7.6.5 Development of Scientific Infrastructures

In common with other research establishments around the world, DREV needed to provide the requisite infrastructures and instrumentation to enable researchers to pursue their scientific activities. Over the past decades, DREV never deviated from the commitment to meet this requirement, which was indispensable to the success of its scientific endeavours. This was especially evident in the case of the Armaments Division and the Energetic Materials Division, the two scientific divisions which required extensive research infrastructures. To improve the conditions for armaments research, the Armaments Division was furnished with an environmental simulation laboratory, an instrumentation and control centre, an open-jet wind tunnel, an in-draft wind tunnel and certain facilities for small- and medium-calibre ammunition of weapon tests. In addition, the precision firing range was extended and the aeroballistic range was renovated. The Energetic Materials Division was equipped with a static test bed for the CRV7 rocket, a recoil simulator, a high-capacity detonation cell, modern facilities for pouring and working explosives, and a pilot plant for producing glycidyl azide polymer (GAP). DREV also provided the Energetic Materials Division with the equipment needed to produce smoke opaque to visible and infrared radiation, and to facilitate characterization of energetic materials.

The type of research conducted by scientists in the two other divisions required less extensive infrastructure. Nevertheless, the Command and Control Division was equipped with a unique laboratory instrument - a command and control tactical data test assembly - which was used to evaluate the latest data processing techniques for application to tactical command and control at the brigade level. The Electro-Optics Division was equipped with a number of facilities such as a high-intensity laser laboratory, ranges for studying atmospheric propagation of 1 and 5.7 km in length, a tactical engagement simulator (missiles, aircraft and countermeasures), equipment for measuring wide-band spectral signatures of targets, and equipment for processing infrared images.

1   Peter Drucker, *Post-Capitalist Society*, New York, Harper Business, 1993, p. 215.
2   Glassco Commission, "Special Areas of Administration", *Royal Commission on Government Organization (Glassco Commission)*, Vol. 4, Ottawa, Queen's Printer, p. 200.
3   *Ibid.*, p. 218.
4   *Ibid.*, p. 233.
5   OECD, *Review on National Science Policy in Canada*, Paris, 1969, p. 63 *et passim*.
6   *Ibid.*, p. 65.
7   Senate of Canada, "Proceedings of the Special Committee on Science Policy", Phase 1, Second Session of the 27th Parliament, 1967-1968, p. 129, cited in *ibid.*, p. 65-66.
8   *Ibid.*, p. 67.
9   *Ibid.*, p. 63 *et passim*.
10 *House of Commons Debates*, 8 October 1970, p. 2.
11 *Ibid.*, 28 February 1972, p. 327.
12 *Interview with Dr. André Lemay*, p. 23-24.
13 Glassco Commission, *op. cit.*, p. 205.
14 *Ibid.*, p. 205.
15 *Ibid.*, p. 257.
16 *Ibid.*, p. 211.
17 Canada, *White Paper on Defence*, Ottawa, DND, 1964, p. 27-30.
18 DRB, *Annual Report of DRB, 1966*, Ottawa, DND, 1966, p. 2.
19 DRB, *Annual Report of DRB 1967*, Ottawa, DND, 1967, p. 3-4.
20 Col P.D. Manson, "The Restructuring of National Defence Headquarters: 1972-1973", *Canadian Defence Quarterly*, Vol. 3, No. 3, Winter 1973, p. 9.
21 Douglas Bland, *The Administration of Defence Policy: 1947-1985*, Kingston, Frye, 1987, p. 142.
22 *Ibid.*, p. 84.
23 *Ibid.*, p. 84.
24 Message, *DRRG 104 291600Z MAR 74*, 1974.
25 DREV, *Annual Report for 1974*, p. 1.
26 Gordon D. Watson, "Why The Bureaucrats Secretly Carved Up The DRB: It Worked Too Well", *Science Forum*, No. 47, October 1975, p. 23.
27 *Ibid.*, p. 24.
28 Douglas Bland, *op. cit.*, p. 143.
29 Dr. O.M. Solandt, "The Defence Research Board's Untimely End: What It Means For Military Science", *Science Forum*, No. 47, October 1975, p. 19.

30 CRAD, *The Research and Development Branch Review: 1976-1986*, Ottawa, Department of National Defence, p. 3.
31 Canada, *Statutes of Canada*, Chapter 5, 1947.
32 Glassco Commission, *op. cit.*, p. 206-207.
33 *Ibid.*, p. 206.
34 *Interview with Mr. E.J. Bobyn*, p. 32-33.
35 DREV, *Annual Report for 1971*, p. 2.
36 DREV, *Annual Report for 1974*, p. 3.
37 DREV, *Annual Report for 1975*, p. 17.
38 DRB, *Annual Review for 1970*, p. 9.
39 DREV, *Annual Report for 1975,* p. 20.
40 *Ibid.*, p. 19.
41 *Interview with Dr. Jacques Gilbert*, p. 15.
42 DREV, *Annual Report for 1975*, p. 20.
43 CRAD, *op. cit.*, p. 13-14.
44 DREV, *Annual Report for 1979*, p. 41.
45 DREV, *Annual Report for 1975*, p. 35.
46 *Interview with Dr. Jacques Gilbert*, p. 15.
47 *Press release*, 8 August 1974.
48 DREV, *Annual Report for 1973*, p. 21.
49 DREV, *Annual Report for 1973, Annual Report for 1975*.
50 LCol H.P. Nielsen, "The CRV7 Weapon System: An Example of Weapon Development in Canada", *Canadian Aeronautics and Space Journal*, Vol. 1, No. 1, 1980, p. 10.
51 D.L. Smith, *The CRV7 Rocket Weapon System*, DREV, Valcartier, 1988, p. 1.
52 *Ibid.*, p. 2.
53 CRAD, *op. cit.*, p. 9.
54 D.L. Smith, *op. cit.*, p. 5.
55 *Interview with Dr. Maurice Gravel*, DREV, 1994.
56 DREV, *Annual Report for 1973*, p. 13.
57 CRAD, *op. cit.*, p. 14.
58 *Interview with Dr. Maurice Gravel*, 1994.
59 Major Gérald Baril, "Une visite dans le monde merveilleux des savants", *Sentinelle*, 1992, No. 1, p. 5.
60 DREV, *Annual Report for 1988*, p. 36.
61 DREV, *Infocentre*, 25 November 1991, p. 25.
62 DREV, *Infocentre*, 29 September 1989, p. 28.

> "Applied sciences and technology are forced to adjust themselves to the highest intellectual standards which are developed in the basic sciences. This influence works in many ways: some fundamental students go into industry; the techniques which are applied to meet the stringent requirements of fundamental research serve to create new technological methods. The style, the scale, and the level of scientific and technical work are determined in pure research; that is what attracts productive people and what brings scientists to those countries where science is at the highest level. Fundamental research sets the standards of modern scientific thought; it creates the intellectual climate in which our modern civilization flourishes. It pumps the lifeblood of idea and inventiveness not only into the technological laboratories and factories, but into every cultural activity of our time."
>
> Why pure science? in the Bulletin of the Atomic Scientists, 1965, vol 21, p. 4-8

8

IMPACT OF DREV'S PARTICIPATION IN DEFENCE RESEARCH

8.1 SOME EXAMPLES OF THE MAIN SPIN-OFFS FROM DREV SCIENTIFIC ACTIVITIES

8.1.1 Patents, Inventions and Licences

Patents are a most revealing indicator of the quality of research conducted by a scientific establishment. During their careers, researchers often devise new ideas on methods, machines, manufacturing processes or even the composition of matter. These ideas may generally be regarded as inventions. When an invention is publicly disclosed, the researcher may obtain a patent provided that the invention satisfies certain conditions (usefulness, novelty, etc.). These conditions determine the patentability of the invention.

A patent is a legal document which constitutes a contract between the State and the inventor. Under this patent contract, the State accords the inventor a 17-year monopoly on the exploitation of the invention. Such exploitation can take the form of either production of goods or use of a procedure.

The value of a patent can be measured by the revenue it

produces, which is indicative of its importance in the marketplace. As patentability applies only in the country in which the patent is awarded, the inventor must obtain patents in other countries if the invention is to be exploited on an international basis.

Once an invention has been disclosed and a patent application has been filed, the inventor can grant a licence to a third party. A licence is a contract which stipulates that the licence holder must pay the inventor a fixed percentage of his profits, called royalties, for the right to manufacture, sell or exploit the invention. In particular, it should be noted that all the rights to an invention conceived by a public servant are ceded to the State. In return, the public servant receives an award and royalties from the State.

In practice, the procedures are relatively simple. Once a DREV invention is formally submitted to the DND Director of Patent Administration, Canadian Patents and Development Limited (CPDL) is automatically informed and asked to examine the potential commercial applications of the invention. When the first patent application is filed, the public servant credited with the invention receives a small financial award. If the patent rights are licensed to a company through CPDL and the invention exploited, the inventor receives part of the royalties paid to the State. Most of the defence scientists and a number of technicians at DREV have disclosed one or more inventions during their careers. However, only a small number of inventions have been licensed for commercial exploitation.

Impact of DREV's Participation in Defence Research 273

FIGURE 10 - Invention Reports Between 1950 and 1994

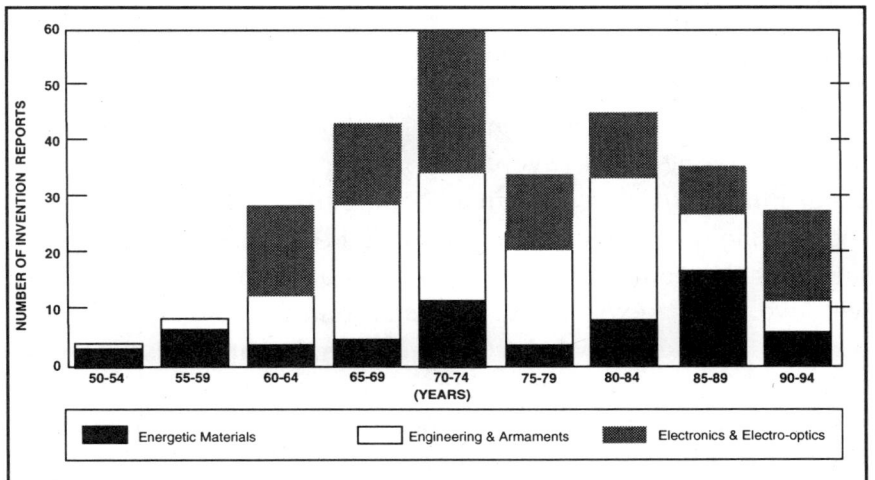

FIGURE 11 - Invention Reports Between 1950 and 1994

	Matériaux énergétiques	Génie & armement	Électronique & électro-optique	TOTAL
1950-1954	3	1	0	4
1955-1959	7	2	0	9
1960-1964	4	10	15	29
1965-1969	6	23	14	43
1970-1974	12	22	25	59
1975-1979	4	17	13	34
1980-1984	8	25	11	44
1985-1989	15	11	9	35
1990-1994	5	6	16	27
TOTAL	64	117	103	284

Source: DREV Compendium of Invention Reports

Since 1950, DREV personnel have submitted 284 patent applications, and no less than 366 patents have been awarded in Canada and in 14 other countries, mainly the United States, Japan, Australia and the former USSR.

As shown in the table and graph above, the patents awarded to DREV concerned inventions related to the synthesis and development of new chemical compositions and research in engineering and armaments. In the field of energetic materials, scientists maintained an invention rate of about 5 every five years, with two notable exceptions; the increase in the 1970-1974 period was due to a series of developments in granular explosives, propellants and smoke generation, while the increase in the 1985-1988 period was due to the development of the glycidyl azide polymer (GAP) binder and of pyrophoric substances. In the field of engineering and armaments, there was a steady rise in reports of inventions up to 1974, then a slight decrease. A new peak occurred in 1984 due to the development of fibre-reinforced polymer rocket launchers and several special pieces of equipment. Subsequently, there was a relative decline in the number of inventions reported. Finally, in the field of electro-optics, there was a significant increase in the invention rate between 1960 and 1970 following the discovery of the TEA-CO_2 laser. After reaching an unprecedented peak following such a scientific breakthrough, the invention rate declined slightly between 1975 and 1979. This trend continued throughout the 1980's, to be followed by a recovery in recent years (1990 to 1994). An analysis of the invention reports reveals that the scientists from all the research sectors at DREV, with each sector progressing at its own pace, enjoyed an unprecedented era of invention between 1970 and 1974. Since that time, DREV has not experienced a comparable period.

8.1.2   The Make-or-Buy Policy

In another vein, the integration of DREV into CRAD

coincided with the implementation of the make-or buy policy established by the Cabinet on 10 February 1972. It was introduced in 1973 "with the objective of increasing the proportion of government research and development requirements contracted out to industry rather than performed in-house."[1]

In 1972, the gross national expenditure on research and development (GERD) expressed as a percentage of gross national product (GNP) was 1.14%. At about that time, the Lamontagne Committee warned the government that, in order to maintain Canada's international competitiveness, national R&D expenditures should be about 2.5% of GNP. On 21 February 1974, Cabinet expanded the original policy to provide for consideration of financing of unsolicited proposals for R&D from the private sector.[2] The policy would thus provide for contracts to Canadian industry for mission-oriented R&D in response to solicited as well as unsolicited proposals from industry.

From the beginning, this policy met with some resistance from scientists who viewed it as a threat to their employment security. According to one person interviewed, the make-or-buy policy had some advantages and some disadvantages. In his view, it was not always easy to find firms in the high-technology sector which could meet all the conditions necessary for the award of an R&D contract. Industrialists were sometimes reticent to become involved if they considered that there was only a slim chance of making a profit, that there were few commercial opportunities or that the venture would only benefit the military. On the other hand, provision was often made within these R&D contracts for the companies to manufacture and market the products that they developed.

This provision, together with the amounts involved and the undeniable advantages of owning the rights to a leading-edge technology, led a large number of firms to seek the advice of DREV scientists in order to understand the requisite criteria for the award of research contracts. In some instances, when a firm received a contract, it would create specialist positions in vanguard fields of endeavour according to DREV's particular needs, such as in the fields of image processing or artificial intelligence. Successive contracts could ensure continuity of research and, *de facto*, contribute to the development of a new technology. Subsequently, the federal government would issue invitations to tender for the technology, production processes or equipment developed by companies, in order to select the particular company that would benefit from the technology transferred. Despite the lead enjoyed by companies that had been involved in the earlier research and development work, it sometimes happened that companies which had conducted the R&D would not be awarded the production contracts. In any event, these contracts allowed companies in Quebec and in Canada to benefit from DREV's material support and intellectual resources; to remain conversant with military requirements and the various standards of the NATO nations; to train technical personnel and obtain computer programs; to set up modern, effective production methods; to engage additional personnel in order to meet the objectives of R&D, engineering or production contracts, and frequently be able to retain these employees for several years; to become leaders in certain fields, develop world-class products and retain a competitive position in the international marketplace; to increase their stature and expand their capacity to undertake work in new fields of activity so as to be eligible to compete for contracts other than those awarded by DND; and, to remain competitive and ensure their survival.

In summary, the objective of the make-or-buy policy was to increase the amount of research undertaken by Canadian industry and promote a stronger synergistic relationship between the public and private sectors. In conformity with this policy, DREV awarded millions of dollars in research contracts and strengthened its links with industry. Over the years, DREV increased its annual expenditures on research contracts and, from 1986/87 onwards, they averaged $6 million/year. The Establishment also joined the *Groupe d'action pour l'avancement technologique et industriel de la région de Québec* (GATIQ) so as to become better known to the industrial participants in the region.

The make-or-buy policy holds the promise of becoming even more effective following the recent announcement by the Department of National Defence that the proportion of R&D contracted to industry would increase from 50% to 70% in the years to come. Accordingly, DREV will have to augment its contracting-out efforts and reorient its program so as to award larger contracts to the private sector and forge strategic alliances with industry and university.

8.1.3   Exploitation of DREV's Research

DREV was well aware of the importance of pursuing the commercialization of inventions and ideas which emerged from research and development activities. Given that its prime role was neither marketing nor production, its personnel had to work closely with representatives of CPDL, the organization responsible for exploiting technology developed by government and owned by the Crown. Technology transfer was effected with and through CPDL in various forms such as brand licensing agreements, patent transfers, franchise agreements, business agreements, sub-contracting, start-up contracts, entrepreneurial ventures or any other action leading to either the sale of patents to companies, patent exploitation or the creation of new industries. Technology transfer also occurred through development or production contracts, exchange of personnel, release of technology, dissemination of DREV publications, and publication of invention reports or patents.

As we have seen throughout the present historical document, DREV has transferred technology to industry on many occasions. Indeed, it played a key role in creating the Canadian missile and laser industries through awards of contracts and several patent licences. R&D contracts have had a major impact in helping several Canadian companies to become established, to develop and to diversify their product lines. Notable examples are: the transfer of propellant and rocket-motor technology to BAL and the subsequent exploitation of this technology in the Black Brant, Metroc and CRV7 projects; the support given to Aviation Electric in designing and manufacturing a gun alignment and control system; assistance provided in creating the Bomem company in Quebec; and the award of a development contract to SPAR for a shipboard passive surveillance system. These are only a few examples of technology transfer from DREV to private enterprise over the last two decades.

In the fields of energetic materials and armaments, contracts have been awarded for the production of hundreds of thousands of smoke-generating and pyrotechnic devices (Hands Fireworks, Astra, IVI), for the production of new explosives (CIL), for viscoelastic analysis of propellants (H.G. Engineering) and for the development of pyrophoric flare technology. Contracts awarded to Béton-Vibrek for the production of targets allowed the company to develop extremely high resistant concrete technology. The interest, support and backing of DREV encouraged Trans-Equip to become involved in powder metallurgy.

Technology transfer has been extensive in the field of electro-optics as follows: detection using passive optics (Optech Inc., Toronto); electro-optical countermeasures (Leitz Canada); infrared signature analysis (Somapro); DF laser construction techniques (Lumonics); design of standard EO instrument for the ADATS system (Oerlikon); Stark cell (MPB Technologies); Gaussian mirrors (INRS Énergie and NOI); large-surface avalanche photodiode operating at 1.54-μm wavelength (RCA); image recognition and non-linear filters (LROL); infrared signature measurement (Davis Engineering); stabilized alignment system (SPAR); maritime applications of ADATS (Oerlikon); multi-sensor data fusion (IR, millimetre wave, radar, acoustic, etc.) by NOI; and, IR detector characterization (Optotek, which became the only manufacturer of IR detectors in Canada).

Contracts in the area of electro-optical countermeasures

awarded to Leitz Canada allowed the company to acquire new expertise and become internationally competitive. Contracts awarded by DREV to Somapro under the "Aerosols and Atmospheric Properties Measuring Stations" project allowed the company to apply expertise acquired to other areas and to win the Octas 90 prize for "Excellence in Informatics". Through contracts in the field of image processing, Computing Devices Company succeeded in forming a highly competent team which subsequently worked on a new sighting system and other DND projects. DREV collaborated closely with Bomem in the development of an infrared spectrometer which was highly successful. As a result, the Establishment consolidated its excellent international reputation in the field of electro-optics, and Bomem sold the product to defence agencies, universities and research institutions around the world. With DREV support over the years, Gentec developed technologies that were directly applicable to its product lines. In 1979, contracts were awarded to Optech in Downsview, Ontario, to develop a cloud-mapping lidar capable of measuring opaque and aerosol clouds with high precision. Through these contracts, Optech was able to remain in operation and to secure a favourable position in this high technology area, especially since Canada was the only nation to market such a product.

In the field of data processing, DREV transferred a number of technologies related to: combat systems simulation (Thomson CSF); parallel computation for processing sequential images (Lyre Instruments); automatic processing of tactical data (Midi-Plus); data fusion systems (DMR); command and control systems for combat engineers (CGI); etc.

DREV contracts to Thomson CSF helped to develop industrial expertise in naval artificial intelligence, and its funded development work awarded to Hart and Page had application to some commercial systems such as the geophysical information systems of Géo Vision. The Establishment's contracts also enabled Computing Devices Company to develop world-class competence in the field of electronic stabilization of images. In summary, most of the state-of-the-art software technologies used in DREV enabled all these companies to develop a wide range of commercial and military applications. In some instances, technology was simply given to companies for incorporation into their products. For example, the expertise acquired by DREV in improving the Fourier-transform spectrometer was passed on to Bomem which exploited it in the company's standard product.

The above is far from an exhaustive list, but it serves to illustrate the importance of technology transfer in helping companies and universities from all regions in Canada to be aware of advanced technology and military requirements, to develop new expertise and, in several cases, to compete internationally. Technology transfer has thus significantly fostered the growth of high technology capability in Canada in a considerable number of areas.

8.1.4   Industrial Benefits

DREV's influence on the private sector has been felt in many ways: through patents and inventions, licences awarded to companies, participation in the creation of new companies (Bomem, for instance), research contracts and other technology transfer.

A few examples of industrial benefit which accrued through defence research activities are given below. In the field of explosives, where the technology is highly complex, Canadian Arsenals and other manufacturers are indebted to DREV for perfecting certain processes which allowed these companies to remain internationally competitive. In the field of propulsion and solid propellants, DREV research established the technology base for Canada's rocket propulsion program. The Establishment played a major role in the development of the Black Brant series of rockets, one of the key elements in the Canadian space program. Similarly, the transfer of a wide range of computer programs to companies such as CAL, BAL and IVI working in the fields of aerodynamics, trajectory prediction, internal ballistics, stress analysis of missiles, rockets and munitions, enabled these companies to become more competitive, offer better products and increase their export sales.

DREV management, aware of the need to increase the technological capability of Canadian industry in an age of market globalization, has recently created the position of Director of Technology Exploitation, with the aim of transferring research results as rapidly as possible from the Establishment to industry. The duties of the incumbent of this position include ensuring that technologies developed by DREV are exploited effectively, promoting the development of requisite technology transfer mechanisms, and fostering linkages between participants from government, university and industry. It was decided to locate the office of the Director of Technology Exploitation in the *Parc technologique du Québec métropolitain* in order to maximize the return on investment from its research and to enable local firms to benefit from the immense potential of its technologies, advanced facilities and scientific expertise. In this way, DREV could maintain close, effective relationships with major research institutes such as CRIQ, NOI and ITM, with large companies such as Asea Brown Boweri and Bell and with over 60 small- and medium-sized businesses. In this same context, the Establishment maintains linkages with MICTQ and IC(Quebec), and also collaborates with NRC (IRAP) and the *Bureau de valorisation des applications de la recherche* (BVAR) of Laval University.

Because of the mounting pressure to transfer technology more rapidly, DREV is making efforts to use DIR (Defence Industrial Research) program funding to maximize opportunities for collaboration, to develop synergistic relationships and to establish partnerships. Already, various mechanisms to stimulate technology exploitation are in place for most of the areas of DREV activity.

At present, emphasis is being placed on sharing project costs, in terms of both human and financial resources. For this reason, partnering between DREV, industry and other organizations is becoming more prevalent. For instance, DREV, the *Centre de recherche informatique de Montréal* (CRIM), ATS Aerospace and PRECARN Associates are jointly conducting research on a series of three-dimensional terrain models using parallel processing computers. The major project to develop leading-edge propulsion technologies, involving DND, Industry Canada and Bristol Aerospace Limited is another good example of successful partnering. Finally, greater use is being made of the DIR program to reduce risks and maximize the return on investments of individual partners.

8.1.5 Scientific Benefits

Technology transfer is only one of the many benefits which accrue to Canada through DREV's activities. There is also a significant scientific impact. Some aspects of DREV's influence in its relationships with other scientific bodies in Canada and abroad are examined below.

Over the years, the Establishment's scientists have published hundreds of scientific articles, including complete chapters of books that subsequently became high technology reference works. The thousands of references to the articles and research work of its scientists which have appeared in foreign scientific journals constitute further evidence, if such were needed, that DREV research results do not go unnoticed by the international scientific community. Many Establishment scientists have received awards of have been honoured for their scientific work and many have achieved international renown in their particular fields.

In this context, it will be recalled that the invention of the TEA-CO_2 laser was featured on the cover page of *Laser Focus*, the definitive reference journal in this field. The disclosure of the new laser propelled DREV to the front page of all the scientific journals. At the time, its researchers were the acknowledged leaders in carbon dioxide molecular lasers, and they were invited to make presentations throughout the world. Some of the world's most prestigious laboratories, such as those of Lawrence Livermore and United Technologies, consulted DREV on laser technologies. A detailed document on this subject has been published and is available for consultation in the DREV Library. In general, DREV researchers have not only presented a considerable number of scientific papers on defence technologies but have also contributed, through their research activities, to the growth of Canada's scientific community. They participated, without hesitation, in research groups and organizations, became members of a multitude of scientific and technical committees within and outside the Department, became members of the councils of certain scientific societies, provided advice and assistance to many industrial organizations, and provided, with their expertise, various review and evaluation committees and committees of experts.

8.2 AN OUTLINE OF THE ECONOMIC BENEFITS TO QUEBEC FROM THE PRESENCE OF DREV AT VALCARTIER

The economic benefits to Quebec stemming from the presence of Defence Research Establishment Valcartier can be estimated based on the portion of its budget expended in the region. Figure 12 gives a more detailed distribution of the amounts expended in Quebec during fiscal year 1989/1990. Although a significant portion of the funds allocated to research contracts and procurement are expended outside the Province, the fact is most of the expenditures on salaries are made in Quebec. Equally, it may be assumed that expenditures on infrastructure maintenance, including many important non discretionary items such as electricity, telephone services, heating and transportation subsidies, are made entirely in Quebec. Similarly, construction contracts make an appreciable contribution to the regional economy.

Because of its reputation and its participation in many international cooperative programs, DREV also has a non-negligeable impact on tourism in the region. DREV receives a large number of visitors annually who participate in meetings and seminars, work on joint research projects or take part in multinational exercises. By way of example, in 1989 about a hundred Americans participated in evaluation trials on smoke screen performance. These trials lasted for 20 days. It is estimated that the US visitors spent some $200 K on local travel and living, and a further $200 K on support services related to these trials. Many participants also rented cars. This one set of trials alone injected about $500 K into the local economy during the three-week period.

Figure 12- Economic Impact of DREV on Quebec (Fiscal Year 1989/1990, in thousands of dollars)

Item	Total expenditures	Expenditures in Quebec
Research contracts	7,571	4,000
Procurement	6,544	4,000
Development	3,246	1,850
Operations and Maintenance	2,957	12,957
Construction	1,474	1,474
Salaries	25,563	25,563
Expenditures by visitors		1,000
Total	**57,355**	**50,844**

The impact of DREV expenditures on the economy can be estimated using the Statistics Canada input-output model of the Canadian economy, which divides the national economy into 602 commodities and 192 industries. Using this model, estimates can be made of the number of jobs created through each Parliamentary Vote, and hence the total number of jobs created in the economy in person-years.

The Operations Research and Analysis Establishment (ORAE) used this model to estimate the impact of various Canadian Forces bases on the local economy, and hence the consequences of closing them.

However, for the purposes of the present study, a simplified method of analysis can be used. According to Dr. Finan,[3] job creation can be determined by using the following figures:

R&D employment:	$60 K
Civil engineering employment:	$35 K
Wage-earning employment:	$25 K

Taking an average figure of $35 K, DREV's expenditures in Quebec would translate into about 1,450 jobs, 25% of which would derive from direct employment (contract work) and 75% from indirect employment (sales of material to contractors) and induced employment (retail store sales). Despite DREV's declining budget, it is estimated that, in 1994, at least 1,000 jobs were created or maintained by the Establishment's presence.

8.3   INTERNATIONAL PARTICIPATION

Canada participates with the NATO nations and other allied nations across the world in a large number of international defence research and development committees. In 1994, over 60 DREV scientists represented Canada as members, heads of delegations or chairpersons of these international allied research committees. Canada participates in a number of multilateral agreements and has also established bilateral agreements on defence R&D with several countries, including the United States, the United Kingdom, France, Germany and the Netherlands.

8.3.1 The Technical Cooperation Program (TTCP)

On 25 October 1957, the President of the United States and the Prime Minister of the United Kingdom signed a Declaration of Common Purpose. In this important document, they recognized that the free nations of the world were interdependent and that they should collaborate in several areas. Canada quickly subscribed to this principle, and the Tripartite Technical Cooperation Program was born. Australia joined TTCP in July 1965, (the name of TTCP was changed to The Technical Cooperation Program), followed by New Zealand in October 1970. The participating nations, recognizing that they could not conduct R&D in isolation across the full spectrum of defence areas, decided to pool their resources and share tasks within many sub-groups established to address a vast number of scientific and technological areas.

8.3.2 NATO

Canada, as one of the first parties signatory to the North Atlantic Treaty Organization, participates in many NATO groups. Because of the importance of defence research, NATO formed a Defence Research Group (DRG, AC/243) which is subdivided into nine Panels which in turn are composed of Research Study Groups (RSG). DREV participates in those Study Groups concerned with electro-optics and infrared, image processing, atmospheric propagation effects on electro-optical systems, missile signatures, military lasers, optical and infrared countermeasures, eye protection, sensors, etc. DREV also participates in NATO Air Force Armaments Group (AC/224), NATO Army Armaments Group (AC/225) and in the NATO Group on Safety and Suitability for Service of Munitions and Explosives (AC/310).

8.3.3 NATO Industrial Advisory Group (NIAG)

The member nations of NIAG advise NATO on their respective defence industrial capabilities, and Canada's participation in NIAG thus assumes this advisory role on behalf of Canadian industry. Canada has participated with other NATO nations in a large number of projects, including the NATO Anti-Air Warfare System (NAAWS), the NATO frigate replacement program, the NATO Sea-Sparrow program, area defence weapons, the 155-mm Autonomous Precision Guided Munition (APGM), the Battlefield Information Collection and Exploitation System (BICES), the Advanced Short-Range Air-to-Air Missile (ASRAAM), etc. DREV scientists actively contributed to the work of these committees as experts in their own particular fields.

8.3.4 The Franco-Canadian Accord

In Paris, on 25 September 1972, Canada and France signed the Franco-Canadian Defence Science Agreement to facilitate cooperation on pyrotechnics, explosives, propellants, atmospheric propagation at 10.6-µm wavelength, operational research, electrical energy sources, human performance in pressurized environments, and human protection in hostile environments. Over the years, DREV scientists participated in information exchange and joint projects and tests in the first four areas. The scope of the Agreement was reviewed periodically over the years, and several other areas were added, including research on lasers, submarine detection and composite materials.

1 MOSST, *The Make-or-Buy Policy 1973-1975*, Ottawa, Ministry of State for Science and Technology, 1975, p. 3.
2 *Ibid.*, p. 3-4.
3 Dr. J.S. Finan, Director Social and Economic Analysis, Operations Research and Analysis Establishment, *Communications Industry*.

PART FOUR

MAJOR DEVELOPMENTS IN DREV ADMINISTRATION

> *"The intellectual's world, unless counterbalanced by the manager, becomes one in which everybody "does his own thing" but nobody achieves anything. The manager's world, unless counterbalanced by the intellectual, becomes the stultifying bureaucracy of the "Organization Man". But if the two balance each other, there can be creativity and order, fulfilment and mission."*
> *(Peter Drucker)[1]*

9

EVOLUTION OF THE ADMINISTRATIVE STRUCTURE OF DEFENCE RESEARCH ESTABLISHMENT VALCARTIER

9.1 ADMINISTRATIVE STRUCTURE OF DREV UNDER DRB

9.1.1 Importance of the "Wing" or "Divisional" Structure in CARDE

As we have seen throughout this history, CARDE management established a flexible organizational structure that could be modified in concert with changes in the types of research activity undertaken by defence scientists. This flexibility was achieved through a structure that permitted some decentralization of power within the organization, coupled with efficient control and coordination of the Establishment's resources by the Chief Superintendent. Under the "Wing" structure, each Wing had its own sections composed of all the necessary scientific and technical personnel needed to undertake the research activities.

Established in 1945, this kind of structure led naturally to some decentralization of power. Since then, the Wing

Superintendent has essentially been responsible for overall management of his Wing, for implementing and executing research and development programs, for directing multi-disciplinary teams in support of projects for which he is responsible, for planning and coordinating the technical activities of the Wing, for planning and developing appropriate facilities, for maintaining effective liaison external organizations, for budgeting and allocating Wing resources, for ensuring safe work practices and safe-keeping of classified information, for planning the careers of his subordinates and evaluating their performance, and for participating in all CARDE committees which require his presence.[2]

Through this organizational structure, the Chief Superintendent "minimized the interdependence between divisions, so that each [could] operate as a quasi-autonomous entity, free of the need to coordinate with the others."[3] Such an organization, subdivided into Wings, Sections and Groups along specialty lines, did not preclude the participation of the administrative units in common research and development programs.

Despite this delegation of powers to the Wing Superintendents, the Chief Superintendent nevertheless remained responsible for ensuring overall management of the Establishment and for coordinating its resources and functions. The Wing Superintendents had, of course, the power to manage and control their operations and, to some extent, to determine and influence the present and future needs of defence in their respective areas and to formulate appropriate strategies. But in the final analysis, the Chief Superintendent determined the major R&D objectives of the Establishment and established research priorities in conformity with the overall research strategy defined in Ottawa.[4] The Chief Superintendent was also responsible, amongst other things, for approving strategic plans, ensuring sound operation and relevance of the financial and administrative systems of the Establishment, endorsing the distribution of overall financial resources and approving the creation, merging or disbandment of administrative units.

In addition, with the assistance of the Administrative Wing and the Deputy Chief Superintendent, the Chief Superintendent was responsible for controlling the overall program, the results obtained, the individual projects within each of the Wings and the internal administrative procedures governing management of resources and projects. It should be noted that the latitude of the Chief Superintendent in these matters was subject to the administrative directives, regulations and procedures of DRB, but these were minimal for most of the period. The Chiefs of the defence research establishments thus retained sufficient flexibility to apply their own style of administration to managing their operations.

9.1.2   Successive Structural Reorganizations

From the 1940s onwards, the Chief Superintendent has been assisted by the Deputy Chief Superintendent who is the second in command of the Establishment and assumes full responsibility for it in the absence of the Chief. He participates fully in the overall management of the Establishment by advising the Chief Superintendent, by assisting him in the coordination of the Establishment's resources and functions and by functioning as Chairman of various committees.[5] The Chief Superintendent, and indeed the whole of CARDE, were also supported by the Administration Wing, consisting of a small staff, whose function was to free the Wing Superintendents from various administrative tasks.

Although this small team was largely sufficient to meet the needs of a relatively modest organization, the situation was totally different when the activities of the Establishment expanded in an unprecedented way with the initiation of the Velvet Glove research project. In 1952, CARDE management anticipated a phenomenal growth of scientific activities with a proportional increase in human, material and financial resources, and in management control. Management thus created a central office for coordinating scientific activities and appointed three project managers responsible for all the Establishment projects who were assisted by administrative support staff. In addition, the staff of the Administration Wing tripled in 1952. When the Velvet Glove project was terminated, the *ad hoc* group was disbanded but the project officer function remained.

As we have seen earlier, the termination of this project led to a reorientation of CARDE activities. In 1958, the Chief Superintendent, Brigadier D. Waldock, reorganized the scientific wings and created the Technical Services Wing. From then on, CARDE had two support Wings for its scientific activities. In 1959, with the signing of joint research programs on ICBMs, CARDE management completely reorganized its research projects. This eased the task of the project managers and facilitated project control. In 1963, the Chief Superintendent, Dr. L'Heureux, made some minor organizational changes to the scientific wings and transferred the Data Processing Section to Technical Services Wing in order to serve the computational needs of the whole Establishment.[6]

In the year following, Defence Minister Hellyer tabled a *White Paper on Defence* which profoundly changed the organizational structure of the Canadian Forces and exerted a strong influence on the future of defence research in Canada. 1964 also marked the termination of the joint Canada/US research programs initiated in 1959. CARDE management undertook a complete review of its research programs and decided to emphasize armaments research and development.

In light of the structural changes within the Canadian Forces, the Chief Superintendent, Dr. L'Heureux, felt the need to rationalize the Establishment's research activities and ordered a detailed review of the administration and management procedures of the Establishment. Following this review, a Project Information Office "was established to assist CARDE and Wing management of projects by supplying current status information in a readily accessible form".[7] This information concerned the status of projects and the human and material resources assigned to them in order to monitor progress and costs. Administrative data was also computerized in order to manage support and research resources more efficiently.[8] CARDE management could thus respond more effectively to changes occurring in the defence sector. This concern for close monitoring of project resource allocations led, in 1967, to a "changeover from Division to Project accounting for manpower and funds."[9]

Earlier, in 1965, CARDE was reorganized to accommodate the increased administrative tasks and the need to better coordinate the various support units. The Chief Superintendent decided to segregate the administrative functions from the scientific functions. First, he appointed an administrative assistant "to each of the superintendents of the four scientific wings so that the latter could devote a greater part of their effort to scientific activities."[10] Second, he introduced a new hierarchical level in the CARDE organization chart and modified the terms of reference of another. The position of Assistant Chief Superintendent was created in order to coordinate and supervise the activities of the Technical Services and Administration Wings, and those of the Project Information Office. Through these changes, the Deputy Chief Superintendent was relieved of the burden of his administrative responsibilities and was able to devote his complete attention to the effective coordination and management of the research and development activities of the scientific wings. This reorganization reflected the growing importance of administration within CARDE through the creation of a separate reporting channel for this function.

In 1967, CARDE management changed the title of Wing Superintendent to Division Director, and the title of Chief Superintendent to Director General. In 1969, following a DRB directive, the Canadian Armament Research and Development Establishment was renamed the Defence Research Establishment Valcartier.

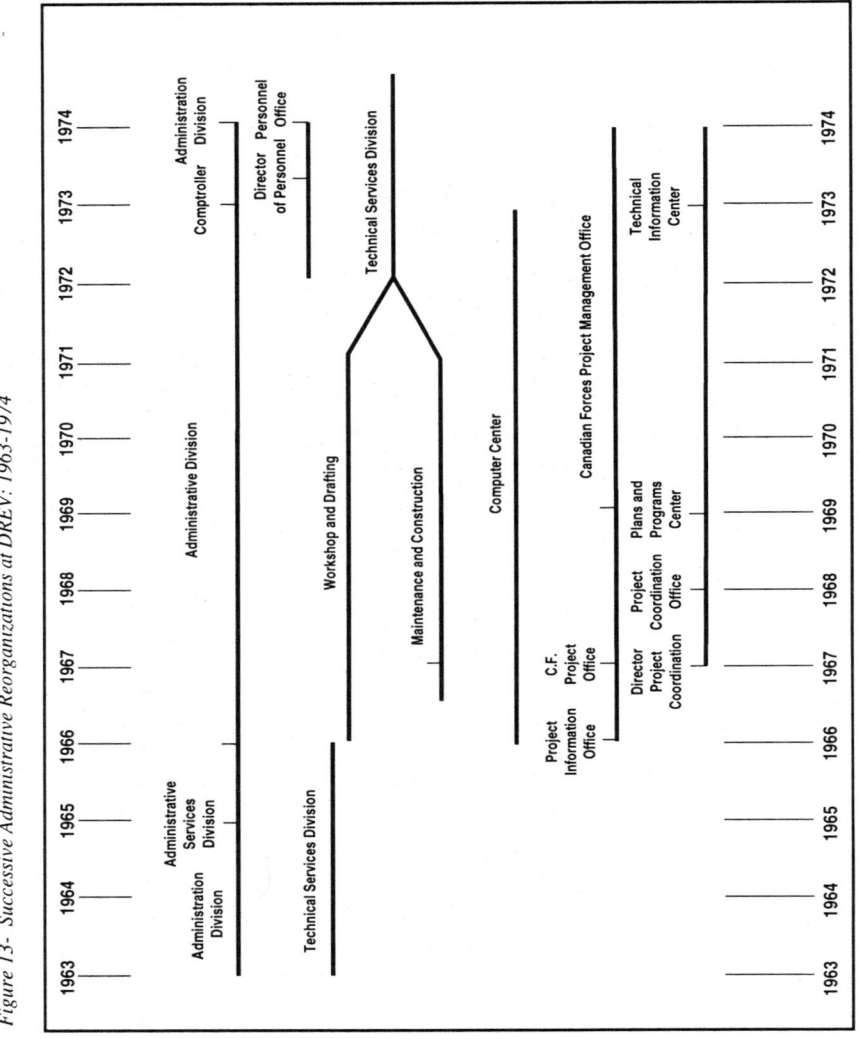

Figure 13- *Successive Administrative Reorganizations at DREV: 1963-1974*

9.1.2.1 Computerization of Administrative Data

The efforts of the Data Processing Section and the Project Information Office had a strong influence on the way that the

Establishment was managed, and some broad description of these two units would seem warranted. Prior to 1964, CARDE scientists frequently used a computer to process and analyze data obtained in their experiments. As they were fully aware of the rapid advances being made in the field of informatics, their requests for computer time progressively increased. As commonly occurs, with progress in computer technology the flow of requests continues until the capacity of a computer becomes exhausted and a more powerful computer is required. Since a very interesting document on the

The staff of the Purchasing and Finance Office in their workplace in 1966, well before the advent of office automation.

introduction of data processing in CARDE will soon be published by DREV,[11] it need only be mentioned that defence scientists had to familiarize themselves with new computer equipment on several occasions.

In 1964, CARDE management decided to create the Data Processing Section to meet the growing needs of the

Establishment's personnel. This small section, headed by T.H. Courtenay, was responsible for responding to requests from scientists and for undertaking the preliminary work needed for "the introduction of a modern electronic data processing system [for] equipment delivery and stores cataloguing by the NATO code."[12] In 1965, work progressed swiftly, but the Establishment's computer (IBM 1620) was used to capacity and plans were being drawn up for the acquisition of a "powerful hybrid analogue-digital computer [to provide for] original research in computer and analysis science as well as to provide the necessary data analysis facilities for other CARDE programs."[13]

By 1966, computerization of records was well underway and identification and cataloguing of the Establishment's entire inventory was virtually complete. Concurrently, to reflect the ever-increasing role that the computer sciences were playing in scientific programs, the Data Processing Centre, formerly a section of the Technical Services Wing, was renamed the Computer Centre and placed organizationally under the Deputy Chief Superintendent.[14] In 1967, computerization of stores management was achieved and 90 per cent of other systems development was completed. Plans were made to train personnel in the use of the COBOL programming language and to write the necessary programs for a fully automated management information system. In 1968, the Sigma 7 digital computer was acquired equipped with a batch processing monitor, magnetic tape and disk storage, and the potential to support a network of terminals.

In the following years, programmers and managers established the Management Information System (MIS) to integrate purchasing, finance, personnel and accounting data, cost records and budgetary data. According to Marcel Letarte, who was responsible for the implementation of administrative data processing at the Establishment from 1971 onwards, the purpose of the system was twofold: "First, to provide management at all levels with accurate cost data for large research programs, scientific projects, tasks and smaller work units as well as technical and administrative overhead costs. Secondly, to provide management and Heads of support services with adequate data so that a more efficient day-by-day management of all available resources may be achieved."[15]

9.1.2.2 Project Coordination

In 1964, CARDE management decided to establish another formal mechanism - the Project Information Office - for administrative control of the Establishment's activities. The purpose of the Project Information Office was to establish a complete information system to facilitate planning and monitoring of research projects. Until such time as a computerized administrative data processing system was implemented, the Project Information Office compiled and classified data manually. Early in the process, the Office introduced the Program Evaluation and Review Technique (PERT) for evaluating projects.

In 1967, the Defence Research Board embarked on a major de-centralization of authority. As a result, CARDE became responsible for four DRB Advisory Committees concerned with grants to universities and coordination of the Defence Industrial Research (DIR) Program. These new responsibilities fell to the Project Information Office, which also had to coordinate the activities of CARDE with those of the DRB Programs Office. In order to reflect the growing importance of the coordination function, the Project Information Office was renamed the Project Coordination Office (PCO).

Despite the broadening of its mandate, in 1968 the PCO was able to prepare, for the first time on a routine basis, an accurate statement of the distribution of the Establishment's manpower and financial resources among its various project activities.[16] In 1969, the Canadian Forces' Project Management Office was merged with the PCO to become the Plans and Programs Centre (PPC). The duties of the PPC thus included "the coordination of military projects as well as DRB activities, Defence Industrial Research on materials, advisory committees dealing with university grants, public relations and visits, and the administration of weekly seminars by DREV scientists and guest speakers, and of computer facilities."[17]

The Director of the PPC reported directly to the Director General of the Defence Research Establishment Valcartier. The PPC continued to improve methods and procedures for preparing regular statements of direct cost and time expended on all DREV projects, tasks, facilities and services, to enable management to base decisions on budgets, program emphasis and service function effectiveness.

In the early 1970's, "the scientific work of DREV was structured into technical programs (a number of projects grouped together into fields of interest), projects and tasks (subdivisions of projects with very specific objectives)."[18] The work of the Plans and Programs Centre was so successful that DRB considered introducing procedures similar to those of DREV for formalizing tasks at all its research establishments. The PPC was also responsible for gathering the necessary data for periodic reviews of projects to ensure that they met defence requirements and that the requisite funds were available. This data was also useful in establishing budgetary forecasts.

9.1.2.3 Reorganization of Administrative Services

A major reorganization of all DREV's activities took place in 1973. This impacted directly on administrative services. The Plans and Programs Centre, which shortly before had been renamed the Technical Information Centre, henceforth would report to the Deputy Chief. The Technical Information Centre consisted of personnel from technical activities management, the Canadian Forces Project Office, and Information Services (Library, Publications and Printing). The Administration Division included "all general administrative functions such as provisioning, accounting, safety and security, transport, and the electronic data processing of accounting data in materiel, cash, and labour."[19] In 1973, the head of this Division was called the Comptroller, but the title of Director was restored during the year following. Because of the increasing complexity of personnel management, DREV officials decided to create a Personnel Division distinct from the Comptroller Division. Finally, a Technical Services Division was formed consisting of the workshops, the design and draughting section, and the maintenance and construction section. All these support services reported directly to the Assistant Chief. In 1973 also, the titles of the three principal officers of DREV were changed: the Director-General became the Chief, the Deputy Director-General became the Deputy Chief, and the Assistant Director-General became the Assistant Chief.

9.2 THE CHANGE OF STATUS FROM SEPARATE EMPLOYER TO AN ORGANIZATION SUBJECT TO THE REGULATIONS OF THE FEDERAL PUBLIC SERVICE

The concept of the Fourth Service arose from military deliberations at the end of the Second World War on the issue of organizing defence science in Canada. The Minister of National Defence, Brooke Claxton, took the advice of the military and decided to create a highly autonomous organization within his Department. Subsequently, in 1947, Claxton introduced a Bill in the House of Commons to create the Defence Research Board, stating "our object is to set up this Board in much the same way as the National Research Council is set up"[20] so that the new organization would be free to establish its own systems and procedures for administration, finance, supply, inventory, safety and security, etc.

Parliament was disposed favourably towards the Bill and adopted it, specifying that DRB would not be subject to the rules and regulations enforced by the Civil Service Commission (later to become the Public Service Commission). Thus DRB enjoyed the status of a separate employer, free to establish its own personnel system and exercise autonomy in position classification, recruitment, hiring, evaluation, promotion, etc. Parliament had given DRB considerable freedom in the management and control of its personnel, its organization and its activities in general.

For its administrative and support positions, DRB elected to adopt a system similar to that used by the Civil Service Commission, but it was not applied to defence scientists and technicians. Instead, it was decided to establish a classification system better tailored to their professional culture. In this way, it was hoped that the Board would have greater flexibility in attracting and retaining a cadre of highly-qualified scientific personnel. Actually, DRB created two distinctly unique classification systems, one for defence scientists and one for technicians, based on individual development and the merit principle.

Scientists were categorized as Defence Scientific Service Officers (DSSO). This category contained eight levels and promotion was based on a merit system. Within the DSSO community, remuneration and promotion depended on the individual's contribution to the scientific projects in progress at the research establishments. Consequently, scientific managers had to set assignments at realistic and achievable levels based on the demonstrated capability of the individual scientist. The intention was "to structure assignments so as to provide tangible evidence of progress and to be able to distinguish the contributions of individual group members."[21] Promotions and salary increments for all DRB researchers within the DSSO structure were determined on the basis of individual professional development and merit through an annual merit review process. In many cases, it was in the interests of defence scientists to expand their knowledge through development programs offered by DRB and through post-graduate studies at the master's, doctoral or post-doctoral level. It was also in their interests to participate in the scientific activities of the defence research community through publications, attendance at seminars and symposia, and applications for patents. As was usual in the scientific world, DRB practice was to fill managerial positions with defence scientists who had about a decade of research experience. This process of promoting researchers to administrative positions probably explains why DRB senior managers and administrative officers were classified within the DSSO category. The one exception was the Chairman DRB who was not classified as a DSSO.

The remuneration and promotion system for technicians was similar to that for the scientists, in that their classification levels and salaries were determined on the basis of individual professional development. Each technician's degree of professional development was assessed annually through the performance evaluation review process, at which time recommendations were made concerning salary increase, promotion or retention at the current level. The separate employer status proved to be important when the *Public Service Staff Relations Act* was passed in 1967. This Act gave accredited public service unions the right to negotiate collective agreements with Treasury Board on the terms and conditions of employment, except those under arbitration.

Because of its separate employer status, DRB assumed all the responsibilities of Treasury Board in respect of its personnel and administrative activities. It retained the exclusive power for classification, selection, appointment and supervision of its employees independent of Treasury Board or the Public Service Commission. Union membership rights did, of course, exist long before the creation of DRB in 1947. There was, however, no legal mechanism for collective negotiation including the right to strike. This legal mechanism was established only in 1967 through an act of Parliament passed under the Liberal administration. Subsequently, there was a strong move towards unionization within the federal public service which involved, of course, DRB employees.

Because of its separate employer status, DRB had the legal authority to negotiate directly with the various unions, whereas this authority was vested in Treasury Board in the case of government departments. As was the case in most other areas of sector bargaining, the collective agreements signed between the unions and DRB took account of the distinctive features of the defence research community. Consequently, the terms and conditions of employment of DRB personnel, and hence DREV personnel, were somewhat different from those which applied generally to the federal public service.

In summary, DRB had the authority to maintain the defence research organization as a distinct entity which was not subject, in many instances, to the administrative regulations of the federal public service or the Department of National Defence. Since DRB had this degree of independence, its personnel developed, over the decades, a keen sense of belonging to their organization. DRB thus possessed a distinct organizational culture.

With the major restructuring of defence science in Canada in 1974, DRB lost most of its prerogatives and ADM(Mat) became the manager of the research establishments. For many who witnessed this transfer of responsibilities, the implications extended beyond a mere reorganization of the defence research sector. It marked the end of an era; for the scientists, restructuring changed the style of operations and the way they viewed defence research in Canada. Many DREV personnel had difficulty accepting this transition and recalled nostalgically the earlier period and the organizational culture that characterized it.

One person interviewed observed that several DREV employees displayed disappointment or resistance to change. When one organizational structure is replaced by another, employees often have difficulty perceiving the benefits but they readily identify the elements that have been lost. One argument used to encourage DREV employees to accept this organizational change was linked to the visibility of DRB's budget. Because DRB was an independent entity, its budget was more exposed to the politician's aim than that of a branch within a larger organization. The new CRAD branch, being part of the ADM(Mat) organization, received a fixed percentage of the Department's budget but it did not appear as a line item in the Public Accounts. Since CRAD's budget was established through formula funding, defence research was better protected within the ADM(Mat) organization which had a significant operating budget. This was true, at least, until the defence budget suffered major cutbacks under budgetary restraints imposed by the Canadian Government.[22]

9.3 RESHAPING OF DREV ADMINISTRATION

The restructuring of the defence research organization in 1974 marked a turning point in the history of DREV. The Defence Research Establishment Valcartier, which until then had been part of an autonomous organization with its own operating procedures, had to conform with the regulations in effect throughout the Canadian Government. DREV had to re-model its organizational structure according to the administrative guidelines of the Department of National Defence. The integration of DREV within DND did not, however, call for fundamental changes in the former's organizational structure since that of the Department was similar, in many ways, to its divisional structure. On the other hand, implementation of the regulations and standards governing work conditions, staff relations and management was quite another matter. From 1974 onwards, work patterns had to conform more closely with the regulations of the federal public service, and the Establishment's administrative standards and procedures had to be more closely harmonized with those of the Department of National Defence. In many instances, the changes were radical. DREV had to abandon long-established policies and procedures or revise them considerably to suit the new organizational environment.

Because of its magnitude, this process was unique in the history of DREV, although the program reconfiguration currently taking place at the Establishment as part of the reengineering of CRAD scientific programs will likely exert a significant impact on the evolution of DREV's administrative structure.

9.3.1   Changes in DREV Management

The year 1974 marked the beginning of a new era. At that time, ADM(Mat) and DRB signed a transitional agreement which allowed DRB administrative procedures to remain in effect until they could be replaced by the rules and regulations of the Department of National Defence. Once the Department's administrative standards were in place, an official directive was issued to annul DRB's procedures. According to Mr. E.J. Bobyn, former Chief of DREV and the first Chief Research and Development, CRAD's main problem at the time:

> "was to retain the unique administrative system that we had developed within the DRB. It was always our policy to try and simplify the administrative procedures both in procurement, personnel management, project management, project assessment and so on, so as to reduce the time and effort required for that activity to a minimum. We always tried to make certain that the number of administrative people involved in any process, in any Establishment, was a very small fraction of the overall scientific and technical resources. We tried very hard to combat a statement sometimes used by the high-powered administrators in the Civil Service, that: "If it was not for all those scientists we could sure run this Establishment very well". That may sound as a bit of a joke but it is essentially what some administrators used to think. That is not the way to run a Research Establishment; it must not be overgoverned

by strict administrative procedures. Now, when we were integrated into the DND, there were two very important systems that needed to be integrated; one was the Personnel Management System and the other one was the Project Management System. My most important objective was to retain control of the scientific program and the resources necessary to carry out these programs. I succeeded in resisting efforts by Departmental personnel, particulary the military people, to adopt their old routines and systems for the management of their military bases. For instance, DREV (Valcartier) could have been subservient to the Valcartier Camp (CFB Valcartier) in all procedures."[23]

This transition involving administrative, financial and supply systems took place smoothly and gradually until the new structure was officially confirmed on 28 October 1980. The organizational structure and legal status of the Defence Research Establishments, including DREV, within the Department of National Defence were approved in a telegram signed by the Deputy Minister of National Defence, Mr. C.R. Nixon, and the Chief of the Defence Staff, General R.M. Withers.[24]

9.3.2 Integration of DREV Staff within the Public Service: A New Classification Structure and Formal Position Descriptions

With the reorganization of defence research, the separate employer status disappeared. All DREV employees became public servants subject to the *Public Service Employment Act* and the *Public Service Staff Relations Act*, as well as all the internal directives and procedures of the Department of National Defence. As often happens in government, however, DREV employment categories and related conditions did not radically change on 1 April 1974, the date of integration into DND. A transition phase was needed to allow for reclassification of all DREV positions and for revision of the grade structure to ensure compatibility with Public Service policies and procedures. According to persons interviewed, the transition phase from the DRB classification system to the Public Service system was somewhat difficult because the procedures to be followed were lengthy and exacting and the agencies involved displayed some disinterest in the special requirements of the research community.

The difficulties of converting employment categories from DRB to the Public Service varied according to category. In the case of administrative and support positions, the transition was relatively easy since there were no major differences between the two systems. It was quite another matter as far as the defence scientist and technician categories were concerned. Following the integration of DRB personnel into DND, the Public Service Commission and Treasury Board revised the DSSO category. During this process it was decided that personnel occupying administrative positions should be reclassified as members of the administrative category of the Public Service. DRB scientists working in fields such as engineering, mathematics, physics, biology and the social sciences were grouped into the Defence Scientist (DS) category, a new category within the Public Service.

Treasury Board and the Public Service Commission established the classification and selection standards for the DS category, developed more detailed descriptions for each of the levels, together with more stringent selection standards and staffing procedures. The performance evaluation system was also modified to ensure conformity with the criteria and requirements of the Public Service. Compared with the former system, the new system was more highly structured, comprising more complete task descriptions and a more formal and rigorous competitive process. Managers had to devote considerably more time to the evaluation process because of its complexity and its stricter rules of application. A document discussing all these issues was prepared in 1976 and introduced in 1977.

Significantly, the classification system for defence scientists preserved the unique characteristic of being personnel-oriented, based on individual development rather than on the work description. Thus, an exception was made since the merit system was not normally favoured by the PSC. According to Peter Devitt, Director Defence Scientist Plans and Programs (DDSPP), the merit system remained essentially intact following the transfer of defence scientists into the Public Service because it was well-structured and well-managed. In addition, abolishing the merit system would have caused too great a disruption in the defence research and development organization.

For the technicians, integration carried more serious consequences than for the scientists. The PSC and Treasury Board considered that their work was equivalent to that of groups already existing within the Public Service and that the rules applicable to those groups would also apply to defence technicians. In other words, the classification system based on individual development was replaced by a system based on the work description.

Consequently, managers and defence scientists, often in collaboration with technicians, set about developing position descriptions for individual technicians and having the positions evaluated against Public Service criteria in order to establish their levels. As a result, technicians seeking promotion had to compete for higher-level positions. This process often led to disruption in operations, particularly when experienced technicians had to change fields and transfer to another division in order to obtain a promotion.

The merit system for technicians was replaced by a lock-step system which provided salary increments for satisfactory performance up to the maximum level within the technician grades as established through the collective agreement. Although it cannot be clearly determined whether this change in the management system was advantageous or otherwise for the technicians, it was viewed as highly detrimental at the time of integration. Following the announcement of the new classification system, 160 technicians submitted requests for review and re-evaluation. Most of these requests were settled through consultation, but 55 technicians remained dissatisfied and submitted classification grievances. At the time, this broke all records for a single administrative unit.

The amount of time devoted to writing position descriptions steadily increased, and those technicians who were still dissatisfied with their classifications exerted enormous pressure to have their statements of duties and position descriptions rewritten and re-evaluated. This whole process consumed a great deal of time and effort, and introduced delays in classification, staffing and performance evaluation. Morale declined significantly and, according to some persons interviewed, technicians began to place their rights and personal needs before those of the organization. In addition, during the period that DREV was part of DRB, the administrative burden on the DS population was kept to a strict minimum, but this was no longer possible following integration.

9.3.3 The Loss of Separate Employer Status and its Impact on Staff Relations at DREV

With the restructuring of the defence research community, Treasury Board assumed authority over collective bargaining for all the Canadian defence research establishments, including DREV. Following the reclassification of its employees, DREV personnel fell into 23 employment groups, of which 21 were unionized. The scientific and most of the other professional groups were represented by the Professional Institute of the Public Service of Canada (PIPSC), while most of the technicians, office personnel and tradespersons were represented by the Union of National Defence Employees (UNDE), a union affiliated with the Public Service Alliance of Canada (PSAC). Finally, the electronics technicians were represented by the International Brotherhood of Electrical Workers (IBEW).

On 1 April 1974, staff relations took a more formal turn with the introduction of well-documented labour-management consultations, and employees began participating in the Labour Management Relations Committee (LMRC), the Safety and Health Committee (SHC) and the Employee Aid Program (EAP). For many, this interaction coupled with union action served to clarify the rights and privileges of employees in various categories, eliminated any possibility of paternalism and ensured that employees were classified on an equitable basis. The committee discussions also led to safer working conditions and to improved methods of operation in hazardous environments. The unions had no hesitation in using the grievance procedure in pursuing their rights. Some groups affiliated with the Public Service Alliance of Canada also exercised the right to strike in 1975, 1980 and 1991, but as part of a general strike within the Public Service. No situations at DREV were ever sufficiently serious to provoke local disputes.

According to some persons interviewed, labour-management relations were generally good despite a few minor incidents. In recent years, relations have even improved, perhaps because of the serious problems faced by all employees in this difficult period of downsizing during which management and the unions have worked together with the common objective of protecting personnel to the extent possible. General downsizing of the Public Service and cutbacks in certain programs obviously exert a strong impact on the morale of all employees, provoking a reaction to change and a sense of insecurity. These problems transcend traditional labour-management relations.

9.3.4 The Attempt to Integrate Certain Establishment Services into the Valcartier Base

Over the years, the organizational structure of DREV has seen few major changes. But this might have been otherwise if a mid-1970's NDHQ decision to regard the defence research establishments as lodger units of Canadian Forces bases had been implemented.[25] The Department of National Defence believed that economies of scale could be realized by integrating the support services of the defence research establishments (transport, supply, construction, maintenance, etc.) with those of their host bases.

In order to comply with this Departmental position, the Canadian Forces Base Valcartier and DREV formed teams to study mechanisms for integrating support services and to establish procedures. After years of study, the Base Commander and the Chief of DREV jointly recommended against proceeding with this integration because of the extensive needs of the Establishment, the lack of available resources at the Base to meet these needs and the fact that the Base support units were often away on exercise. Following a series of discussions, this recommendation was finally accepted by ADM(Mat) in 1980.[26]

9.4   ADMINISTRATIVE STRUCTURE OF DREV DURING THE 1980's

During the 1980's, there were no major changes in the administrative structure of DREV, despite the proliferation of new theories which have surfaced in management science since 1975. ADM(Mat) and DREV managers nevertheless attempted to derive maximum advantage from theories such as management by objectives, incentive theory (for example, the Merit Award Program), organizational theory and matrix management. Computerization of administrative data, which was pursued during the 1960's and 1970's, was further expanded. Electronic data processing as a management tool continued to grow in importance, and the Informatics Centre was formed in 1987 to provide an integrated capability for administrative and scientific data processing. Finally, as will be seen in the Conclusion, DREV is currently pursuing a major management initiative through

Evolution of the Administrative Structure
of Defence Research Establishment Valcartier   313

Figure 14 - DREV Organization Chart for 1974.

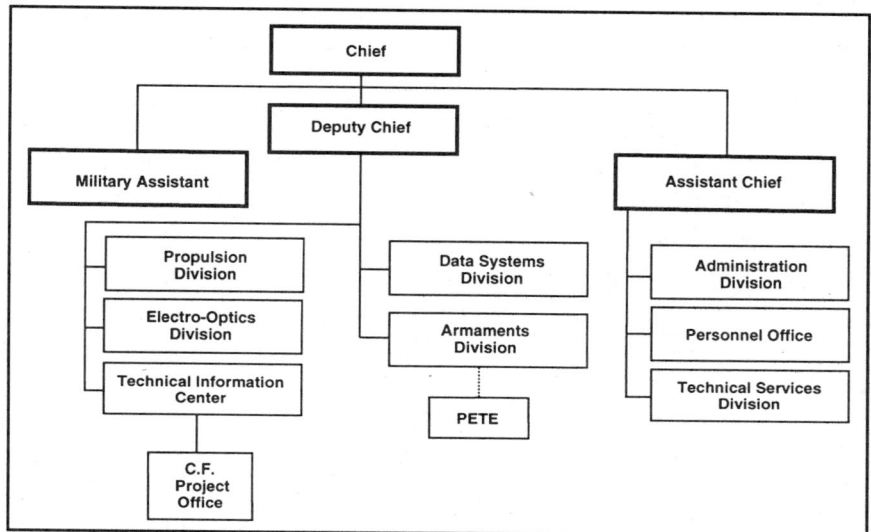

Source: *DREV Annual Report, 1974, p.4.*

Figure 15 - DREV Organization Chart for 1980.

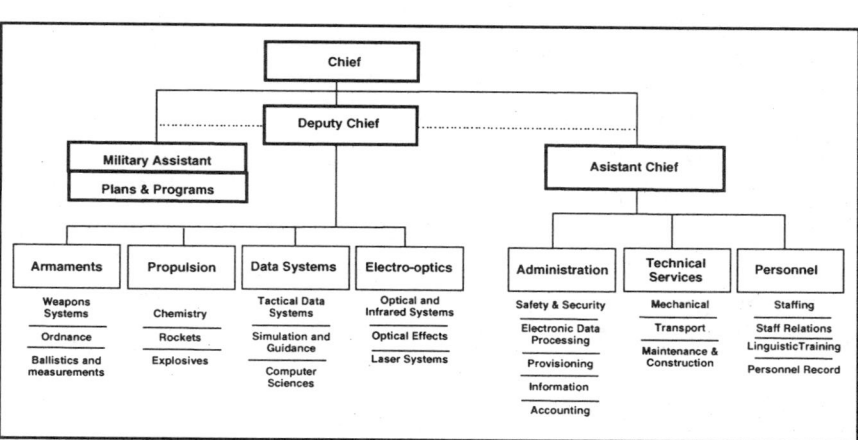

Source: *DREV Family Day Brochure.*

organizational reengineering of its scientific programs.

Aside from the current reorganization, there were no major

structural reorganizations at DREV during the past two decades.

As we have seen, the divisional structure was tailored to the scientific program in that it divided scientific activities along the lines of the four defence technology areas under development at the Establishment. Apart from changes in names to better reflect the fields of activity, the current divisional structure (Command and Control, Electro-Optics, Energetic Materials and Armaments) corresponds essentially to that existing in 1974.

Over the past 20 years, the organizational structure for support services at DREV has experienced a number of major changes which cannot be described in detail herein. The DREV annual reports from 1975 onwards do not provide a systematic account of the main reasons for organizational changes made during the specific years. More importantly, no annual reports were produced between 1975 and 1979. After 1979, the reports describe only the main scientific activities undertaken at DREV. Finally, DREV has not published an annual report since 1989-1990. Despite the lack of information on administrative matters, a number of related documents have been published which help to fill some of the gaps in DREV's corporate memory. Even so, it remains impossible to provide a detailed description of the decisional process underlying the changes which have appeared in DREV's organizational chart over the past twenty years.

After 1974, the first document to appear describing the various divisions of the Establishment was produced on 20 September 1980 on the occasion of Family Day. A comparison of this document with the 1974 Annual Report shows how the organizational structure changed during those years. The DREV organization charts for 1974 and 1980 are shown in Figures 14 and 15 respectively. As will be noted, the only major change was the partitioning of the Technical Information Centre in the late 1970s. Information Services (Library, Publications and Printing) was transferred back to the Administration Division, and the Canadian Forces Project Office was disbanded. The Military Assistant retained his position with all the prerogatives and responsibilities inherent to his function, while the Plans and Programs Office retained its mandate for information coordination, management of intra- and extra-mural research programs, processing of patent applications, provision of information to the public, etc.

In 1980, the organization of the Assistant Chief was as shown in Figure 15. "The Administration Division [was] divided into five services: Safety and Security, Electronic Data Processing, Provisioning, Accounting and Information Services. [...] The Safety and Security Services [were] responsible for controlling access to the Establishment, [...] for records, mail delivery and accident prevention, the Health Centre and first aid stations, organized visits and information security especially in sensitive areas of national security".[27] "The Electronic Data Processing Services [provided] human resources necessary for the development, support and scheduled processing of a wide range of business data processing applications; these [included] an integrated management system used in decision-making by managers and in the performance of regular duties by personnel of other services."[28] This reflected the realization of a decade of effort in computerizing administrative information. "The Provisioning Services [included] the Purchasing and Stores Services. The Purchasing Services [had to] take the necessary action for the procurement of goods and services required for the efficient operation of DREV; these [were] obtained through Supply and Services Canada or, in some cases, from the suppliers themselves."[29] At the time, the Stores Services operated "six material and equipment distribution points". It was responsible for controlling equipment distribution and ordering the materiel needed to maintain adequate stocks pertinent to DREV needs. "The Accounting Services [included] the Financial and Inventory Services. [Financial Services was] charged with the management of public funds and the gathering of relevant data, the payment of accounts to suppliers and all travel arrangements; the Inventory Service [ensured] control and audit of all equipments used or stocked by DREV. [Finally...]the Information Services [included] the Library, Publications and [characteristic of the times] Word Processing Services. The Library Service [was] tasked with the acquisition of technical and scientific documents, manuals and periodicals for use by DREV personnel. The Publications Service [was] involved in all aspects of the preparation of documents published by DREV thus ensuring their high standard."[30] Word Processing Services was responsible for formatting the final versions of the Establishment's documents.

In 1980, the Personnel Directorate became the Personnel Office. With only 12 employees, it was the smallest administrative unit in the Establishment. The Personnel Office administered "the salaries of all employees, maintained personnel records and provided information concerning pension plans, insurance plans, etc". Because of the complexity of these functions, the Director of Personnel assigned officers exclusively to fulfil the duties of staffing and staff relations. The main task of the staffing officers was to fill all permanent and temporary non-scientific positions at DREV and "to provide management with information concerning job descriptions and classification."[31] As previously noted, staff relations had become increasingly important for the Establishment and a staff relations officer was appointed to the Personnel Office to advise management on employer and employee relations. He also acted as "liaison officer for all training programs and [organized] courses in personnel administration. He [was] further responsible for the bilingualism program and [advised] management in this regard."[32]

In the early 1980's, the Technical Services Division continued to provide design, draughting, maintenance, construction, transport and workshop services. Through its highly sophisticated workshop, the Mechanical Section designed, draughted and manufactured "defence weapon prototypes and various equipments for research requirements."[33] The Construction and Maintenance Section provided "engineering services, [tailored] the laboratories to the requirements of research projects, [carried] out new construction and [took] care of the maintenance"[34] of infrastructures. The Technical Services Division also included the

Transport Section which, in 1980, had 65 vehicles including 14 heavy trucks. Technical Services also operated a printing press and a photographic laboratory on behalf of Information Services. Printing and graphic arts services would later be moved from this Division to the Administration Division.

Figure 16- DREV Organizational Chart for 1989

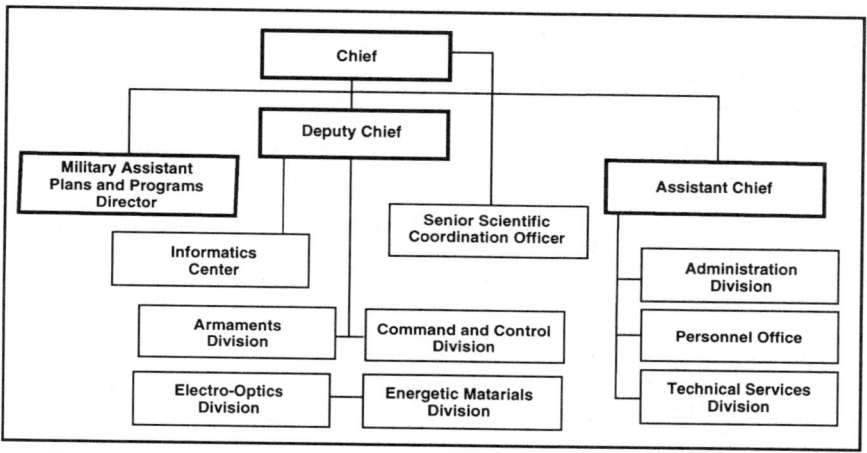

Source: *DREV Annual Report 1989, 1990, p. 77.*

As shown in the organization chart for 1989 (Figure 16), DREV management made two significant changes by creating the position of Senior Scientific Coordination Officer DREV and regrouping all data processing functions within the Informatics Centre under the Deputy Chief. The Senior Scientific Coordination Officer DREV reported directly to the Chief and assisted "in coordinating the Establishment's R&D activities"[35] and in conducting strategic planning for the Establishment.

The Informatics Centre was equipped with two central computers, one for processing unclassified data and the other for classified work. The computer used for processing classified scientific and administrative data was housed in a shielded room (Faraday cage) with controlled access. Aside from the two exceptions noted, DREV's organizational structure remained essentially unchanged throughout the 1980's and early 1990's during which period only minor changes occurred in the missions and responsibilities of the various administrative units and support services.

As shown in Figure 17, the DREV organization of 1994 was similar to that of 1989. The four scientific divisions, reflecting four defence technologies, continued to report to the Deputy Chief. In 1994, with the aim of improving technology transfer to industry, DREV management established the position of Technology Transfer Advisor reporting to the Deputy Chief. Another position, that of Explosives Safety Officer, was also established following the unfortunate accident of June 1990 involving two members of the Armaments Division, one of whom died. As for support services, the Informatics Centre was placed under the authority of the Assistant Chief who was responsible for the other three administrative divisions. In sum, the DREV organization remained essentially unchanged between 1974 and 1994. But the current reengineering of DREV will undoubtedly lead to significant changes. Before discussing the future of DREV, some commentary on the changing pattern of human and financial resources would seem appropriate.

9.5   DREV HUMAN RESOURCES

9.5.1   Recruitment of Scientists

At the end of the Second World War, CARDE experienced some difficulty in recruiting the scientific staff required for its mission. Many scientists conscripted during the war returned to their civilian occupations and the British scientific advisors progressively returned home. Nevertheless, CARDE was able to retain some uniformed scientists. The Department of National Defence pondered over the form that defence research should take. Colonel W.W. Goforth then proposed the creation of an organization supervised by civilians which could better attract pre-eminent scientists and young graduates. The proposal was accepted by Parliament and DRB was created in 1947.

Figure 17- DREV Organizational Chart for 1994 (April)

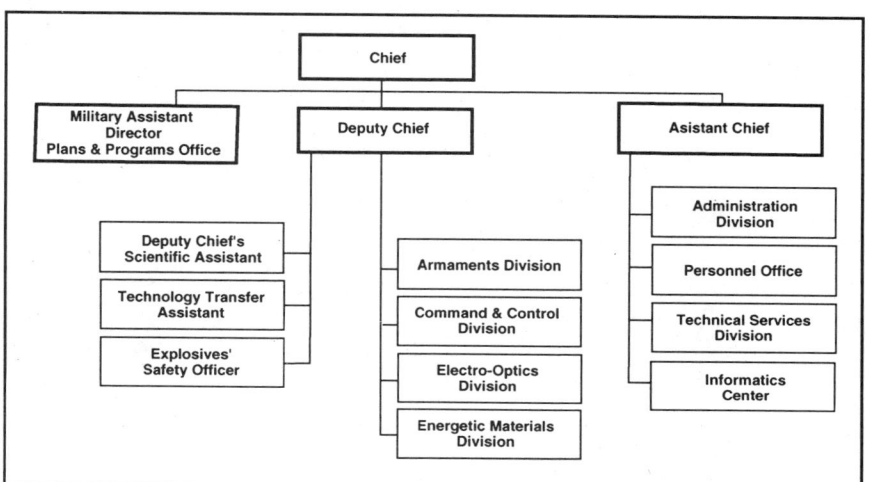

Like most Canadian scientific organizations, DRB faced a difficult challenge in recruiting scientists. The Canadian scientific community was small and there was an insufficient number of researchers and technicians to meet the needs of Canadian science. DRB met the challenge in two ways, first by recruiting from abroad and, second, by hiring young scientists and sending them to the United Kingdom and the United States to acquire the requisite expertise. DRB also funded university research in Canada, and contributed significantly through grants to the development of the University of Toronto Institute of Aerophysics (UTIA). Created in 1948, UTIA's mission was "to teach and conduct research in supersonic aerodynamics."[36] DRB's efforts came to fruition with the initiation of the Velvet Glove project. Many young scientists formed part of the research team for this important project, and the team included at least one UTIA graduate in the person of Dr. Gerald Bull.

Figure 18 - Fluctuation in Human Resources of the Establishment: 1952-1953 to 1996-1997

FISCAL YEARS	SCIENT. & PROF.	TECHNIC.	OTHER	MIL OFF.	MIL OTHER	TOTAL
1996-97*	120	99	121	7	6	353
1995-96*	130	115	190	7	7	449
1994-95	146	131	224	8	12	521
1993-94	144	145	254	8	12	563
1992-93	143	157	257	8	10	575
1991-92	141	152	261	7	10	571
1990-91	145	164	272	7	9	597
1989-90	148	168	284	7	9	616
1988-89	136	161	287	7	9	600
1987-88	136	163	256	6	10	571
1986-87	143	166	256	7	9	581
1985-86	143	160	264	5	10	582
1984-85	142	166	267	5	9	589
1983-84	151	171	299	6	11	638
1982-83	145	174	301	5	9	634
1981-82						
1980-81						
1979-80	134	200	311	9	11	665
1978-79						
1977-78						
1976-77						
1975-76	130	200	350	9	11	700
1974-75	130	202	350	8	10	700
1973-74	145	300	238	7	10	700
1972-73	145	300	212	13	30	700
1971-72	145	310	210	15	30	700
1970-71	140	62	302	16	32	800
1969-70	151	61		17		
1968-69	121	59		18		
1967-68	119			18		
1966-67						
1965-66	115	62		26		900
1964-65	109					825
1963-64	98					780
1962-63	111					845
1961-62	140			27	111	1000
1960-61	135			27	111	1000
1959-60	135			27	143	1000
1958-59						
1957-58						
1956-57						
1955-56	112	173	493	29	115	922
1954-55	101	175	494	24	95	889
1953-54	90	160	474	26	66	816
1952-53	76	145	461	22	66	770
1951-52						
1950-51						
1949-50						
1948-49						
1947-48						
1946-47						
1945-46						

* *Estimated values*
Source: Johanne Cantin, Plans & Programs Office.

During the 1950's, when CARDE's need for scientific and technical personnel was growing rapidly, CARDE management started to benefit from Canada's efforts to develop a strong scientific community. As shown in Figure 18, the Establishment experienced fewer difficulties in recruiting scientific and technical personnel. The very existence of CARDE was an influencing factor, for the growth of the defence research organization contributed to the critical mass needed to induce some of Canada's most brilliant scientists to remain and work in their home country. In other words, the creation of organizations such as DRB strengthened the Canadian scientific community and substantially reduced the brain drain to other nations. In parallel, there was an increase in the number of doctoral graduates and a greater enrolment rate for junior university training. According to Chartrand, this growth promoted the "rapid development of [university] research during the 1950's and 1960's [at least in Quebec, for] an increasing number of newly-hired professors held doctoral degrees. In addition to teaching, they sought to pursue research activities and this led to a greater diversification of research. During this period, every faculty wanted to offer a full spectrum of specialties in its discipline."[37] Thus, the scarcity of scientists and technicians became progressively less problematic during the 1950's. This remarkable growth in the Canadian research community enabled CARDE to recruit the highly-qualified manpower needed for its research program.

As shown in Figure 18, recruitment ceased to be problematic and the growth in CARDE's human resources kept pace with the implementation of major research projects such as Velvet Glove and the applied research projects on ballistic missile defence and lasers. Scientific personnel recruited by CARDE during the 1950's and 1960's included chemists, specialists in electronics, computer scientists, mathematicians, statisticians, aerophysicists and physicists, as well as chemical, metallurgical, electrical and mechanical engineers. The Establishment also recruited technicians skilled in most of these disciplines to assist the scientists. In addition to scientific an technical personnel, CARDE hired a number of support personnel, such as administrators, secretaries, desk officers, skilled workers, photographers, librarians, security officers, etc.

The records are somewhat obscure following the integration of DREV into the Department of National Defence up to fiscal year 1979/1980 for which data is available. During that year, the number of defence scientists was up slightly even though the overall establishment strength was slightly lower. The situation was similar in 1982/1983. This trend continued for a further year before the DS population started to decline in the same way as for the other employment categories. Apart from slight fluctuations, the total establishment strength no longer oscillated around 700 as in the early 1970's, but dropped to between 630 and 570 during the 1980's and the early 1990's. Since the DREV budget remained sensibly constant, the explanation of this phenomenon must be found elsewhere. Part of the explanation lies in the increased use of computerization (for example, simulation instead of experimentation) and of office automation for some of the administrative tasks of the Establishment. This led to a decrease in the ratio of support personnel to scientific personnel from 7:1 in 1974, through 6:1 in 1982 to 4:1 in recent years. Another contributing factor was the demise of the major projects which had absorbed a large number of scientific and technical personnel. As we have seen in Chapter 6, the Canadian government embarked on a major re-equipment program in the early 1980's which spawned additional research requirements, but it appears to have had little effect on the number of personnel employed at the Establishment. Since then, the trend to reduce government expenditures has exerted a major impact on the Establishment strength. This is clearly evident in Figure 17. The principles of "do more with less" and then of "do less with less" led directly to a steady decline in DREV personnel which will continue markedly through fiscal years 1995/1996 and 1996/1997.

9.5.2 The Women of DREV

During the Second World War, Canada looked to the women of the country as well as the men to assist in the war effort. Although war production did not call for qualified personnel, defence research certainly did. There were only a few female graduates in the pure and applied sciences, and correspondingly only a few who took part in the war effort as military researchers. Although the pool of potential candidates was limited, the Inspection Board of the United Kingdom and Canada succeeded in hiring nine female scientists (test and evaluation) as follows: Mabel Hunt, Margaret Jackson, Barbara McGuire, Dorothy Peers, Joan and Margaret Pettipher, Catherine Synge, Patricia Timmins and Lorraine Wilkinson. At least three of these women started their work in 1941, and all nine remained until the end of the war. There is no information on female scientists who may have worked in facilities that were eventually integrated into CARDE. Equally, there is no information on women who may have provided support services in scientific research.

At the end of the war, government activities in munitions inspection diminished significantly with the decline in need. The female scientists working at Valcartier, in common with the majority of scientists working on the war effort, returned to their civilian careers. The Army merged the various elements of the military technological complex at Valcartier to form CARDE, but over twenty years passed before women again occupied scientific positions at the Establishment. Women nevertheless occupied other positions at the Establishment during this period, particularly secretarial and support positions. There was a marked absence of women in management or other non-traditional careers. One year after CARDE was formed, Helen Rojeska was hired as a technician and remained with the Establishment until 1972. For five years she was the only woman working directly on defence research projects, and was thus a pioneer in her field. In 1951, Jocelyne O'Donnell joined the scientific and technical staff of

CARDE as a technical officer.

Another 16 years passed before the Establishment recruited its first female defence scientist, a chemist by the name of Joan Armour (1967-1980). Ten years afterwards, the Establishment hired Madeleine Bousquet (1977-1982), a graduate in computer science (see Figure 18). Evidently, this situation resulted from the paucity of female graduates in the applied sciences and engineering. But this was not the only explanation, for the proportion of women in the scientific community started to increase during the 1960s, but there was no proportionate increase in the CARDE scientific population. Perhaps this anomaly was due to the particular nature of defence research and the fact that there were many other employment opportunities for scientists at the time.

In 1977, Parliament passed the Canadian Human Rights Act which led DREV management to intensify its efforts to increase the proportion of women employed in the Establishment. After this law was passed, the Public Service Commission of Canada introduced affirmative action programs (later called employment equity programs) to promote employment of women, visible minorities, native peoples and the handicapped.

In parallel with other federal government organizations, DREV made affirmative action an integral element of its hiring programs. As we shall see later, DREV had some success in hiring visible minorities and also in hiring women in non-traditional occupations. DREV management took the pro-active step of publishing a promotional booklet entitled "Women and Science at DREV" aimed at encouraging women to pursue non-traditional careers as defence researchers and technicians. This booklet described the daily work and the aspirations of seven women employed in various specialized fields at DREV. The Public Service Commission subsequently awarded a Certificate of Merit to DREV management in recognition of its efforts. DREV management was also aware of the need to offer women interesting career prospects and to provide opportunities for their promotion within the organization. Although there were relatively few women amongst DREV's personnel, some rose to managerial positions, for instance Madeleine Pelletier and Claudine Lussier of Information Services, and Julienne Dionne and Jana Viens of the Pay Office.

As we have just seen, the first female defence scientist was hired in 1967 and the second in 1977. From 1977 to 1980, five other women were hired by the Establishment in the field of

DREV female staff Christmas dinner, 17 December 1970. At the head table, from left to right: Mrs. Madeleine Pelletier, Julienne Dionne and Eileen Coss, Nurse Carmelle Morin, and Mrs. Andrée Delisle, Francine Gaudreault, Louise Butler, Monique Paquet, Alice Laroche, Constance Bleau and Mary Sturton.

computer science. In 1984, the Establishment hired its first female mechanical engineer. In 1985, DREV employed 13 female defence scientists: a mechanical engineer, an electrical engineer, four chemists and seven computer scientists. In summary, the Establishment hired its first female scientist in 1967 and 22 other

Figure 19 - List of Women Occupying Managerial or Scientific Positions at DREV

SCIENTIFIC WOMEN AT DREV

Name	Taken on / Struck off Strength	Discipline	Research Field
JOAN ARMOUR	02-10-67 to 02-07-80	PhD Phys. Chemistry	Chemical Lasers
MADELEINE BOUSQUET	22-08-77 to 21-08-82	BSc Comp. Science	Data Bases
HÉLÈNE MEUNIER	10-07-78 to 26-05-79	BSc Math	Data Bases
LYNE DESGROSEILLERS	01-05-79 to 04-01-95	BSc Math/Comp. Science	Decision Aids
CLAIRE GIRARD	26-05-80 to 07-03-87	BSc Comp. Science	Data Bases
SUZANNE CLOUTIER-MARQUIS	09-06-80 to 07-08-87	BSc Comp. Science	Display Systems and Decision Aids
LINDA DRUET	08-10-82 to 25-11-94	BSc Chemistry MSc Organic Chemistry PhD Physics/Chem.	Formulation and Stability of Gun Powders and Propellants
MARLÈNE GAUVIN	12-09-83	BSc Comp. Science/Math	Automated Intelligence Functions
JOSÉE MAILLETTE	02-04-84 to 12-07-91	BASc Mech. Eng. MSc Mech. Eng.	Internal Ballistics
FRANCE BEAUPRÉ	21-05-85	BASc Chem. Eng. MSc Chem. Eng.	Gun Powders
PROTHIBA TOMAR	03-06-85 to 29-04-88	BASc Chem. Eng.	Infrared Decoys
JOSÉE MORIN	12-06-85 to 05-01-95	BEng. Elec. Eng.	Infrared Imaging
FRANÇOISE REID	12-08-85	BSc Comp. Eng. BSc Math	Simulation of IR Guidance Systems
MICHELINE BÉLANGER	04-05-87	BSc Math/Comp. Science MSc Comp. Science	Decision Aids
AGNÈS LEE	11-01-88 to 10-01-90	MSc Chemistry	Composite Materials Rheology
IRENE HOOTON	28-03-88 to 04-07-95	BSc Chemistry PhD Solid State Chem.	Composite Explosives
MANON BOLDUC	09-05-88	BASc Mech. Eng MSc Comp. Mat.	Materials and Terminal Ballistics
IRENE ABI-ZEID	16-05-88 to 14-10-92	BSc Math MSc Math	Weapons Effectiveness
SYLVIE VILLENEUVE	13-02-89	BSc Chemistry MSc Polymer Chem.	Rocket Propellants
SONIA THIBOUTOT	23-11-89	PhD Chemistry	Composite Energetic Materials
ANN BRADFIELD	09-07-90 to 03-06-94	BA App. Math	Simulation and Weapons Effectiveness
SOPHIE LAROCHELLE	25-06-92	BSc Eng. Phys. MSc Physics PhD Optics	Laser Detection and Optical Countermeasures
SYLVIA LAM	01-09-92	BSc Comp. Science MSc Surveying	Geomatics

FEMALE MANAGERS AT DREV

Name	Taken on / Struck off Strength	Research Field
JOAN KANE	01-04-74 to 15-01-92	Program Manager
MADELEINE PELLETIER	18-01-43 to 20-08-80	Chief, Information Services
CLAUDINE LUSSIER	04-05-87 to 30-03-95	Chief, Information Services
JULIENNE DIONNE	01-07-48 to 16-10-74	Chief, Pay Services
JANA VIENS	18-11-80 to 29-03-96	Chief, Pay Services

female defence scientists during the 1977-1992 period. Of this total, 13 left for various reasons (promotions outside DND, transfers within DND, family reasons, etc.), and in 1994 10 were still employed at the Establishment.

According to one person interviewed, DREV was fortunate to have been able to hire and retain such a large proportion of the relatively few women who have graduated in engineering over the years. This same person considered that several factors impeded DREV in its attempts to hire and promote women. One was the linguistic situation in Québec which induced some anglophones to relocate to other provinces. But the most important factor was the massive cutback in the public service which led several women to leave voluntarily with the attendant loss of any re-hiring possibility (see Figure 19). In any event, of the 4,406 people who worked at the Defence Research Establishment Valcartier during its fifty-year history, 840 were women who were employed as clerks, secretaries, personnel officers, librarians, technicians or defence scientists.

9.6 DREV FINANCIAL RESOURCES

As seen earlier, the Establishment's budget between 1945 and 1956 grew significantly with the development of infrastructure and the implementation of the Velvet Glove project. In 1956, the CARDE budget experienced further growth with the inception of the ballistic missile defence program. Between 1956/1957 and 1960/1961, the budget grew by almost two million dollars. During this period, actual expenditures were greater than forecast expenditures and supplementary funding was required to cover the projected deficits. This was due mainly to underestimates of the total payroll for three of the five years in question. In this context, CARDE hired 200 employees between 1956 and 1960 (see Figure 17), an increase of almost 20% in establishment strength. As a result, the total payroll soared by almost one million dollars and its share of actual expenditures increased by 8% to reach 58% of CARDE's actual budget in 1960/1961. Aside from salaries, the other contributors to the overruns during this period were supplies, equipment and miscellaneous items.

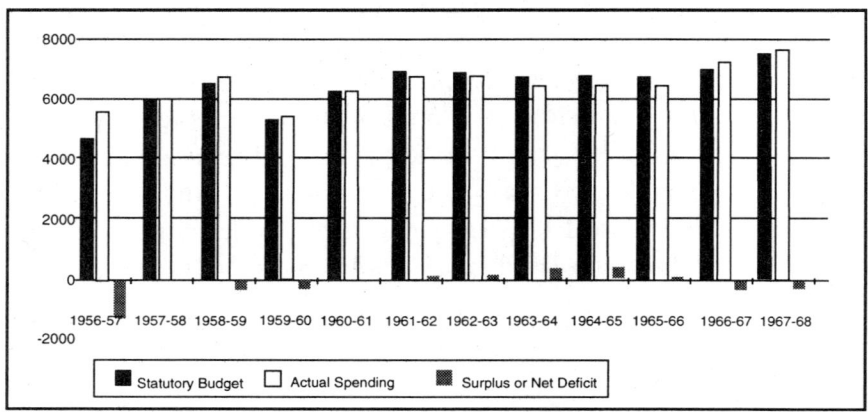

Figure 20- *Establishment Budget for Fiscal Years 1956/1957 to 1967/1968 Actual Expenditures and Net Surplus or Deficit (Thousands of Current Dollars)*

During the period 1961/1962 to 1965/1966, budgetary allocations were always higher than actual expenditures. As a result, the budget grew only slightly ($69,000), but this represented a decline in real terms since the inflation rate remained constant at about 1.2% from 1962 onwards. During these years, the budget appears to reflect the slack period following the termination of Project Lookout and Black Brant and the re-assignment of researchers from these projects to other activities, as well as the greater importance accorded to conventional armaments in the Establishment's research programs. This resulted in a slight decline in salary and supply expenditures in 1963/1964 and a surplus of 6.4% of allocated budget ($429,206 out of $6,699,700). A similar situation occurred during the following year when CARDE expended less than its allocated budget and showed a surplus of almost 6.1%. In 1965/1966, expenditures on Establishment activities increased and only 1.2% of the allocated budget was under-utilized.

As the largest DRB establishment, CARDE received a significant share of DRB's resources. As we have seen, salary and equipment costs increased during the 1960's[38] and, in order to accommodate the increased salary costs, CARDE elected to reduce expenditures in other areas, including equipment acquisition. Thus, the total payroll, which was 60% of CARDE's budget in 1961/1962, rose to 62% of the budget four years later. What, at first glance, can seem like a marginal increase, is, in fact, considerably more than that. Pay rises were higher than the actual rise in expenditures, but that came at a cost since funds had to be found elsewhere, and cuts were made in other expenditures, including in equipment procurement. In 1966, CARDE received 25.2% of DRB's budget, which was almost as large as the combined budgets of the second and third largest DRB establishments, namely the Defence Research Telecommunications Establishment (16.2%) and the Suffield Experimental Station (11%).

Figure 21- Percentage of DRB Funds Allocated to DREV

1966/1967	25.2%	1969/1970	24.8%
1967/1968	21.3%	1970/1971	26.8%
1968/1969	*Not Available*	1971/1972	25.9%

In 1966/1967, the Establishment entered a new phase of growth which again resulted in cost overruns. A similar situation prevailed during the following year when actual expenditures amounted to $7,993,153 representing a cost overrun of $107,599 relative to the budgetary allocation of $7,825,554. Salary costs continued to rise slowly, amounting to 63.5% of total expenditures in 1967/1968. This was the last year for which budgetary information for the Establishment is available prior to integration into DND. Data is available, however, for DRB as a whole. Expressed as a percentage of DND's budget, DRB equipment expenditures fell from 7% in 1967/1968 to 5.3% in 1975/1976, while scientific operations fell from 4.8% to 3% of the DND budget during the same period.

The relative decline in DRB's budget was due to Canada's new defence policy, and correspondingly this impacted on DREV's budget. Nevertheless, DREV's budget in 1979/1980 was still roughly the same as in 1967/1968, or slightly over 7 million dollars.

According to one person interviewed, the budgetary situation improved following the integration of the DRB establishments into DND, since CRAD's capital budget was fixed at 5% of Departmental capital. Because equipment suppliers rarely met their contract deadlines, Departmental capital funds were usually under-expended, and this was a recurring phenomenon. As a result, some of these surplus funds were made available to CRAD and hence DREV. In later years, however, as public funds became scarcer, the Department's capital acquisition budget was insufficient to meet requirements, and DREV could no longer count on supplementary amounts to meet unexpected expenses.

Starting in 1987/1988, the Canadian government has progressively made cutbacks in the defence budget, making it increasingly difficult to invest in equipment and infrastructure for the future. This posed a particularly difficult problem for the laboratories since scientific equipment needed for leading-edge research became increasingly sophisticated and expensive. Budgetary cuts also led to a reduction in personnel and in travel, and this impacted on the degree of DREV's participation in the scientific committees of NATO and TTCP. For these reasons, DREV is currently reengineering its programs and developing strategies to manage downsizing.

Evolution of the Administrative Structure of Defence Research Establishment Valcartier

Figure 22 - DREV Expenditures from 1982/1983 to 1996/1997 (Thousands of Dollars)

Fiscal Year	Development	Research	Equipment	Construction	Operation & Maintenance	Salaries	Total
1982/83	675	2,852	4,251	1,490	7,783	N.A.	17,051
1983/84	668	2,291	4,850	1,347	8,679	N.A.	17,835
1984/85	1,455	3,650	10,447	1,981	9,687	N.A.	27,220
1985/86	1,084	5,194	6,416	1,070	9,395	20,700	43,859
1986/87	344	5,328	5,767	1,348	9,559	22,100	44,446
1987/88	1,062	6,496	3,047	733	11,132	22,200	44,670
1988/89	1,903	6,152	7,614	1,361	12,300	22,700	52,030
1989/90	3,246	7,571	6,544	1,474	12,957	25,563	57,355
1990/91	3,480	5,874	6,151	1,886	11,666	25,100	54,157
1991/92	2,974	6,037	3,376	1,708	9,309	24,000	47,404
1992/93	3,214	6,107	3,550	1,866	11,478	25,000	51,215
1993/94	3,979	5,817	1,453	1,150	10,461	24,800	47,710
1994/95	3,842	6,273	2,392	978	9,815	23,685	46,985
1995/96*	3,500	4,300	1,200	900	9,400	20,500	39,800
1996/97*	3,500	4,300	1,200	900	9,400	16,100	35,400

*Estimated   N.A.: Not Available

Source: Yvon Noël, Plans and Programs Office.

1. Peter F. Drucker, *Post Capitalist Society*, New York, Harper Collins Publishers, 1993, p. 215.
2. *Summary of Duties*, Wing Superintendent.
3. Henry Mintzberg, *The Structuring of Organizations*, Englewood Cliffs, N.J., Prentice-Hall Inc., 1979, p. 381.
4. *Summary of Duties*, Chief Superintendent.
5. *Summary of Duties*, Deputy Chief Superintendent.
6. CARDE, *Annual Report for 1963*, p. 3.
7. CARDE, *Annual Report for 1966*, p. 3.
8. CARDE, *Annual Report for 1964*, p. 3.
9. CARDE, *Annual Report for 1967*, p. 1.
10. CARDE, *Annual Report for 1965*, p. 3.
11. The document entitled *Computing at DREV: The Early Days* was completed by Don Galbraith in September 1992 and was included in Dr. Henri Tardif's book *Recollections of CARDE/DREV 1945-1995*.
12. CARDE, *Annual Report for 1965*, p. 3.
13. *Ibid.*
14. CARDE, *Annual Report for 1966*, p. 3.
15. Marcel Letarte, *DREV Management Information System*, Valcartier, 1974, p. 1.
16. CARDE, *Annual Report for 1968*, p. 5.
17. DREV, *Annual Report for 1969*, p. 47.
18. DREV, *Annual Report for 1970*, p. 3.
19. DREV, *Annual Report for 1973*, p. 6.
20. Canada, *House of Commons Debates*, 13 February 1947, p. 383.
21. DND, *Careers in Defence Science*, Department of National Defence, p. 2.
22. *Interview with Dr. Jacques Gilbert*, pp. 51-52.
23. *Interview with Mr. E.J. Bobyn*, pp. 31-32.
24. Telegram, 1901-99TD295 DGDAS, 28 October 1980.
25. NDHQ/ADM(Mat) Instruction 4/76, 25 August 1976.
26. Letter-Telegram, *op. cit.*
27. DREV, *Family Day 20 September 1980*, Valcartier, DREV, unpaginated.
28. *Ibid.*
29. *Ibid.*
30. *Ibid.*
31. *Ibid.*
32. *Ibid.*
33. *Ibid.*
34. *Ibid.*

35   Summary of Duties for Position Number ND-73266-07681, Senior Scientific Coordination Officer DREV.
36   Normand Lester, *L'affaire Gerald Bull: Les canons de l'apocalypse*, Montreal, Méridien, 1991, p. 62.
37   Luc Chartrand et al., *Histoire des sciences au Québec*, Montreal, Boréal, 1987, pp. 426-427.
38   DND, *Defence Research Board: The First 25 Years*, Ottawa, DND, April 1972, p. 13.

CONCLUSION

Aside from the efforts of the National Research Council, military research in Canada was virtually non-existent prior to the Second World War. NRC contributed not only to developing national expertise in specific defence science fields, but also developed Canada's scientific potential in terms of personnel and infrastructure. Canada mobilized all its resources to ensure Allied victory during the Second World War, and NRC, as the nation's foremost scientific organization, was designated by the Canadian Government as the arm responsible for sustaining, stimulating and coordinating the national scientific and industrial research effort. The task was not easy, but NRC performed it brilliantly as evidenced by the many successes achieved by Canada in the field of military research. The decision to develop a scientific front in Canada contributed to the creation of a military technological complex at Valcartier formed of the Artillery Proof and Development Establishment, the Small Arms Proof and Experimental Establishment, the Explosives Experimental Establishment, the Internal Ballistics Research Laboratory and the Army's Field Trial Wing.

Towards the end of the war, the Army viewed with some consternation the fateful moment when the scientific machinery so painstakingly developed during the conflict would have to be dismantled. Action was needed to identify those elements of the scientific infrastructure viewed as essential for the nation. Amongst the priority elements to be retained, the Army quickly identified the various research establishments at Valcartier. In 1944, the Army took the necessary steps to regroup these various components into a single unit. On 1 October, the Department of National Defence issued a ministerial directive to form the Canadian Armament Research and Development Establishment (CARDE) at Valcartier. Implementation of this directive was, however, delayed by the civilian aspects associated with regrouping the various elements. While the Privy Council deliberated this matter, the Director of Artillery developed plans for the future organization and made efforts to preserve the integrity of the scientific teams and infrastructure which existed at the time.

On 8 March 1945, the government authorized the formation of CARDE by Order-in-Council and the new research establishment embarked on its mission in the field of armaments science under the direction of the Army. The Army had the difficult task of integrating within the new establishment three components each having its own organizational culture. The Army elected to adopt a divisional structure which offered the advantage of allowing each division to function as an independent entity while remaining under centralized control. The resulting organization consisted of five divisions, known as the Ballistics Wing, the Chemistry Wing, the Design Wing, the Trials Wing and the Administration Wing. The process of starting up the Establishment was not easy, for the Army had to define a research program responsive to its needs, construct the necessary infrastructure and recruit the requisite personnel. A construction program was soon implemented and development began on three new weapon systems, but recruitment proved to be problematic for CARDE's first Chief Superintendent, Dr. Rose.

The problems of recruiting civilian scientists for key positions were not unrelated to the broader issue, under study in Ottawa, of determining the form that defence research should take in the immediate post-war period. In this context, Colonel W.W. Goforth argued that the formation of a research organization administered by civilians would ease the difficulties of recruiting civilian scientific staff and reduce the risk of duplication of effort within the military research structure that existed in 1945. Goforth advocated that defence research and development should be segregated from the existing Service and reorganized under the authority of a Fourth Service of the Department of National

Defence. His proposals came as a bolt from the blue, and almost two years passed before the concept received official approval. On 28 March 1947, the Act to Amend the National Defence Act received royal assent authorizing the creation of a Defence Research Board. On 30 April, CARDE was officially transferred to DRB, but a transition period was needed for full implementation of all the DRB rules and regulations. During this period, the Chairman of DRB, Dr. Solandt, assessed the future role of the Establishment. At first, Solandt seriously considered relocating the Ballistics Laboratory to Ottawa and transforming CARDE into an Explosives Research Establishment, but later abandoned this idea and decided that CARDE should remain as an armaments research and development establishment.

Even following CARDE's integration within DRB, the Establishment continued to encounter difficulties in recruiting civilian scientists to fulfil its mission. These difficulties were eased somewhat by hiring scientists from abroad. At the same time, DRB implemented a program to train promising young scientists in the new technologies with the intention of creating a new generation of scientists to meet its particular needs. During this period, CARDE progressively developed the infrastructure needed to support the work of the scientists whose efforts were focused on the development of conventional weapons and their derivatives. In 1949, the Chemistry Wing obtained promising results with a new process for manufacturing nitroguanidine. This first success was a precursor of future CARDE achievements. Some years later, Solandt concluded that the best year in CARDE's history was 1950, when the Establishment succeeded in developing a much improved 17-pounder anti-tank weapon.

The year 1950 also marked the beginning of the Korean War which many believed was the fore-runner of a general war between the Soviet Bloc and NATO. Since the end of the Second World War, the two superpowers had progressively confronted each other at all levels without actually coming to blows. The polarization of the world into two camps and the Cold War climate which pervaded international affairs strongly influenced Canada's defence policy. According to Coulon, Canada, as a close neighbour of the United States, found itself torn between the two imperatives of ensuring national security through alliances and of maintaining national sovereignty. This dichotomy largely explains why Canada appeared to be a cautious supporter of the United Nations and why Canada was somewhat apprehensive of pursuing a common continental defence policy with the United States. This quest for independence was also the main reason why Canada played a major role in the formation of NATO. Because of the crisis situation in Eastern Europe and the technological advances made by the Soviets, Canada intensified its military effort and consequently its defence research efforts.

Canada's defence scientists sought constant collaboration with their American and British colleagues, and considered that priorities should be established amongst the various research fields. For its part, DRB advocated that scientific work should be divided amongst the allies. Even though Canada identified priority areas of research, the other areas could not be totally neglected. In this context, DRB undertook a study in 1947 on guided missiles to meet the future needs of the Canadian Armed Forces. It was considered that the enormous costs of developing a guided missile system precluded such a venture. As it happened, the venture was only delayed, for two years later the Royal Canadian Air Force asked DRB whether Canada should develop a guided missile or purchase one from another country. The members of the Board met with their British and American counterparts to deliberate this question. Shortly afterwards, a Tripartite Committee concluded that Canada should undertake the development of a missile based on a relatively simple concept, proven technology and existing know-how.

With this endorsement, DRB asked CARDE scientists to undertake a feasibility study on the development of a Canadian guided missile. The resulting study report recommended that the ultimate aim of the program should be to develop scientific personnel capable of designing and developing guided missiles and to allow Canadian Armed Forces and industry personnel to become familiar with the problems and technical aspects of air-to-air missiles. DRB approved the project in June 1950 and, in March 1951, the members of the Tripartite Guided Missile Committee endorsed the technical approach proposed by CARDE. Mr. G.D. Watson was appointed Project Manager and CARDE embarked on the Velvet Glove Project to develop a relatively small tactical missile. Although the missile was only 10 feet long and less than one foot in diameter, its development was a first-ever venture for Canada.

In the years that followed, CARDE, as responsible manager of the Velvet Glove program, enjoyed unprecedented growth both in terms of facilities and personnel. Although the government eventually abandoned Velvet Glove, the project was viewed as a major success for CARDE. First, the missile was virtually perfected by 1955 and its development was a true technical triumph. Second, it was an organizational success in that CARDE was able to develop creative synergistic relationships with the various partners in the project. Finally, through the expertise transferred to its industrial partners, CARDE succeeded in developing a technological capability within Canadian industry where none had previously existed.

In 1955, with the pending cancellation of the Velvet Glove project, CARDE found itself at a crossroads. The project had dominated the Establishment's activities since 1951, and DRB asked CARDE management to define a new program in the guided missile field. Based on lessons learned from Velvet Glove, Establishment researchers considered it vital that the new project should span at least a decade. At about that time, the United States realized that the Soviet Union had a significant lead in the field of ICBMs. The Soviets had made a major technological breakthrough and, in September 1955, the President of the United States accorded top national priority to ICBM research. In Canada, the problems of continental air defence also assumed prime importance. This was the context in which CARDE scientists proposed that the new research program should focus on surface-to-air missiles and particularly on effective protection against ICBMs.

In the years that followed, Canada made significant contributions to the development of ICBM defensive systems and research in the area of ballistic missile defence became an increasingly important activity. It had three major orientations: missile propulsion, infrared detection and aerophysics. CARDE research activities in these three areas attracted the interest of US research organizations and the US Armed Forces. US General Trudeau, for instance, was keenly interested in the light-gas gun technology developed by the research team of the Aerophysics Wing under the direction of Dr. Bull. Other US agencies were equally interested in CARDE atmospheric research using sounding balloons and research on the Black Brant sounding rocket.

In 1959, US Government agencies signed three major master agreements with CARDE. The first was an agreement between ARGMA and the Aerophysics Wing to develop large-scale hypersonic ranges and to study certain phenomena associated with the physics of re-entry of ballistic missiles into the Earth's atmosphere. The second was a formal invitation from the US Air Force to the CARDE infrared research team to participate in a joint program to measure radiation emitted by ballistic missiles on re-entry into the atmosphere. This was a vast US/Canada program, and CARDE participated in the Canadian portion, known as Project Lookout. The third agreement was between the US Army and the CARDE rocket-propellant research team to undertake pilot-production of a new rocket propellant. Through these agreements, CARDE again experienced phenomenal growth, consolidating, increasing and diversifying its research activities in these three major areas and acquiring new infrastructure, such as hypersonic ranges.

In 1964, Project Lookout and the Black Brant project were

nearing completion, and a new White Paper on Defence was tabled before the House which marked an important step towards unification of the Canadian Armed Forces. For CARDE's Chief Superintendent, Dr. L'Heureux, the new defence climate and the administrative changes occurring within the Department of National Defence had a positive impact, causing DRB to adopt a more integrated approach in responding to existing and future military requirements. This was an important factor given that Canada, at the time, was developing a five-year plan for re-equipping its Armed Forces. CARDE management then started to place greater importance on conventional armaments in the Establishment's research programs, but the Establishment still pursued its mission of advancing science for purposes of defence, proffering advice to the Department of National Defence and providing technical assistance to the Canadian Armed Forces. CARDE continued to make an effective contribution to national security through its broad program of analysis, evaluation, research and development in several different fields, such as lasers, armaments and surveillance.

Despite this return to basics, CARDE did not abandon those areas which had contributed to its remarkable growth over the previous ten years. Research continued on the chemistry of propellants, the design of rocket-motors, the phenomena of hypersonic physics and the detection of infrared radiation. New agreements were signed with the United States, demonstrating CARDE's desire to rationalize and consolidate its research activities. These agreements included the Cold Can project and the hypersonic wake program which was aimed at determining the properties of turbulent wakes behind projectiles travelling at hypersonic speeds.

At the same time, researchers across the world became fascinated with the laser. This invention is considered by many today as the most sensational discovery of modern times after the atomic bomb. Defence departments around the world quickly recognized the potential applications of the laser. In Canada,

CARDE scientists appeared to be well positioned to exploit the potential of the laser, having developed solid expertise in the areas of microwaves and optical and infrared spectroscopy. After experimenting with a number of prototype lasers using other types of active medium, CARDE researchers focused their efforts on the carbon dioxide molecular laser.

In the mid-1960s, the main problem encountered in developing the CO_2 laser was the size required to obtain high output. Scientists throughout the world elected either to lengthen the laser cavity or to increase the mass of the lasing medium. CARDE scientists at first experimented with these techniques, and with laser modules in cascade, but then pioneered a new approach to overcome the impasse. The new design consisted of electrically exciting the lasing medium in a direction transverse to the optical axis of the laser (defined by the two end mirrors). In late 1967, Dr. Jacques Beaulieu conducted basic studies of the transverse excitation mechanism, and developed a multiple parallel pin electrode configuration for exciting the lasing medium. The feasibility of the Transversely Excited Atmospheric Carbon Dioxide (TEA-CO_2) laser was demonstrated in early 1968, and DRB allocated funds for the construction of a laser laboratory at CARDE. Project Lotion was born, and researchers set about solving all the problems which impeded the development of a practical laser. In 1970, Dr. Beaulieu publicly disclosed the invention of the TEA-CO_2 laser and DREV became renowned as the world's leading laboratory in the field of lasers.

The media coverage of this invention enhanced DREV's reputation beyond the confines of defence science circles to the Canadian public and the international scientific community. The private sector was particularly interested in obtaining licences to manufacture the laser, and DREV was a major contributor to the birth and development of the laser industry in Canada. DREV researchers continued their work to improve the performance of the TEA-CO_2 laser and to develop military applications in the areas of laser radar (rangefinders), surveillance and target identification.

At the same time, DREV researchers were interested in chemically-excited lasers which also attracted world interest with the discovery that several chemical reactions proceeding at atmospheric pressure could produce lasing action. In 1974, following these successive breakthroughs in pure and hybrid chemical lasers, DREV scientists embarked on studies to develop military applications of experimental pulsed hybrid HF/DF lasers. As in the case of TEA-CO_2 lasers, the most promising applications appeared to be rangefinders, tracking devices and target designators. As this laser work proceeded, there began a progressive phase-out of the major projects that had mobilized the majority of DREV scientists around common objectives and common-core research, and which had led to a greater diversification of DREV's research activities. Defence scientists continued to devote a large part of their effort to developing the technology base, although from then on they appeared to be increasingly occupied with short-term applications.

In 1974, a major change occurred in the way that defence research was organized in Canada, and this exerted a significant influence on DREV's research activities. During that year, responsibilities for research activities were redistributed within government. DRB lost all its administrative and executive responsibilities for the defence research program and all responsibility for personnel at the various defence research establishments across Canada, including the Operations Research and Analysis Establishment in Ottawa. The role of DRB was restricted to that of scientific advisor to the Minister on research of interest to the military. This administrative shake-up was due to a number of factors, including the reorganization of the Department of National Defence, the new science policy in Canada, increased bureaucratization of the Public Service and the move towards centralization which posed a challenge to autonomous organizations such as DRB.

Responsibility for DRB's defence research program was

transferred to the Chief Research and Development (CRAD) who headed a new branch within the Assistant Deputy Minister (Materiel) (ADM(Mat)) Group. This reorganization had the advantage of regrouping all research and development activities under CRAD who could exercise budgetary control and ensure coordination of these activities. As a result, R&D planning within the Department of National Defence was facilitated since research objectives and results could be better aligned with the existing and future requirements of the Canadian Forces.

The reorganization of defence research had a significant influence on DREV, for it led to a progressive change in organizational culture at all levels. DREV was no longer a separate employer and its personnel became subject to all the rules and regulations of the Public Service Commission. As a result, personnel management and staff relations in the Establishment changed significantly. DREV also had to conform with the administrative regulations and procedures of the Department of National Defence, and many of the habits and customs prevailing under the DRB administration had to be abandoned or changed.

Since 1974, defence scientists have, of necessity, worked very closely with the military, since their mission was to develop requisite technology, provide advice and technical support and enable the Department to be a smart buyer. This mission was not new for DREV, but the integration of the Establishment into DND gave the technical directorates of the Canadian Forces more direct access to DREV's expertise. For its part, DREV intensified its efforts to undertake projects of direct interest to the Canadian Forces and participated in the planning of new projects with the CF technical directorates. DREV nevertheless continued to devote an appreciable effort to long-term research aimed at developing the technology base needed to respond to emerging military requirements. Most of these projects were conceived by scientists, but always after consultation and agreement with the military. In other words, a client-oriented approach prevailed.

A brief review of DREV's research activities over the past

twenty years reveals that no major projects were undertaken but rather a stream of minor projects geared to the immediate or projected requirements of the military. This reorientation of activity impacted on the way that scientific activities were structured at the Establishment. These activities were grouped along the lines of four major defence technologies: energetic materials, armaments, information technologies and electro-optics. But stabilization of the program in no way implied stagnation, for DREV had to make choices to keep pace with scientific advances and progressive budgetary restrictions. Some traditional programs were downsized to accommodate more promising technologies. Informatics was increasingly used in all aspects of command and control and management information systems, and research in electro-optics was pursued at a consistently high level. On the other hand, the priorities in armaments and energetic materials research declined relative to other programs.

Budgetary policy has impacted on all government operations. Consequently, Canada's defence policy has been strongly affected, which in turn has had direct effects on military research. This impact has been particularly apparent since the late 1980s, as evidenced by the latest White Papers developed by the Department of National Defence. Defence policy is now predicated on geopolitical realities as well as on Canadian budgetary constraints. While budgetary policy is oriented towards the long term, it exerts an immediate influence on the future of DREV and the whole of defence research in Canada. The budgetary decisions taken by the government form the essential guidelines for the future management of its machinery. Deficit reduction has become the prime objective in the latest budgets, and the government has had no hesitation in bringing under scrutiny all aspects of its operations and in implementing a program of major downsizing of the Public Service.

In this new environment, CRAD management is studying the possibility of applying the recent concept of business reengineering to its operations. Michael Hammer, one of the creators of the concept, defines business reengineering as "the fundamental rethinking and radical redesign of business processes to achieve dramatic improvements in critical, contemporary measures of performance."[1] Hammer identifies three types of situation where reengineering is warranted: first, where a company is in serious financial difficulty; second, where company management has the foresight to see trouble coming; and third, where a company in a leading position sees reengineering as an opportunity to consolidate its lead over its competitors.[2]

Given the difficult budgetary situation in Canada, it would appear that the whole apparatus of government finds itself in the first of these situation categories, and this is particularly true for the defence sector which has been strongly affected by recent budget cuts. In particular, the defence research organization has suffered the impact and DREV, as its main component, has experienced considerable budget reductions following the tabling of the 1990, 1992 and 1994 federal budgets. Reductions in DREV personnel between 1992 and 1996 amount to some 30 to 40% of establishment strength, and these reductions will have "a direct negative impact on all aspects of its scientific program."[3] In short, the defence research organization has to develop a plan for balancing the budget which takes account of anticipated major budgetary reductions resulting from government cuts to the Departmental budget.

This is the climate in which CRAD and establishment managers alike must review their long-standing procedures and take a fresh look at ways of re-shaping the defence research program while continuing to satisfy the requirements of the program's only client, the Canadian Forces. In 1994, CRAD formed a committee to define "a new framework for the management and delivery of its R&D program. [DREV management is playing a major role in this exercise,] by which [it] has been able to establish the parameters for the Establishment's future scientific activities."[4]

During this period it was decided to re-categorize scientific activities along the lines of R&D thrusts, which would group activities corresponding to military capability areas, so that they become more visible and more easily identifiable by the military, industrial and academic partners of CRAD, and hence of DREV. Consequently, DREV is proposing a series of research activities structured into thrusts "around which its future scientific program would be shaped. These thrusts have been developed in response to the technology emphasis in the CRAD Strategic Plan and as a result of [DREV's] interpretation of client priorities. While it remains to obtain client feedback on these proposed thrusts, the initial indication is that a rebalancing of the scientific effort at DREV is necessary."[5]

Because of budgetary pressures, downsizing in the Public Service, development of the next five-year plan and the new nomenclature of R&D, DREV must take immediate action to restructure its scientific divisions. For the Chief of DREV in 1995, Dr. Jacques Gilbert, the objectives of this reorganization are to establish closer links with the client and the various partners of DREV, to promote stability of the organization, to align R&D thrusts with core competencies, to rationalize the organization in view of the planned reductions in personnel and to minimize "the requirement for staff re-deployment and re-training across divisions."[6] To achieve these objectives, it was decided to reduce the number of scientific divisions from four to three, and then rationalize the organization of these three divisions by April 1995.

With this schedule in mind, DREV management adopted a four-stage plan to establish a new organizational structure. At the end of this exercise, the missions of the three divisions will be defined and the scientific programs distributed amongst them. For example, the Armaments Division and the Energetic Materials Division will be merged into a new Weapon Systems Division whose mission (see Figure 21) encompasses the respective activities of the two current divisions. The missions of the other divisions will also be revised. The Command and Control Division will be known as the Command and Control Information

Systems Division, while the Electro-Optics Division will become the Electro-Optics and Surveillance (EO&S) Division. For the first of these divisions, the change in name "more accurately defines the actual scope of division activity than does the present name. [For the other division], the addition of the word surveillance is intended to indicate a broadening of the mission to include other than EO sensors, and to stress the defence application of the Division's activities."[7] To be consistent, DREV management also decided to assign responsibility for the superconductor and tactical surveillance programs of the Armaments Division and the chemical countermeasures characterization program of the Energetic Materials Division to the new EO&S Division.

Figure 23- Missions of the New Scientific Divisions at DREV

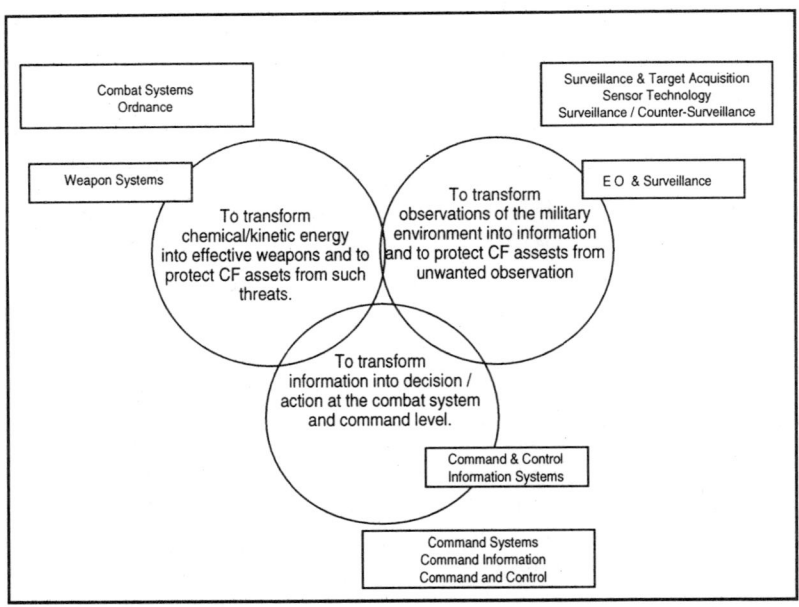

Source: DREV, "A Plan for the Re-organization of DREV's Scientific Divisions: Annex B", Manager's Guide to DREV Scientific Re-organization, p. 5.

Once the organizational nomenclature has been established, DREV management will undertake the delicate operation of redistributing staff across these new divisions in conformity with all the Public Service rules and regulations that apply to such situations. This is a complex exercise even under normal circumstances, but it will be even more difficult in light of the downsizing program of the Federal Government. DREV management will have to strive to find solutions that meet national objectives and simultaneously provide the necessary staff complement to ensure smooth operation of its scientific divisions. The challenge is not easy, since the number of personnel has dropped from 500 in 1994 to 430 in April 1995. Despite this additional difficulty, DREV management is succeeding in reconfiguring the scientific divisions to meet forecast needs, specifically 235 employees distributed amongst the three scientific divisions.

At the time of writing, DREV management is continuing to restructure its organization, and has started the reengineering of its administrative support services. Here again, DREV is faced with the challenge of managing a major reduction in its material, financial and human resources while pursuing the objectives set by the organization at the beginning of this major organizational restructuring exercise. In meeting this challenge, DREV management is making every effort to protect the integrity of the Establishment's mission while adapting its organization to meet the imperatives of tomorrow. Undoubtedly DREV will succeed, for one of the major themes which has characterized the Establishment's history is the ability of its personnel to adapt to change and to overcome difficulties so as to preserve the integrity of this important government research institution.

At this point in time, when DREV stands at a crossroads, personnel could well draw on the lessons of the past from the Establishment's rich heritage to inspire their thinking on the best way to build its future.

1. Michael Hammer and James Champy, *Reengineering the Corporation: A Manifesto for Business.*
2. *Ibid.,* p. 34.
3. DREV, "A Plan for the Reorganization of DREV's Scientific Divisions: Annex B", *Manager's.*
4. DREV, "A New Scientific Organization for DREV: Annex A", *Ibid.,* p. 1.
5. DREV, "Annex B", *Ibid.,* p. 2.
6. *Ibid.,* p. 3.
7. *Ibid.,* p. 4-5.

ANNEX

SENIOR MANAGEMENT
CARDE / DREV 1945 - 1995

CHIEFS
Dr. D.C. Rose	May 1945	- October 1947
Dr. W.B. Littler	October 1947	- February 1949
Dr. C. Craig	June 1949	- October 1952
Dr. H. Barrett	October 1952	- November 1955
Brig. D.A.G. Waldock	November 1955	- May 1959
Dr. J.J. Green	September 1959	- July 1963
Dr. L.J. L'Heureux	August 1963	- March 1967
Dr. W.N. English	March 1967	- July 1968
Mr. E.J. Bobyn	September 1968	- November 1972
Dr. A. Lemay	November 1972	- November 1976
Dr. W.G. Brownlee	November 1976	- August 1984
Dr. H.P. Tardif	September 1984	- December 1989
Mr. K. Peebles	January 1990	- June 1992
Dr. J. Gilbert	June 1992	- July 1995
Dr. R.S. Walker	July 1995	- Present

DEPUTY CHIEFS
LCol T.R. Gemmel		- 1952
Col D.A.G. Waldock	1952	- 1954
Dr. L.J. L'Heureux	1955	- 1960
Mr. R.F. Wilkinson	1960	- 1964
Dr. W.N. English	1965	- 1967
Dr. J.L. Boivin	1968	- 1970
Dr. A. Lemay	1971	- 1972
Dr. W.G. Brownlee	1972	- 1976
Dr. H.P. Tardif	1977	- 1984

Dr. R.S. Thomas	1985	- 1988
Dr. J. Gilbert	1990	- 1992
Dr. R. Walker	1994	- 1995

ASSISTANT CHIEFS

Mr. E.S. Guy	1965	- 1973
Dr. H.P. Tardif	1973	- 1977
Mr. M. Letarte	1978	- 1980
Vacant	1981	- 1982
Mr. J.-P. Lafrenière	1983	- 1988
Mr. A. Morency	1988	- 1993
Mr. J.-C. Ratté	1993	- 1995

MILITARY ASSISTANTS

LCol T.R. Gemmel	1950	- 1952
W/C E.L. Baudoux	1952	- 1955
W/C E.A. Smith (Air)	1956	- 1960
Col H.J. Lake (Land)	1958	- 1964
LCdr J.B. Boase (Sea)	1960	- 1962
LCdr D.R. Whittemore (Sea)	1963	- 1964
S/L D.W. East (Air)	1961	- 1963
Col J.S. Dunphy	1965	- 1967
Col P.J. Patterson	1968	- 1969
Col (L) J.C. Boughton	1969	- 1971
Col (A) E.J. Kuffner	1971	- 1973
Col (A) R.I. McDowell	1974	- 1976
Col J.A. Bordeleau	1976	- 1979
Col M.J.F. Braün	1979	- 1983
Col W.M. Osborne	1983	- 1985
LCol J.R. Gérard	1985	- 1990
LCol N. Jodoin	1990	- 1992
LCol J.M. Coderre	1992	- Present

DIRECTORS - ARMAMENTS DIVISION
Maj J.S. Dunphy	1947	- 1950
Maj G.W. Donaldson	1950	- 1952
Mr. B.O. Baker	1953	- 1959
Mr. R.P. Blake	1960	- 1965
Mr. C.R. Iverson	1966	- 1969
Dr. H.P. Tardif	1969	- 1972
Mr. P. Solnoky	1973	- 1976
Mr. P.N. Brooks	1976	- 1979
Mr. A.K. Roberts	1979	- 1983
Mr. M. Laviolette	1983	- 1986
Mr. M. Clark	1987	- 1995

DIRECTORS - COMMAND AND CONTROL DIVISION
Mr. W.G. Thistle	1971	- 1977
Dr. G. Giroux	1978	- 1988
Vacant	1988	- 1989
Mr. J. Gilbert	1989	- 1990
Mr. D. Smith	1990	- 1995

DIRECTORS - ELECTRO-OPTICS DIVISION
Dr. L.J. L'Heureux	1952	- 1954
Mr. E.J. Bobyn	1955	- 1958
Mr. R. Chinnick	1958	- 1964
Dr. W.N. English	1964	- 1965
Mr. J. Hampson	1965	- 1970
Dr. C. Cumming	1970	- 1975
Dr. J. Gilbert	1975	- 1986
Vacant	1986	- 1987
Mr. K. Peebles	1987	- 1989
Mr. R. Corriveau	1990	- 1995

DIRECTORS - ENERGETIC MATERIALS DIVISION
Dr. H. Poole	1943	- 1945 (EEE)
Dr. D.C. Rose	1945	- 1948
Dr. W.B. Littler	1947	- 1949
Mr. A.L. Lovecy	1949	- 1950
Mr. A.M. Pennie	1951	- 1952
Mr. R.F. Wilkinson	1953	- 1959
Mr. I.R. Cameron	1959	- 1966
Dr. J.L. Boivin	1967	- 1967
Dr. W.G. Brownlee	1968	- 1971
Mr. J.Y. Bélanger	1972	- 1978
Dr. G.H. Kimbell	1978	- 1982
Mr. A.K. Roberts	1983	- 1985
Dr. J. Gilbert	1985	- 1988
Mr. M. Laviolette	1989	- 1994

DIRECTORS - "E WING"
Maj G.E. Baxter	1947	- 1951
Maj A. Pennie	1952	- 1954
LCol R.C.D. Stewart	1955	- 1957

DIRECTORS - "B WING"
Dr. K.J. Laidler	1945	- 1946
Mr. G.D. Watson	1946	- 1947
Maj C.M. Wright	1947	- 1949
Mr. G.D. Watson	1949	- 1952
Mr. E.W. Greenwood	1952	- 1957

DIRECTORS - "AEROPHYSICS WING"
Dr. G.V. Bull	1958	- 1961
Mr. G.H. Tidy	1961	- 1967
Dr. A. Lemay	1968	- 1971

DIRECTORS - "SYSTEMS WING"
Mr. E.J. Bobyn	1958	- 1960
Mr. C.R. Iverson	1961	- 1963

DIRECTORS - "EXPERIMENTAL WING"
Mr. A.L. Lortie	1966	- 1971
Mr. P. Solnoky	1971	- 1972

DIRECTORS - "F WING"/TECHNICAL SERVICES
Mr. E.S. Guy	1952	- 1964
Mr. A.L. Lortie	1965	- 1966
Mr. M. Letarte	1972	- 1973
Mr. P. Croteau	1973	- 1978
Mr. J. Dufour	1978	- 1995

DIRECTORS - ADMINISTRATION DIVISION
Maj McAulay	1945	- 1947
Mr. J.P. Giroux	1947	- 1962
Mr. W.G. Mylett	1962	- 1973
Mr. M. Letarte	1973	- 1977
Mr. J. Lavigueur	1978	- 1985
Mr. P. St-Onge	1985	- 1992
Mr. J. Lavigueur	1992	- 1995

MAJOR RESTRUCTURES

On January 1, 1953, two new divisions were created, namely "F" (Fabrication) and "G" (Guided missiles) wings. These divisions were an outgrowth of the activities of "B" and "D" Wings, and of the need to split their operations to refocus their mandates around very specific functions. In this way, the workshops and production engineering cell were separated from "D" Wing to form "F" Wing, whereas most of the research fields associated with the guided missiles of "B" Wing were brought together under "G" Wing.

In 1957, the Aerophysics Section was established and placed under the administrative responsibility of the deputy chief. The section's first director was Dr G.V. Bull. Most of the staff of the new section were drawn from "B" Wing, but it also had on its establishment members of "D" and "E" Wings.

On April 1, 1958, new directions in the field of research carried out at CARDE led management to undertake a major administrative restructure of the establishment. The functions of "B" Wing were assigned to two new wings: Systems and Aerophysics. The system analysis and computer components of "G" Wing went to the new Systems Wing and the Electronic Section of "G" Wing was renamed the Electronics Wing, which would later become the Electro-Optics Division. Finally, "F" Wing amalgamated all technical support services provided to the scientific divisions.

Between 1966 and 1972, the various components of "F" Wing reported directly either to the Assistant Chief or to the other directors.

In 1971, on completion of the hypersonic wake study project, the Aerophysics Wing became the Informatics Division, which would later be called the Command and Control Division, and was entrusted with responsibility for the computer centre. The Ballistics and Aerodynamics cell of this division were transferred to the Experimental Wing the following year.

In 1972, "F" Wing was established and amalgamated the workshops, design, maintenance and construction sections.

In 1973, the Experimental Wing was fused with the Armaments Division. The Pyrotechnics Group became part of the Propulsion Division and the Weapon Systems Section was integrated into the Informatics Division.

In 1987, the Informatics Section was restructured to bring together administrative and scientific support. Responsibility for the Informatics Section went from the Command and Control Division to the Deputy Chief.

BIBLIOGRAPHICAL SCOPE

This bibliography includes manuscripts and printed documents as well as a selective list of other sources and government publications consulted. It also includes a list of the major studies and specialized articles related to defence and defence science used in researching the book.

Sources
Manuscripts and Printed Documents

Defence Research Establishment Valcartier

Administrative Documents

Infocentre 1990 to 1995

Annual Reports:

1948-1975, 1979 to 1989-1990.

In 1948, the *Survey of Organization, Facilities and Programmes of Work; September 1947 to September 1948* served in lieu of annual report since CARDE had been issuing this as an annual report starting in 1949. CARDE became DREV in 1969, but the Establishment had been publishing a bilingual report since 1965. Following the 1975 report, DREV stopped producing annual reports and did not resume until 1979, producing a report every year after that for the next ten years or so.

National Archives of Canada

At Ottawa:

> Privy Council collection (RG 2), Volumes 1629 and 1978.
>
> Orders in Council related to CARDE.
>
> Department of National Defence collection (RG 24), Volume 4238 of the Headquarters Records Registry; Volumes 11995, 11997 and 11998 of the Defence Research Board series; and reel C-5170 of the microfiche section collection.

This collection holds the relevant administrative documentation on the establishment of CARDE and on the first years of its existence as well as the annual and administrative reports of the DRB.

Munition and Supply Department collection (RG 28), Volume 1.

Private archives and records of Mathew Hower Somers Penhals (MG 31 G 21), Volumes 5 and 6.

This collection holds a certain number of documents related to the principles that guided the Canadian government in organizing defence research in Canada, notably the writings of Goforth and Foulkes.

Government of Canada Publications

>*Canada Year Book,* Ottawa: Dominion Bureau of Statistics and Department of Trade and Commerce, 1932 to 1947.
>
>Glassco Commission, "Special Areas of Administration", *Royal Commission on Government Organization (Glassco Commission),* Vol. 4, Ottawa: Queen's Printer, Chap. 20, p. 55 to 98 and Chap. 23, p. 187-334.
>
>DRB, *Research and Development Bureau: Review 1976-1986,* Ottawa: National Defence, 1987, 36 p.
>
>DRB, *A Brief History of the Office of the Defence-Research & Development Advisor London (DRDA[L]) 1940-1943,* Ottawa: DRB/DND, 1994, not paginated.
>
>DRB, *Defence Research Board: The First 25 years,* Ottawa: DND, April 1972, 46 p.
>
>*House of Commons Debate,* 1940, 1947 to 1950, 1951, 1956, 1957-1958, 1964, 1966, 1970, 1982, 1989, 1990.
>
>Minister of State for Science and Technology, *The Contracting-Out Policy 1973-1975,* Ottawa: Minister of State for Science and Technology, 1975, 44 p.
>
>Department of National Defence, *Careers in Defence Science,* National Defence, undated, 26 p.

Department of National Defence, *White Paper on Defence,* Ottawa: DND, March 1964, 34 p.

Department of National Defence, *Challenge and Commitment: A Defence Policy for Canada,* Ottawa: DND, 1987, 89 p.

Department of National Defence, *Canadian Defence Policy,* Ottawa: DND, 1992, 44 p.

Department of National Defence, *1994 Defence White Paper,* Ottawa: DND, 1994, 55 p.

DRB, *Annual Reports of the Defence Research Board,* 1966 to 1973.

Department of National Defence, *Annual Reports of the Department of National Defence of Canada,* 1939 to 1952 and Defence, 1971 to 1990.

Canada, *Statutes of Canada,* Chap. 21, 1940, and Chap. 5, 1947.

Illustrated Documents

Private collection of Gordon D. Watson.

DREV Collection

Oral Sources

Interviews with Drs Jacques Gilbert and André Lemay as well as with Messrs. Eddy Bobyn and Marcel Letarte in the Fall of 1994. Transcripts were produced.

Video Documents

Caméra 62, Radio Canada.

General Works

CHARTRAND, Luc et al., *Histoire des sciences au Québec,* Montreal: Boréal, 1987, 487 p.

LINTEAU, Paul-André et al., *Histoire du Québec contemporain: Le Québec depuis 1930,* Montréal: Boréal, 1986, 739 p.

MORTON, Desmond, *A Military History of Canada: 1608-1991,* Toronto: McClelland & Steward, 1992.

STANLEY, George F.G., *Canada's Soldiers, 1604-1954: The Military History of an Unmilitary People,* Toronto: Macmillan, 1954, 327 p.

Specialized Works

Defence Policy and Military History

BLAND, Douglas, *The Administration of Defence Policy: 1947 to 1985,* Kingston: Frye, 1987, 252 p.

COULON, Jocelyn, *En première ligne: Grandeurs et misères du système militaire canadien,* Montréal: Éd. du Jour, 1991, 277 p.

CUTHBERTSON, Brian, *Canadian Military Independence in the Age of the Superpowers,* Don Mills Ont.: Fitzhenry and Whiteside, 1977, 282 p.

FORTIER, Rénald, *Intervention gouvernementale et industrie aéronautique: L'exemple canadien 1920-1945,* Doctoral Thesis, Quebec City: Université Laval, 1990, 669 p.

FORTMAN, Michel, "La politique de défense canadienne", in Paul Painchaud et al., *From Mackenzie King to Pierre Trudeau: Forty Years of Canadian Diplomacy, 1945-1985,* Quebec City: Presses de l'Université Laval, 1989, 507 p.

FOULKES, Charles, *Canadian Defence Policy in a Nuclear Age.* (Behind the Headlines, Vol. XXi, no. 1) Toronto: Canadian Institute of International Affairs, 1961, 20 p.

GRANATSTEIN, J.l., "The Defence Debacle, 1957-1963", *Canada 1957-1967: The Years of Uncertainty and Innovation,* Toronto: McClelland & Steward, 1986, p. 101 to 133.

HITSMAN, J. Mackay, *Military Inspection Services in Canada 1855-1950,* Ottawa: Department of National Defence Inspection Services, 1962, 122 p.

MCNAUGHTON, Andrew George Latta and MACKENZIE, Chalmers. *The Mackenzie-McNaughton Wartime Letters*, Toronto: University of Toronto Press, 1975, 177 p.

STACEY, C.P., *Arms, Men and Governments: The War Policies of Canada 1935-1945*, Ottawa: Queen's Printer, 1970, 747 p.

Defence Science and History of Science

BROWN, J.J., *Ideas in Exile: A History of Canadian Invention*, Toronto/Montreal: McClelland & Steward, 1967, 372 p.

CHAPMAN, J.P. et al., *Upper Atmosphere and Space Programs in Canada*, Ottawa: Science Secretariat/Privy Council Office, 1967, 258 p. (Special Study No. 1)

EGGLESTON, Wilfrid, *Scientists at War*, London: Oxford University Press, 1950, 291 p.

GOODSPEED, D.J., *A History of the Defence Research Board*, Ottawa: Queen's Printer, 1958, 259 p.

HECHT, Jeff, *Beam Weapons: The Next Arms Race*, New York and London: Plenum Press, 1984, 363 p.

OCDE, *Examens des politiques scientifiques nationales: Canada*, Paris, 1969, 479 p.

Other Subjects

ADAMS, Benson D., *Ballistic Missile Defence*, New York: American Elsevier Pub. Co., 1971, 274 p.

CAMPBELL, Robert Malcolm, *Grand Illusions: The Politics of the Keynesian Experience in Canada, 1945-1975*, Peterborough: Broadview Press Ltd., 1987, 270 p.

HAMMER, Michael and CHAMPY, James, *Le Reengineering [réinventer l'entreprise par une amélioration spectaculaire de ses performances]*, Paris: Dunod, 1993, 247 p.

MINTZBERG, Henry, *Structure & Dynamique des organisations,* Paris: Les Éditions Agence d'ARC, 1982, 439 p.

PURVIS, Douglas and SMITH, Constance, "Canada's Fiscal Policy, 1963-1984", in John Sergent (ed.), *Fiscal and Monetary Policy,* University of Toronto in cooperation with the Royal Commission on the Economic Union and Development Prospects for Canada, and the Canadian Government Publishing Centre, Ottawa: Supply and Services Canada, 1986, p. 1-50.

SAVOIE, Donald J., *The Politics of Public Spending in Canada,* Toronto: University of Toronto Press, 1960, 433 p.

Articles

Defence Policy and Military History

BLAIS, Jean-Jacques, "The Defence Budget: Goals, Piorities and the Allotment of Funds". *Canadian Defence Quarterly,* Vol. 4, No. 1 (Summer 1984), p. 8-12.

BYERS, R.B., "Defence for the Next Decade: The Forthcoming White Paper", *Canadian Defence Quarterly,* Vol. 7, No. 2 (Autumn 1977), p. 18-22.

MANSON, P.D., "The Restructuring of National Defence Headquarters - 1972-1973", *Canadian Defence Quarterly,* Vol. 3, No. 3 (Winter 1973), p. 8-14

ORR, John L., "The Defence Industrial Research Programme", *Aircraft,* December 1961, p. 8-10 and p. 48.

ROY, Reginal H., "Canadian Defence Policy 1945-1976", *Parameters,* Vol. VI (1976), p. 60-70.

Defence Science and History of Science

"The Weapon that Almost Was" (Velvet Glove), *Aircraft,* 19 (March 1957), p. 53-54 and 102.

BARIL, Gérald, "Une visite dans le monde merveilleux des savants", *Sentinelle,* 1992, No. 1, p. 4-6.

"New Anti-Tank Weapon is Developed for Canadian Army", *Canadian Army Journal,* April 1955, (n.p.).

FLEURY, Jean-Marc, "Laser québecois: un succès éblouissant", *Québec Science,* Vol. 12, No. 3 (Dec. 1973), p. 32-39.

FLEURY, Jean-Marc, "Les canons de Valcartier", *Québec Science,* Vol. 11, No. 10 (Dec. 1973), p. 32-39.

MERKLINGER, Harold, M. *Canada's Historical Involvement with Ballistic Missile Defence,* Ottawa: DND, 1994, (n.p.).

NIELSEN, H.P., "The CRV7 Weapon System: An Example of Weapon Development in Canada", *Canadian Aeronautics and Space Journal,* Vol. 1 No. 1 (1980), p. 10-19.

PENNIE, Archie M., "The Defence Research Board: A Quarter-Century of Achievement", *Canadian Defence Quarterly,* Vol. 1, No. 4 (Spring 1972), p. 6-16.

PENNIE, Archie M., "DRB Quarter-Century Mark", *Sentinel,* Vol. 8, No. 4 (April 1972), p. 19-23.

"Un laser à gaz accessible aux petites industries", *Québec Industriel,* February 1970, p. 31-35.

SMITH, D.L., The CRV7 Rocket Weapon System, A Xerox copy of a text for publication in *Forum.*

SOLANDT, O.M., "Defence Research in Canada", *The Engineering Journal,* August 1951, p. 765-768.

SOLANDT, O.M., "Defence Research in Canada", *Address... CBC,* Jan. 1947 (n.p.).

SOLANDT, O.M., *Science as It Relates to Defence,* Kingston: The Royal Military College of Canada/The John Waddell Lecture, 1977, (n.p.).

SOLANDT, O.M., "Scientific Research in the Modern World", *Dalhousie Review,* No. 37 (Summer 1957), p. 141-153.

SOLANDT, O.M., "The Defence Research Board's Untimely End: What It Means for Military Science", *Science Forum,* No. 47 (October 1975), p. 22-25.

WATSON, Gordon D., "Why the Bureaucrats Secretely Carved Up the DRB: It Worked Too Well". *Science Forum,* No 47 (October 1975), p. 22-25.

ZIMMERMAN, A.H., "Defence Research Programs", *Air University Review,* March-April 1967, p. 14-17.

Other Subjects

MANN, Paul, "Budget Deficits Constrain Canadian Defence Efforts". *Aviation Week & Space Technology,* Vol. 124, No. 26 (June 1986), p. 44-47.